The Enemy Within the Gate

In
memory of
my father,
Andrew McKee,
'Sweet singer in Israel,'
and of
my mother,
Martha McKee,
'Doctor' in the Church.

The Enemy Within the Gate

The Catholic Church and Renascent Modernism

by

John McKee

LUMEN CHRISTI PRESS
Houston, Texas 77019

First Printing: May 1974

Library of Congress catalog card number: 74-80023

ISBN 0-912414-16-2

Printed in the United States of America

Contents

There are those among us, as it must be confessed, who for years past . . . . having done their best to set the house on fire, leave to others the task of putting out the flame.

J. H. NEWMAN, Letter to the Duke of Norfolk

1

The Graveyard of Heresies

The Modernists claimed that Catholic thought needed reviving—and no doubt it did. But did anything they wrote do much to revive it?

MAISIE WARD, "Insurrection versus Resurrection"

Both of them can rest together in the graveyard of heresies.

A. F. LOISY, referring to his "L'Évangile et L'Église" and FR. TYRRELL'S "Christianity at the Cross-Roads"

In Book IX of the Confessions, St. Augustine looked back on the fresh Spring of his Catholic life, on the days following his baptism and that of his son Adeodatus and friend Alypius, when he first sang the Church's hymns and listened to the teaching of her Apostles when the gospels were read out in the church at Milan, and he recalled how deeply he had been stirred and gladdened, and wrote: "How sorely I wept at those hymns and songs, how often was I melted by the moving founders of the Church! Into mine ear poured those voices; and *the truth shone warm* into my heart, and kindled in it the flame of adoration. My tears flowed, and upon me blessings poured."

The truth shone warm into his heart, as the same truth shines warm into ours. Fifteen hundred years after Augustine, Pope Pius XII gave voice to the same mixture of faith and joy which they call today 'triumphalism': "If those who were under the Old Law could sing this song of their earthly

1

city: 'If I forget thee, O Jerusalem, let my right hand be
forgotten . . .':   how much more ought we to glory, how
much more exuberantly rejoice, in being citizens of a City
built upon the holy mount with living and chosen stones,
'Jesus Christ himself being the chief corner stone.' " He
went on to stress the breath-taking wonder of being a Catholic: "For no greater glory, no higher dignity, no honour
more sublime, can be conceived than that of belonging to the
Holy, Catholic, Apostolic and Roman Church, wherein we
become members of this one venerable Body, are governed
by this one august Head, filled with the one divine Spirit,
and nourished during this earthly exile with one doctrine and
with one Bread of Angels, until at last we come to enjoy in
heaven one everlasting happiness." (*The Mystical Body*)

Pope John, in the speech with which he opened Vatican
II, joined his voice to the triumphant voice of the past,
"whose echo we like to hear in the memories of the more
recent Pontiffs, our predecessors," and showed how deeply
he was moved by their voices "which proclaim in perennial
fervour the triumph of that divine and human institution,
the Church of Christ."

The Vatican Council took up the triumphal song of
the Church warmed by truth and love. The radiance of
the Holy Spirit, it taught, brightens her countenance. She
is the "spotless spouse of the spotless Lamb," the unique
Church of Christ which "transcends all limits of time and
of race," and is "strengthened by the power of God's grace
promised to her by the Lord, so that in the weakness of the
flesh she may not waver from perfect fidelity, but remain a
bride worthy of her Lord." Moreover, she is not a questing
Church as some would have her. "Blessed be God!" said
Cardinal Newman, "We have not to find the Truth, it is put
into our hands; we have but to commit it to our hearts, to
preserve it inviolate, and to deliver it over to our posterity,"[1]
and the Council echoed him, proclaiming that "the very fullness of grace and truth" is already in the Church's hands,
and that she has a monopoly of "the fullness of the means

[1] *Parochial and Plain Sermons*, vol. 11, Sermon XXII.

of salvation"—though both Cardinal and Council would have us always study to penetrate more deeply into the meaning of the truth committed to us.

A true Catholic is, then, by definition a blessed and happy man. According to the measure in which his faith possesses him, he approximates to the legendary lay-brother, nicknamed 'the Smiler', who, when asked why he always smiled, replied, "I smile because no man can take my God away from me!" But listen now to Bishop Christopher Butler speaking of the Church of today:[2] "I think there's an awful lot of worrying about oneself among the younger generation of the present day. . . . I was talking to a priest the other day who in his time has done a fair amount of parish mission work and he was saying to me that you occasionally come across an advanced progressive in the congregation. You could always spot them, he said, because they never laugh." They never laugh . . . . and they see nothing to smile about, and little to love in the Church. And it awakens echoes of seventy years ago. Here is Fr. Gabriel Daly, O.S.A., writing on *The Character of George Tyrrell* in *The Heythrop Journal* for July, 1969: "Religion . . . was rarely for him a thing of joy. . . . Miserable honesty is a very fair description of his fundamental state of mind at least in the face of religion and conscience."

God bless God's great Church, but the tiny stage-army of Sad Men is back among us! Their damp presence is detectable in almost every country. Monica Furlong wrote in *The Sunday Times* (August 4, 1968): "There is often a kind of shattered honesty about the utterances of the radicals. . . . 'The current has been switched off, and we find ourselves a bunch of men living in a cold and featureless house, hardly knowing each other, and wondering what we are doing and why,' said the Benedictine Sebastian Moore. . . ." while the German Bishop Kampe lamented in 1965 that for certain Catholic 'reformers' "absolute triumphalism has given way to a scepticism as absolute."[3] And the result? Mr. Hugh

---

[2] *Catholic Herald,* August 2, 1968.
[3] *Herder Correspondence,* August, 1965.

Kay set it down in this way: "We are supposed to be preaching the gospel message to every creature, but nobody knows
what it is."[4] "Count us out of that generalization!" the
great body of the faithful would rightly cry.

LADY BLENNERHASSETT'S
WASHERWOMAN

"The current has been switched off," Sebastian Moore
said. Yet the Holy Spirit is the 'current' which energises
and warms the Church and this Spirit does not switch off;
thus the "bunch of men living in a cold and featureless
house" must be re-assessed as a small bunch of men grown
cold to the warm House of God. These men are mainly
Modernists, and a Modernist (leaving a definition until later)
must be described as a Christian mutation who tries to ease
his tragic abnormality by claiming to voice a *consensus
fidelium* or at least a consensus of the educated or the 'theologians of any standing.' Yet the simple rank-and-file Catholics, those to whom, Jesus said, the Father reveals His
secrets, scorn a consensus which flouts common-sense. At
the time of the first wave of Modernism, Lady Blennerhassett, though a disciple of Döllinger and therefore pre-
disposed to look coolly upon Rome, delighted Chesterton by
saying, "I must have the same religion as my washerwoman,
and Father Tyrrell's is not the religion for my washerwoman."

Maisie Ward, in *Insurrection versus Resurrection* (p.
569), Appendix C., prints a letter from her father, Wilfrid
Ward, to Lord Hugh Cecil (1911), which reveals how normal
Catholics were able to discern spirits in the Church. He
writes of an agnostic lady who had become a Catholic, and
of the way in which she was able to hold to the truth during
the Modernist turmoil: 'Two things she specially noted, one
was that in practice the individual Catholic gets ample sanc-
tion in authoritative quarters for such breadth of view as is
required; the other was that the Modernists and extreme
Liberal Catholics lost that high ethical tone which was to

---

[4] *The Scottish Catholic Observer,* June 6, 1969.

her one great evidence of the truth of the Catholic religion. She found the priests at Chartres, though persons of little education, far more congenial to her own broad Catholicism than the Liberal Catholics and Modernists she met, because the spiritual quality and obedient temper which were essential to her own broad views were conspicuously absent from the view of these Modernists, though they professed to be broad. On the other hand the simple Chartres priests had this side most fully developed, and she found their incidental narrowness to be only the limited view of a child which has in it nothing repulsive." It is educative to turn from that story to the *Catholic Herald* editorial of 59 years later (April 17, 1970) and read its comment on 38 proposals made by a group of progressive priests of the Liverpool diocese (one of the proposals being that a parochial priest should no longer be obliged to provide a daily Mass): ". . . the petitioning priests . . . have introduced this trade union element . . . and . . . seem bent on turning the Church into a tired branch of the Civil Service . . . What is most depressing about it is the negative nature of the proposals in so far as they concern the spiritual side of a priest's life . . . the priesthood would obviously be changed . . . from being, admittedly, hard, into being soft."

WHAT IS MODERNISM?

History, then, is repeating itself and both the doctrine and the impoverished ethos of Modernism are coming back. But what is this Modernism, so often mentioned, so rarely defined? If theology is faith seeking understanding, modernism is disbelief seeking repose. A Modernist is a man who has lost faith in the Church and her doctrines but cannot steel himself to admit it; therefore he has to fill the traditional dogmas with new content, chanting as he does so the Modernist hymn *Plus ça change, plus c'est la même chose.* The early Modernists have, of course, their champions and heirs. Fr. Thomas Corbishley, S.J., who holds that "it is the conservatives who evince self-righteousness to an almost Phar-

isaical degree,"[5] judged: "What Loisy, Tyrrell and the rest
were concerned to do was to find a manner of presentation
of the faith which, by taking into account the findings of
modern scholarship, would make it intellectually acceptable
to their contemporaries. In principle they were trying to
do what John XXIII recognised as necessary, to bring the
faith up to date . . . if, in the end, they became somewhat
embittered, this was in no small part due to the total failure
of those in authority to appreciate what they were trying to
do";[6] "But in the early years of this century, when orthodoxy was equated with a rigidly defined philosophical method . . . to embark on such pursuits . . . was to enter into a
veritable minefield . . . if the authorities had been . . . less
obsessed with a mechanical view of religious truth, they
need not have driven men to such desperation."[7]

This kind of judgment, of course, is disarmed by the admissions which come peeping through . . . "trying to do" . . .
"in principle." He is wrong, of course, in writing that the
authorities did not appreciate what they were trying to do.
The authorities did appreciate it, at least when the Modernists came out into the open; but the real concern of the
Church's magisterium was not with the 'in principle' but with
the 'in fact'; not with what they were trying to do, but with
what they were doing. Like Lady Blennerhasset's washerwoman, the magisterium was not propelled by a 'mechanical
view of religious truth' but by faith in God's revelation.

Again, Fr. Henry St. John, O.P., wrote in *The Tablet*
(September 30, 1967): "This new movement was met by
an absolute authority, fearfully demanding a submission that
was not and could not be freely given. It failed, as such
authority always will fail, to serve truth, because it greatly
inhibited freedom." There is more than one point to be made
here. First, there is the submission which "could not be
freely given." Newman once wrote of a gentleman named
Henry Formby, "He is only half a man if he can't put his

[5] *The Tablet,* April 3, 1971.
[6] *Catholic Herald,* November 10, 1970.
[7] *Catholic Herald,* May 26, 1972.

book into the fire when told by authority." Alas, few of us measure up to Newman's standard but his standard, exacting as it is, is the supernatural one. Again, Fr. St. John has suggested that Pius X "failed to serve truth," but, in fact, we have only to look at the tattered creeds of other Churches to see how well he served it. "Learned Catholics," wrote Père de Grandmaison, "were warned, the younger clergy preserved, the future saved." A Christian is unworthy of the name if he will not submit to lawful authority fulfilling its duty. It was a Presbyterian, Professor W. Barclay, who reminded us that "A Christian is a man who has accepted the fact that he can never again do what he likes; and that he must for ever after do what God likes." And, at the time of a far greater crisis, the Reformation, it was, as Wilfred Ward reminded the Modernist Fr. Fawkes (who subsequently left the Church), St. Thomas More who said that he would burn his criticisms of authority, *however just*, rather than that they should be used to help rebellion.

As we have seen, in quotation from Fr. Corbishley, the early Modernists attempted to adjust the Church's doctrines to what they considered were the 'findings of modern scholarship.' In the process, they changed the content of the doctrine, and therefore worked to destroy Christianity. *That* is why the Church reacted with such firmness, indeed over-reacted. That the Modernists were working to destroy the Faith was evident even to a non-believer like Professor George Santayana. He wrote in *Winds of Doctrine*, Chapter II, *Modernism and Christianity* (1913): "The modernists think the church is doomed if it turns a deaf ear to the higher criticism or ignores the philosophy of M. Bergson. But it has outlived greater storms. . . . The biblical criticism and mystical speculations of the modernists call for no special remark; they are such as any studious or spiritual person, with no inherited religion, might compose in our day. But what is remarkable and well-nigh incredible is that even for one moment they should have supposed this non-Christian criterion in history and this non-Christian direction in metaphysics compatible with adherence to the Catholic Church.

That seems to presuppose, in men who are in fact particularly thoughtful and learned, an inexplicable ignorance of
history, of theology, and of the world."

'ALL THEOLOGIANS OF ANY STANDING'

We stop there for a moment to consider the paradox in
that last sentence. First, we are told that the Modernists
were especially learned, and then we are told that they were
inexplicably ignorant of history, theology and men. Are the
statements compatible? They are to those who have digested what Chambers' Dictionary says about 'intellectual',
that it is "often used to suggest doubt as to practical sagacity,"
and to those who perceive the realism of what I wrote some
years back, that 'intellectual' "is often used to indicate an
educated odd-bod whose sense of reality is in inverse ratio
to his self-conceit."[8] The truth is that the Modernists were
talented men, with enormous blind-spots and a special talent
for shutting their eyes to reality. Here is Michele Ranchetti,
passing judgment in his *The Catholic Modernists* (1961; pp.
viii & 6): "the modernists cared nothing for the historical
order, for historical reasoning, or for any event in the history
of the Church, however it was understood . . . Loisy's flaw
lay in his sense of history . . . a fact proved by his almost
total lack of understanding of what inspired the most important event in the history of the Church in his day: the
Vatican Council. This lack of an historical sense was found
in nearly all the modernists and religious philosophers who
came after him." Especially, we may add, in Teilhard de
Chardin who was impatient of historical facts.

One understands now why that talented man, Father
Martindale, said that Modernism was the one heresy to which
he could extend no intellectual respect. Indeed, modernism
is likely to flourish mainly when there is a dearth of talent.
Giants like Newman or Chesterton can hold up an ancient
doctrine in the light of their intelligence and make a thousand
facets sparkle, turning what had become a truism back into

[8] *The Scotsman,* March 21, 1967.

a dazzling truth. It is lesser men who can be original only by practising brinkmanship or Bultmannship, and there is irony in the fact that Fr. Tyrrell, reviewing Chesterton's introduction to the Book of Job, should have shaken his head sadly: "What a pity, then, that Mr. Chesterton . . . should don the heavy armour of the abstract philosopher and critic, and descend into the dusty arena of their interminable discussions. Why do able men always prize their second-best talent most dearly?" (*The Nation*, June 15, 1907.) Four months later, Tyrrell was forbidden the sacraments, and, the next year, Chesterton's great *Orthodoxy* appeared.

The moral is that we must not accept the self-evaluation of a Modernist, Tyrrell or Schillebeeckx, Loisy or Küng.[9] First of all, the early Modernists were naive in their scholarship. As Fr. Bevenot remarked in his review of John Ratte's *Three Modernists:*[10] "They mistook the bare beginnings of the scientific study of the Bible for a mature and infallible discipline." Second, there was a strain of intellectual defeatism in Tyrrell. Father Crehan wrote: ". . . Tyrrell professed interests in literary and speculative matters, but not in historical research. . . . Tyrrell had not the inclination or the equipment to make of himself a scholar. . . . He wrote (to Thurston): 'However much researches like yours would be according to my taste, I am afraid they are out of my power.'" The result was that, while Fr. Thurston tackled objections and showed superior scholarship, Tyrrell "came to the conclusion that there was no way through these enquiries that would allow him to keep his faith, and therefore a new foundation for faith must be sought."[11]

Third, there was, at least in Tyrrell, a positive dislike for clarity; clarity tied a man down, clarity made it a matter of 'Yes' or 'No'. Fr. Gabriel Daly wrote (*Art. cit.* p. 272): "He believed that clearness was a snare for the unwary . . . and that the snare is avoided as long as one *distrusts* clear-

---

[9] "My dear Küng, you are very sure of yourself. Are you not pushing the valuation of your theological gift very far?" Fr. Yves Congar, O.P., *The Tablet*, July 25, 1970.
[10] *The Heythrop Journal*, July, 1969.
[11] *Father Thurston*, pp. 51-52.

ness and recognises it as a note of inadequacy." This dislike of clarity is prevalent in radical circles again today, as a letter in the *Catholic Herald* for April 28, 1972, showed by opposing clarity in Eucharistic statements, but it sets at naught all the work of the Councils and the theologians. Listen to Newman attacking the same error in his day: "It is a fashion of the day to suppose that all insisting upon precise Articles of Faith is injurious to the cause of spiritual religion, and inconsistent with an enlightened view of it. . . . Accordingly, instead of accepting reverently the doctrinal Truths, an attempt is made by the reasoners of this age to refashion them—to scrutinize them, with a view of separating the inward holy sense from the form of words, in which the Spirit has indissolubly lodged them. Such a one asks himself, what is the *use* of the message? He proceeds to assume that there is some end, such as to be ascertainable by him; next he measures all the doctrines by their respective tendency to effect this one end. He goes on to discard or degrade this or that sacred truth as superfluous in consequence, and throws the stress of his teaching on one or another, which he pronounces to contain in it the essence of the Gospel. Lastly, he reconstructs the language of theology to suit his (so-called) improved views of doctrine." This, of course, is an attack upon the Liberal Protestantism which in turn appeared in the Catholic Church as Modernism, and it is ironic, in view of Newman's resounding words, that, when *Pascendi* appeared, many read it as a condemnation of Newman, simply because the Modernists had parodied his doctrine of development.

Fourth, there was deliberate ambiguity in the writings of the Modernist clique. They made their doctrines appear tentative and vague, Pius X said in his encyclical, "when on the contrary they are firm and constant." "Tentative and vague . . ." And today again some Catholics do not assert but play the role of the earnest enquirer, getting as much across as if they had forcefully asserted. Consider this passage from *Search* (November, 1966) and note how the Faith is pensively unravelled:

"Following the logical consequences of re-interpreting Original Sin, the thinking Catholic will have to face even more fundamental changes. . . . If there is no Original Sin, what does the Immaculate Conception mean? Just what can it *possibly* mean to say that Mary was conceived without sin? . . . . In an evolutionary context an immaculate conception is meaningless. And this brings us up against the infallibility with which this dogma was pronounced in 1854. What does infallibility mean if it issues in meaningless statements? . . . . The assembled bishops of the world in Vatican I declared that the Pope was infallible, and how valid is their judgment if they themselves are not collectively infallible—and how does one determine the necessary quorum for infallibility?"

Tentative, indeed; the gentleman was only asking! And, when Dr. Küng was careful to put a question mark after *Infallible* when he published his recent book, how did a non-Catholic reviewer, Dr. Cecil Northcott, come to write bluntly: "Dr. Küng scorns the infallible idea whether it is the Pope and Church, Bishops and Church, or Bible and Church"[12] and a Cardinal write to me this very week: "I am sure that Küng has long ceased to be a believing Catholic"?

CARDINAL MERCIER

Careful ambiguities are to the fore again today, since a man who has lost his faith tries to lose, not deny, doctrine, if he wishes to stay in his niche. I quote the technique of writing admitted to by a contributor to *The Experience of Priesthood* who is determined to keep down-wind of the censor: "One learns the use of the double meaning, the tortuously complex sentences and paragraphs which conceal meaning rather than reveal it." The complete un-christianity of such behaviour puts us in a better position now to continue with Santayana's analysis: "Modernism . . . is the love of all Christianity in those who perceive that it is all a fable. It is the historic attachment to his church of a Catholic who has discovered that he is a pagan . . . they (Modern-

[12] *Daily Telegraph*, July 1, 1971.

ists) are men of the Renaissance, pagan and pantheistic in their profounder sentiment, to whom the hard and narrow realism of official Christianity is offensive just because it presupposes that Christianity is true. . . . As to modernism, it is suicide. It is the last of those concessions to the spirit of the world which half-believers and double-minded prophets have always been found making; but it is a mortal concession. It concedes everything; for it concedes that everything in Christianity, as Christians hold it, is an illusion."

The judgment that Modernists are basically pagan rests on the fact that they reject both Christian doctrine and fixed Christian morality; more on this later. To the 'half-believers and double-minded' Catholics of his time, Cardinal Mercier made a call for honest speaking, in his Lenten Pastoral following on *Pascendi:* "The excommunication pronounced by the Pope against obstinate Modernists, which our enemies represent as an act of despotism, is the most simple and natural thing in the world."

"My Brethren, we have here merely a question of honesty. Yes or No? Do you believe in the divine authority of the Church? Do you accept exteriorly and interiorly what, in the name of Jesus Christ, she proposes to your belief? Yes or No? Will you consent to obey her?"

"If Yes, then she puts the sacraments at your disposal and undertakes your safe conduct to Heaven."

"If No, you deliberately break the bond that united you to her, of which she had tied and blessed the knot. Before God and your conscience you belong to her no more. Honesty forbids you to pass yourself off any longer as one of her sons; and she who will not and cannot be an accomplice in your sacrilegious hypocrisy requests you, and if necessary summons you, to leave her ranks."

Yet the faithless sons, the Sad Men, were singularly reluctant to leave then as now. Jacques Maritain writes in *The Peasant of the Garonne* (p. 6) of today's "immanent" apostasy, but it is also yesterday's, and the reasons for the Modernist's wishing to remain in the Church are not all discreditable. Loisy, writing in *Choses passées* of the period c.

1886, explained: "I had been able for several years to half-blind myself in regard to the true state of my mind, to the implication of the essential conclusions of biblical criticism, to the manner of reconciling these with traditional dogmas without abandoning the substance of these latter. Now I could no longer hide from myself that the position was other than I had imagined, that I was outside the current of Catholic thought; that, if one wished to interpret dogmas in keeping with science and the modern outlook . . . a recasting of the whole Catholic system was indispensable. . . . Highly logical people will wonder why not only the idea, but the obligation, of leaving the Church did not present themselves then to my mind. The idea could not fail to occur, but the obligation which I thought that I understood was to remain in the Church. The true reason was that I remained attached to her from the bottom of my heart. . . . Almost in spite of myself, I kept trying to do the impossible, and it needed the Church to teach me, by sharp, repeated blows, that a priest has no right to be half-Catholic, that . . . as Cardinal Merry del Val wrote to the Bishop of Langres, in January, 1908, my 'remaining in the Church' was an 'insupportable scandal'."

The very fact, of course, that the Modernist has lost any idea of the true nature of the Church and her teaching can make it easier for him to remain. Here is Tyrrell writing *A Letter to a University Professor* (the professor, as he admitted later, being entirely fictional, though at one time he tried to claim that he was real): "As to the reasons you have put down on paper, I might quarrel with some of them in detail; but taken all together they constitute a massive objection against received theological positions which, frankly, I am unable to solve. . . . Let it be granted, for argument's sake, that things are quite as bad as you say, and that the intellectual defence of Catholicism breaks down on every side . . . does it straightway follow you should separate yourself from the communion of the Church? Yes, if theological 'intellectualism' be right; if faith mean mental assent. . . . No, if Catholicism be primarily a life. . . . Where do we find

Christ insisting on the spiritual necessity or advantage of beliefs that perplex or do violence to the senses and intelligence of His hearers. . . ?"

His final question is loaded and septic, but the passage serves to reveal the way in which Modernists insist on speaking of *theology* when it is in fact a matter of fundamental doctrine—which is precisely what they still do. "Catholic college head denies one theology" ran a recent newspaper headline,[13] relating to Fr. Hubert J. Richards who has since resigned from his post as principal of Corpus Christi College of Catechetics, London; it will later appear that Fr. Richards rejects one Lord, one Faith, for one tattered Modernist theology. But, to give Tyrrell his due, he does not give the impression of tossing a coin as does Fr. Richard P. McBrien today: "Pope John is one of the many good reasons for remaining within the Roman Catholic communion, and Charles Davis has capably enumerated some of the many reasons for leaving or remaining apart from the Roman Catholic Church. Neither side has an absolute claim in terms of the evidence adduced. Neither side need be embarrassed or unsettled by the decision taken or reaffirmed."[14]

ORTHODOXY

Again, Tyrrell has revealed in this 'apologia' for immanent heresy the low value which his group set on *truth*. Maisie Ward related in *Insurrection versus Resurrection* (p. 491) how the concern of her wonderful father for religious truth served only to irritate Baron von Hügel, the godfather and telephone-exchange of the early Modernist movement: "As early as 1899 von Hügel wrote irritably to Loisy about my father's mania for discussing the orthodoxy of points of view and methods 'when what is needed is to bring our people to look at the reality of things and the legitimacy of scientific methods.' Wilfrid Ward, he said, 'manoeuvres to get air for us,' but 'meanwhile he is always tending to trace

[13] *Daily Telegraph*, January 17, 1972.
[14] *Do We Need the Church*, p. 189.

limits, to set up no-thoroughfare signs, *ce qui n'est que nous enfermer dans la vieille cage.'* "

Who would ever have ever thought that the concern for truth, in Wilfrid Ward's shining intelligence, would have been met by a grumble, when not one doctrine but the whole of Christian belief was at stake? Professor Jean Rivière, in *Le Modernisme dans L'Église* (1929), the classic work, quotes on p. 11 a contemporary Protestant authority, K. Holl (*Der Modernismus*, p. 3): "The struggle no longer revolves on an isolated dogma . . . but on the totality of the Christian faith as the Catholic Church has understood and proclaimed it. A group, of note because of the names of its leaders, has tried to make, between Catholic faith and modern thought, a reconciliation which would end in reality in the complete overthrow of the whole theological and hierarchical system of Catholicism." Thus it was that Tyrrell confessed: "It is not, as they suppose, about this or that article of the creed that we differ; we accept it all; but it is the word 'credo'; the sense of 'true' as applied to dogma; the whole value of revelation that is at stake." That this is still valid will appear from the July (1972) number of the Corpus Christi College magazine, *The Sower*, the swansong of Fr. Hubert Richards and his group when they resigned their posts after differences with Cardinal Heenan; it tears the creed to shreds.[15] It will be referred to hereafter as *that* issue of *The Sower*.

Finally, 'immanent' heresy was defended on the grounds that the Catholic Church was at least the best of a dreadful bunch, and the Modernists might still be able to save her. When an ex-Catholic ex-Dominican wrote to Fr. de Chardin and asked why he also did not shake the dust of Rome off his feet, the Jesuit did not reply with a profession of faith in the divine institution of the Church but with: ". . . I still do not see any better means of bringing about what I antici-

---

[15] It is regrettable and perplexing that Cardinal Heenan should have stressed that "I have never made any objection to what is taught at Corpus Christi . . . I have never thought that the teaching . . . was unorthodox . . ." (*Catholic Herald,* January 4, 1972.)

pate than to work towards the reformation (as defined above)
from within: that is, by remaining sincerely attached to the
'phylum' whose development I expect to see. . . . I find that
only the Roman stem, taken in its entirety, can provide a
biological support vast enough. . . ."[16] Tyrrell phrased it less
scientifically: "The Roman communion may be no more
than the charred stump of a tree torn to pieces by gales and
rent by thunderbolts; she may be and probably is more responsible for all the schisms than the schismatics themselves,
yet, unlike them all, she stands for the principle of Catho-
licity, for the idea of a spiritually united humanity centred
round Christ in one society."[17] This is what Tyrrell himself
called the "grub view" of the Church, in a letter dated January 25, 1905. Just as Judaism could be regarded as "the
larval form, the lowly grub," from which came Christianity,
so true Christianity might grow out of the present Church;
this Church is not the reality, the spotless Bride of Christ.
Here again we hear today vague echoes of Tyrrell. Just as
Magdalen Goffin, in *Objections to Roman Catholicism*, dismissed the doctrine of hell, the doctrine which prompted
Tyrrell's early "A Perverted Devotion" and ensuing trouble
with Rome, so her father, Professor E. I. Watkin, wrote in
The Future of Catholic Christianity, of the Third Kingdom
of the Spirit which will replace the Catholic Church, as she
succeeded the Synagogue.

The enemy of true Christianity was, of course, Rome.
"Will the Roman bureaucracy, that exploits even the Papacy,
ever resign their revenues and their ascendency? Modernists
do not believe it for a moment. Their whole hope is in the
irresistible tide of truth and knowledge, which must at last
surround and overmount the barriers of ignorance, buttressed up by untruthfulness; and, above all, in such inward
and living Christianity, as may still be left in a rapidly dying
Church. . . . While such hopes, be they ever so elusive, live
in him why should the Modernist leave his Church? . . .

---

[16] Cf Fr. G. H. Duggan, *Teilhardism & the Faith,* p. 68.
[17] *A Letter to a University Professor.*

Deliverance comes from below, from those who are bound, not from those who bind."[18]

It is drearily familiar. The Modernist, said Santayana, "feels himself full of love—except for the pope." (*Op. cit.*, p. 48.) He prefers to speak, however, of Roman bureaucracy or the Curia rather than the Vicar of Christ; *tu es Petrus* still petrifies him. "The Roman bureaucracy, that exploits even the Papacy" equals Dr. Küng's "this bureaucratic apparatus, with its wealth of traditions and stratagems, considered to have little love for the present Pope as well as the Council . . . backward-looking, ghetto-bound" (*The Changing Church*, Chapter X). "Untruthfulness" recalls the title of another Küng book and a hundred of his complaints, but the word came ill from Tyrrell who admitted to Laurence Housman, "I never claimed to be more than indifferent honest." And the "rapidly dying Church"? "The Catholic Church is breaking up," Charles Davis told us as he bowed out. Really, it has been an unconscionable time a-dying, especially when we remember that, when Pius VI died in 1799, it was widely supposed that the papacy had come to an end, and that, in the years before 1829, Sydney Smith supported Catholic Emancipation on the frank grounds that the Church was moribund.

A PRIDE OF MODERNISTS

It is far from my intention to deal with the many *personae* of the First Act of the Modernist tragedy, with such priests as Marcel Hébert, who left the Church in 1903, Albert Houtin (left 1912), Hyacinthe Loyson (who married), Fawkes (who also left), and Murri (excommunicated in 1909). The following chapters will centre on Loisy and Tyrrell, the priests whose errors will be repeatedly laid beside their modern counterparts. And yet we have something important to learn from the story of such men before passing on. Hébert published one of the earliest Modernist manifestos, bringing out in 1900-1901 a booklet under the innocuous title *Souve-*

---

[18] *Christianity at the Cross-roads,* Chapter VI.

nirs d'Assise. In it, he made clear that the 'modern spirit'
could accept some dogmas purely as symbols. This may have
seemed to many a cloud on the horizon no larger than a
man's first, but wise heads were already alert to danger. In
1900 the English hierarchy felt constrained to bring out a
joint pastoral distinguishing between the *ecclesia docens* and
the *ecclesia discens*, since the role of the *magisterium* was
already being questioned. When his book came under attack,
it was a case, as so often in the Modernist story, of "Pale
Faith speaks with forked tongue." Hébert wrote to Cardinal
Richard of Paris: "I believe in the *objective value* of the
idea of God, in the *objective value* of the Resurrection of
Christ," and there followed the usual complaint that it was
all a misunderstanding: "People have misunderstood me or
have not chosen to understand me and they have confused
the fact with the explanation of the fact. . . ." He had carefully avoided saying that he believed in God or in the *fact*
of the Resurrection; and this man had written, not long before, of the divine personality as "the last of the idols."

The Abbé Loyson is worth a passing mention for more
than one reason. First, it was he perhaps who fathered a
now well-known Modernist distinction between Roman and
Catholic or Roman and Christian. Writing in 1869, he protested against "doctrines which are called Roman, but are
not Christian"; it is the precise distinction made in Dr.
Küng's *Infallible?* Next, Fr. Loyson was one of the first
priests of this period to marry, and seemed to expect that
many others would hasten to exchange their set of vows. Not
many did, and his act had the opposite effect to what he
intended.

Baron von Hügel, in the second volume of his *Essays and
Addresses*, Chapter IV, related how his wife, at that time
non-Catholic, was visiting the Episcopalian Bishop of Argyll
and the Isles. One morning he appeared deeply distressed
and, in the course of a walk, explained what had so perturbed
him. He had thought that the Abbé Loyson would help to
bring about a 'reform' of the Catholic Church, and neither
his expulsion from the Carmelite Order nor his excommunication had dashed that hope. That morning, however, he had

learned of the ex-priest's marriage, and the Bishop felt that
this act ruled him out as an effective agent of reform. Why?
The Baron, himself at the centre of the Modernist Movement,
remarked that he had often "wondered at the insensibility
of many, even otherwise highly gifted and sincerely religious
persons . . . with respect to this, surely not very abstruse or
very difficult point. For Christianity is—is it not?—centrally
a religion of renunciation, of heroism."

PRIESTLY CELIBACY

He went on to say that he trusted that the Bishop understood the deep feeling shared by Catholics regarding priestly
celibacy, "that here was not simply a strong prejudice which
wise men would not unnecessarily affront, but a high aspira-
tion, a heart of nobility, which good men ought to respect,"
a form of "that renunciation, that asceticsm" which every
religion must in some way inculcate. Fr. Loyson had acted
in a human manner, though he had contracted to live by
supernatural, not natural, standards, and had broken his
contract. Thus he had made a mockery of his own claim to
work for reform.

The Baron added more evidence of the acuteness of the
Protestant Bishop's perception. Fr. Murri, the Christian
Democratic leader, had married an American lady and many
non-Catholics innocently supposed that this would further
his 'reform' work. Yet, the Baron recounted, the Christian
Democratic League, having expressed their appreciation of
Murri's high qualities, went on to insist that "if Christianity,
the religion of heroism, is to be solidly sustained, still more
if it is to be seriously renovated, this can be done only by
maintaining, indeed increasing, the heroism present at the
time of the attempt at reform. . . ." and expelled him from
the organisation. Finally, von Hügel contrasted with Murri's
defection the unfaltering celibacy of the Abbé Huvelin[19]—"he
willed, used and loved this renunciation as an instrument,

---

[19] It was the Abbé Huvelin who advised von Hugel: "Never read
religious papers. They will expose you to all sorts of temptations
and do you no end of harm."

condition and price of the tenderest love of souls in God and of God"—told how the Abbé rushed to the side of the ex-Carmelite when the latter's wife died, and extended to him all the sympathy of a warm heart, but added that the Abbé never relaxed "his sense of the heroic spirit of Christianity, and his deep regret that a priest and a friar had not somehow been able, or been willing, to hold out in the particular kind and degree of heroism he had at first undertaken, and to which the very best instincts in the best Roman Catholics rise in reverent respect and profound trust."

These words bear pondering when so many 'reformers' are mouthing deep respect for celibacy and then crying for the option which would sweep it away. It is a cry against the cross, a cry for a smaller love to replace a greater; that is why a man tinged with the Modernist spirit tends to write of priestly celibacy without ever mentioning the love of God. Looking back, I see that, when Charles Davis wrote in 1966 on *The Meaning and Privations of Celibacy*, without ever mentioning the priest's love of God, I wrote in the *Catholic Herald* (November 25): "To write of celibacy, with reference to the Tremendous Lover only in terms as impersonal as an algebraic symbol . . . is to cry with a vengeance for Hamlet without the Prince of Denmark. . . . Ophelia tends sooner or later to become the main object of interest." A month later, Davis announced his intention to marry.

"The modernism of Pius X's time," wrote Maritain (*Op. cit.*, p. 5), "was only a modest hayfever" compared with today's delirium. In April, 1972, the Vatican released the news that 13,440 priests had left the ministry between 1964 and 1970. Undoubtedly this was due in the main to a fever in the Church. And yet, paradoxically, the haemorrhage was a token of returning health, of reform. The spirit of Modernism bears within itself the seeds of its own destruction, and a priest affected by the modern spirit can be likened to the item in a well-known TV series—"this tape will self-destruct within five seconds of giving its message." The priest of today, not of eternity, mouths his sterile message and then he is gone. And when the faint of faith or heart have left, the Church can do God's work, the truth shine warm. In-

stead of the young priests whom, in some places, we have
come to know to our sorrow, the men of 'non serviam' for
all their love of the vernacular, we shall have again Chesterton's "Young priests with eager faces bright as eagles." They
may be priests according to the numbers of Gideon, but they
will also be according to the heart of Christ.[20]

[20] *The Scottish Catholic Observer* for December 11, 1970, carried the
report of an address by a seminary rector who stated that his seminary aimed at producing men, not 'mice' as in the past. But a not
inconsiderable number of 'men' have gone off after women, while
the 'mice' remained Church mice until their holy death. A senior
seminarist wrote of seminary life (*Catholic Herald,* November 5,
1971), stating that consultation and dialogue were key words in the
students' vocabulary, but not mentioning obedience.

2

The Abbé Loisy

He is speaking more particularly of modernists whose bringing up has been literally Catholic, who have remained Catholics in sentiment but not in belief.

HARVEY WICKHAM, The Unrealists

Alfred Firmin Loisy was born in 1857 and died in 1940. He was ordained priest in 1879, but was off-course in his spiritual life since he noted in an exercise-book in 1882 that he was suffering from great fevers, not only the fever for knowledge and the fever for work—highly commendable— but also the fever for glory, which is in dismal contrast to Père Grandmaison's prayer for "un coeur tourmenté de la gloire de Jésus Christ." His express ambition was to become a Father of the Church; he ended up as the Father of Modernism in France. He entered the Institut Catholique in Paris in 1881, where he came under the influence of Monsignor Louis Duchesne, Professor of Church History. The influence was detrimental since, though Duchesne was a pioneer in the field of critical historical research, he was, as those who have read *The Beginnings of Temporal Sovereignty of the Popes* know, an adept at the cultivated sneer. Loisy was affected by the atmosphere of superior criticism and carried it into the field of Biblical research, but, at the same time, he was to become aware of his teacher's limitations. In his *Mémoires* he wrote of "the Voltairian manner which he assumed . . . An excellent sailor, he took in his sails as the storm grew wilder." Ernest Dimnet, in *My New World*, passed a similar verdict: "I never liked him. I did not like

23

his tendency to combine the advantages of boldness with the profits of orthodoxy. I did not like his wit which I thought semi-professional and suspected of being a convenient screen." Duchesne, however, did not reap all possible profits of orthodoxy. The unlucky man was suspended from teaching for two years for the simple reason that he had advanced the opinion that Mary Magdalen did not land in France. The rector of a seminary is said to have growled in consternation: "He will next attack Scripture itself."

The attack on Scripture, was, however, to come from his pupil Loisy; one is reminded of the dictum that Luther hatched the egg which Erasmus laid. In the same year that Loisy came under the influence of Duchesne, he was appointed lecturer in Hebrew and the Old Testament. Then, from 1882 to 1885, he attended the lectures of Renan whose *La Vie de Jésus* had appeared in 1863. Loisy acknowledged now a new master—"le premier maitre des modernistes français," he called him; he was drawn towards pantheism, and, by July, 1901, was admitting that "the question of God was a problem for him and that the attribution of personality to God seemed to him anthropomorphism." This was two years before the appearance of *L'Évangile et L'Église* which was to cause many intellectual Catholics to hail him as a defender of the Faith. Meanwhile, his critical approach to Scripture was shredding Catholic belief. "My attentive reading of the Gospels immediately destroyed the idea I had been given of them. Faith told me that these writings were wholly divine; reason showed me that they were wholly human, in no way exempt from contradictions. . . ." (*That* number of *The Sower*, p. 68, echoes: "The gospels are entirely human documents, and therefore no more free from historical error than any other ancient document.") Loisy, we note, began with a faulty supposition of what faith inculcated, and replaced it with a worse conclusion. Once again, one experiences the minor shock that is always imparted when the confident expert proves himself naive. One must bear in mind what Ranchetti wrote of Loisy: "his whole personal and intellectual development, his entire religious experience, were marked by an irrevocable refusal to obey. . . . Loisy was remarkably uncritical, and for this reason remarkably intransigent; nowhere in the *Mémoires* is there the slightest doubt or uncertainty, either intellectual or moral . . ."[1] *The Oxford Dictionary of the Universal Church* passes a different judgment but it is even more destructive of the Modernist's claim to be taken as a serious scholar: "Much of his Biblical work does not seem, however, to have convinced even himself, and he readily abandoned his theories without misgivings." The tragedy is that his Faith should also have been abandoned on the basis of such ephemeral guesswork. Little remains of all his labours, but the dying Church endures.

L'ÉVANGILE ET L'ÉGLISE

In 1893, Loisy brought out a bi-monthly magazine, *L'Enseignement Biblique,* and published in it two articles on 'The Biblical Problem and the Inspiration of Scripture.' Gasquet wrote highly of them, but the outcome was that the author was dismissed from the Institut and the encyclical *Providentissimus Deus* was brought out to vindicate the inspiration and inerrancy of the Scriptures. Loisy was sent to Neuilly, to be chaplain to a convent of Dominican nuns. He wrote in *Choses passées* (1913): "How much wiser the bishops would have been if they had kept me at Hebrew grammar and cuneiform texts! During my five years at Neuilly, my mind was in perpetual travail over Catholic doctrine, working to adapt it to the needs of the contemporary mind. It would be a gross error to imagine that this was no more than an idle diversion or even a work of pure speculation. I had not refound, for my own benefit, the naive faith of my childhood. I did not accept literally one article of the creed, save that Jesus was 'crucified under Pontius Pilate'; but religion appeared in my eyes more and more as an immense force. . . . In spite of what the Church had made me suffer, I remained sincerely devoted to her." These were the years in which *L'Évangile et L'Église* was brewed, and here is his own description of the frame of mind which lay behind it. . . .

[1] *The Catholic Modernists,* p. 37.

"I was far from having lost all moral faith. What I had lost was the fire of enthusiasm which had sustained me in so many difficulties since the day I entered the seminary. That beautiful and juvenile trust collapsed with the idea which had at first inspired it. I had managed, for several years, to half-blind myself to my true state of mind, to the import of the necessary conclusions of biblical criticism, to the method of reconciling them with traditional dogmas without jettisoning the substance of these latter. Now I could not hide from myself that the position was not as I had imagined; that I was outside the current of Catholic thought; that, if one wished to interpret dogmas in keeping with science and the modern mind, a more or less broad, new interpretation—one which, in the case of doctrines like the virgin birth of Christ or his resurrection, would crumple with the reality of their content—would not do; that a recasting of the whole Catholic system was essential."

Harnack had published in 1902 *Wesen des Christentums* in which he tried to uncover authentic Christianity by stripping from the teaching of the historic Christ what he held to be dogmatic accretions of later centuries; this was to be a 'liberalisation' of theology. (Chesterton, in *The Everlasting Man:* "There will be no end to the weary debates about liberalising theology, until people face the fact that the only liberal part of it is really the dogmatic part.") Two years later, Loisy brought out *L'Évangile et L'Église* which seemed to be a Christian answer, though the author wrote carefully: "The aim of the work, as a matter of fact, is just to catch the point of view of history. In no sense is it an attempt to write an apologia for Catholicism or traditional dogma. Had it been so intended, it must have been regarded as very defective and incomplete, especially as far as concerns the divinity of Christ, and the authority of the Church. It is not designed to demonstrate the truth either of the gospel or of Catholic Christianity, but simply to analyze and define the bonds that unite the two in history. He who reads in good faith will not be misled."

But what about him who writes in bad faith? Will he not mislead? Dimnet said that he never saw any Machiavellianism in Loisy, but we have seen that he was concealing the loss of his Catholic Faith, and Maisie Ward asks, in *Insurrection versus Resurrection*, p. 163, "How was the reader to suspect that the words 'It is not my aim to prove the truth either of the Gospel or of Catholic Christianity,' were literally true because the author did not believe in either?" "In 1902," she wrote, "he was still in the eyes of the world a sincere Catholic priest and *savant*. . . . Did it seem *likely* that he would write a book condemning Our Lord's God-head? For that is what *L'Évangile et L'Église* really attempted." (p. 162.) It did not, and many were fooled by his move to find true Catholicism in the faith of the developed Church, and not even perturbed at first sight by his suggestion that Christ did not found a Church or give us the seven Sacraments.[2] And, having only half-digested Newman's doctrine of dogmatic development, they did not see the chasm which yawned between Newman's orthodoxy and Loisy's teaching in Section V, *The Christian Dogma*: "Though the dogmas may[3] be divine in origin and substance, they are human in structure and composition. It is inconceivable that their future should not correspond to their past. . . . it is no less natural that the creeds and dogmatic definitions should be related to the state of general human knowledge at the time and under the circumstances when they were constituted. It follows that

[2] From Douglas Woodruff's review (*Catholic Truth,* Spring, 1969) of Fr. Gregory Baum's *The Credibility of the Church Today. A Reply to Charles Davis:* "He is anxious to argue, following Hans Küng, that the claims of the Church cannot be vindicated from the New Testament, since modern scholarship has made us increasingly aware that the records which make up the New Testament are not only scrappy but are literary, in the sense of not trying to be straight history. They reflect feelings and ideas in the generation in which they were drawn up . . . . one is driven to think it is so uncertain what our Lord actually said and did, that the immense claims made for Scripture as the touch-stone for Christian Churches can hardly be maintained." Fr. Baum's reply to Davis seems to be much the same as Fr. Loisy's to Harnack.

[3] Note the careful 'may.' The charitable or innocent Catholic took it, without thinking, to mean 'is.' One has to watch for similar elusiveness today.

a considerable change in the state of knowledge might render necessary a new interpretation of old formulas, which conceived in another intellectual atmosphere, no longer say what is necessary, or no longer say it suitably . . ." A first, quick reading of the above might suggest that it is nothing more than common-sense; but the new interpretations that were desired were denials of the timeless truths. From now on, Loisy was to lay down terms the fulfilment of which, he thought, would make the Church 'habitable.' The modern version of his term is 'credible'; his call for re-interpretation was echoed by Tyrrell, and is voiced again today. Basically, it amounts to: "I have lost my Catholic Faith and can no longer believe in the Church or her teaching, but I will stay in her fold if you will change the teaching to my taste. Then it will be credible and she will be habitable." When one hears talk of the inadequacy of dogma, there is reason to take a hard look at what is being proposed in its place . . . as we shall see.

REACTIONS TO THE BOOK

The book was hailed by many leaders of Catholic thought. Even before its publication, the author had shown it to Archbishop Mignot who urged him to publish. Fr. Herbert Lucas gave it almost unqualified approval in *The Month*, while Dom Cuthbert Butler lauded it in *The Tablet*. Tyrrell, however, found it "too indiscriminately conservative," while Minocchi, it is said, passed on a copy to Cardinal Sarto, the future Pius X, who "expressed great satisfaction with it with the exception of certain passages he found obscure."

Baron von Hügel became Loisy's champion-at-arms and defended him for the next fifteen years, and this in innocence, since Loisy was writing in his journal at the time: "M. von Hügel who defends me so bravely believes very differently from me in the divinity of Jesus Christ. Setting aside metaphysical phraseology, I do not believe in the divinity of Jesus any more than Harnack . . . and I look on the personal Incarnation of God as a philosophic myth." There is something contemptible about this playing of theological poker. In June,

1904, poor von Hügel was battling against Blondel and defending Loisy's orthodoxy in *Du Christ éternel et de nos Christologies successives* in *Quinzaine*. The baron was a man of prayer, but it is evident that he was a bad judge of character and of 'ethos'. In addition, he was warped against authority, and had a facility for closing his eyes. Maisie Ward wrote that "His letters and his actions both during the years preceding *Pascendi* and those immediately following upon it are impregnated with a trust in the new learning and its exponents, and as profound a distrust of authority. . . . He positively encouraged any rebellion against it. . . . Loisy's gaining Catholic support for *L'Évangile et L'Église* must be largely attributed to von Hügel. Several letters in the *Mémoires* consist entirely of accounts of his propaganda. Almost all the favourable reviews that appeared in England were arranged for him both in Catholic and non-Catholic papers." (*Op. cit.*, p. 492.) Thus is a consensus of learned opinion framed. Later she writes: "Subconsciously he *would* not look at the gradual extinction of faith in his friend's mind."

But, if von Hügel had to defend Loisy, it meant that keener intellects were seeing the true nature of the work. Duchesne wrote to the author that Catholics would not understand the book, and "You may hope that they do not, for that is your only chance of escaping the fate of Giordano Bruno." Père Lagrange, the great Dominican scholar, spoke of the need of condemnation, while Batiffol called the book "a work of mystification," which was exactly what it had been intended to be. (Batiffol published, the following year, *L'Enseignement de Jésus* which dealt with the points raised in *L'Évangile et L'Église*, while Lagrange took up the fight in a series of articles in *La Révue Biblique* of 1905 to 1906. Père Léonce de Grandmaison joined in and published some years later his great work *Jésus Christ*.) There was some plain speaking. Lagrange wrote in the *Révue Biblique* (April, 1903): "It is strictly speaking true that M. Loisy's critical theories are as deadly to Christian faith as those of M. Harnack . . . who would consent to accept the yoke of the Church—and it is a yoke—if it had not been founded by

Jesus Christ and if nothing proves that Jesus Christ is God?" *Civiltà Cattolica* condemned the works of both Harnack and Loisy, and Dom Romolo Murri (himself condemned by *Civiltà Cattolica*, and to be suspended in 1907 and excommunicated in 1909) wrote, "Many acute and learned men say that Loisy's book in reply to Harnack may do more harm to unprepared Catholics than Harnack himself. We are of the same opinion." An Italian could see in Loisy's 'answer' to Harnack the defence of "the passionate Catholic against the free Protestant," but the passionate Catholic was soon to confound such idiocy by writing in *Choses passées*: "I insinuated discreetly but firmly the need for a fundamental reform of biblical exegesis, of the whole of theology, and even of Catholicism in general."

The upshot of honest evaluation of the book was that Cardinal Richard of Paris, under pressure from Rome, condemned the book (January 17, 1903) because it endangered faith in:

(a) The authority of Scriptures and tradition.
(b) The divinity of Christ.
(c) Christ's universal knowledge.
(d) Redemption through His death.
(4) The Eucharist.
(5) The divine institution of papacy and episcopacy.

THE EEL

Loisy could now have made an honest break with Rome and have proclaimed his true opinions. Instead he wrote to Cardinal Richard: "I bow before the judgment which your Eminence has given in accordance with his episcopal right. It goes without saying that I condemn and reprobate all the errors which can be found in my book by one who, interpreting it, takes a point of view quite different from the one which I felt duty-bound to adopt, and did adopt, in writing it." When the game was up, he wrote of this in *Choses passées:* "It was little, and yet it was too much. I did not bow before him very profoundly; but I could now be asked to bow more. Besides, my trick of imputing to the censors of my book the errors which the Cardinal had wished to condemn was a piece of rare cheek."

The Cardinal, he says, who had interpreted his letter with "greater simplicity than it was written, invited me very kindly to come and see him. The almost cloying gentleness of the good cardinal in such circumstances never failed to exasperate me." Loisy was not going to be won over so easily. He wrote back: "In withdrawing my book from the market, and in letting your Eminence know in advance that I would withdraw it, I thought to act as ecclesiastical discipline demanded; and I felt that I was in accord with the wishes of the Sovereign Pontiff. But I definitely reserve my personal opinion on all that has come about in connection with this history book in which people try to find theological errors. Your Eminence will permit me to shelve meanwhile the invitation which you so kindly sent me. In present circumstances, the meeting which it proposes would be too painful for me and, I fear, also for your Eminence." "This letter," he commented, "cut down to its true worth, that is, nothing, the previous 'submission.' "

How hard to pin such a man down! Grandmaison had written of *L'Évangile et L'Église* that the author "nuançait jusqu'a l'equivoque et balançait jusqu'a l'ambiguité ses affirmations religieuses,"[4] while Rivière described it as "a strange and disconcerting book which had the knack of insinuating his conclusions throughout without ever expounding them *ex professo*. The whole thing was calculated to make dupes, and the dupes, at the start, were countless."[5] Loisy was to continue to baffle and to make dupes for some time yet. In October (1903) he produced the second of his "petits livres rouges", *Autour d'un petit livre*, to defend and explain the first. "The first condition of scientific work," he wrote, "is freedom. The first duty of a scholar, whether Catholic or not, is sincerity. The author of *L'Évangile et L'Église* dealt with Christian origins in accordance with a historian's rights." Cardinal Richard had condemned his book because it dis-

---

[4] *Recherches de science religieuse*, 1919, t.X., p. 405, quoted from Rivière, *Le Modernisme dans L'Eglise*, p. 166.
[5] Rivière, *ibidem*, p. 166.

turbed the belief of the faithful regarding fundamental dogmas. "What *does* disturb the minds of the faithful," Loisy
now countered, "in regard to the divinity of Christ and to His
infallible knowledge, is the impossibility of reconciling the
natural meaning of the most authentic Gospel texts with what
our theologians teach or seem to teach in the matter of the
consciousness and knowledge of Jesus. . . . The divinity of
Christ is a dogma which grew in the Christian consciousness,
but which was not expressly formulated in the Gospel; it
existed only germinally in the idea of the Messiah, the son
of God. No theological principle, no definition of the Church,
forces one to admit that Jesus had made a formal declaration of it to His disciples before His death. . . ." (Compare
today: *Catholic Herald* report of lecture by Fr. Hubert
Richards: "Father Richards emphasised there is no text in
which Christ said he was God and several which suggested
the opposite, and no text during his life in which his disciples
call him God" [September 29, 1972] and *that* issue of *The
Sower*: "The title the Son or the Son of God was attributed
to Jesus by the first Christians" [p. 71]; "Nowhere does
Christ ever say: 'I am God,' and only once, perhaps twice,
in the text of the New Testament do his disciples say he is
God. So the teacher should reserve the term 'God' for the
Father" [p. 72].)

However, though Loisy was still slow to break out his
true colours, the truth was beginning to appear. Bishops
might, and did, praise his second little red book, but it was
no longer possible to pretend that Loisy was concerned only
with history and not with doctrine; what he was demanding
was a complete re-casting of Christian belief. His writings
were placed on the Index in December of that year, 1903,
Pius X now being Pope. Writing to *The Times* early the next
year, the Abbé declared: "I was a Catholic, I remain a
Catholic. I was a critic, I remain one" and on January he
wrote to Cardinal Merry del Val, reserving his rights of conscience. More was demanded, and he wrote to the Cardinal
again on January 24: "I accept all the dogmas of the
Church." He wrote in this vein after consultation with von
Hügel, but his real thoughts were set down in his diary:

"I have not been a Catholic in the official sense of the word for a long time. . . . Roman Catholicism as such is destined to perish, and it will deserve no regrets."

It was all very well for the Abbé Bremond (who got permission to leave the Jesuits that year) to write from London that the Holy Office's decree was as trivial as a decree which regulated the number of candles required for a High Mass, and to extol Loisy for shattering the prejudice, shared by so many good people, "that they must submit blindly when a Congregation spoke, and that there was no happy medium in the Church between blind submission, which was clearly impossible,[6] and rebellion." Loisy, however, was coming to know that the facts could not be out-stared as simply as that. In his diary for May 10, he wrote: "Do I still believe enough to call myself Catholic? I am staying in the Church, not for reasons of faith but for reasons of (moral) expediency." On May 12: "There are times when I begin to long for something which would make me leave the Church. . . . Pius X, the head of the Catholic Church, would excommunicate me most decidedly if he knew that I hold the creation to be a purely metaphysical symbol, the virgin birth and the resurrection to be purely moral symbols, and the entire Catholic system to be a tyranny which acts in the name of God and Christ against God himself and against the Gospel."

After reading such blunt, if (at the time) secret, honesty, it is difficult to be patient when one comes across the patently ridiculous defence of Loisy's Modernism given by Fr. Mark Schoof, O.P., Dr. Schillebeeckx's assistant, in *Breakthrough* (p. 59): "Later, he (Loisy) wrote about this period in his life, saying that the only statement that he still accepted in the twelve articles of faith was 'Jesus was crucified under Pontius Pilate.' This confession did not mean what was all too easily accepted in the later polemics, that is, that Loisy had lost his faith and was acting as a hypocrite by deliberately continuing his work of undermining the faith of others

---

[6] The reader should look again at the words of Fr. Henry St. John, printed on page 6.

within the Church. It is quite clear from all kinds of data that he only doubted the current interpretations of scholastic theology." This essay in 'blurmanship' brings home exactly what we are facing today, and I hope that I am not lacking in charity when I say that it recalls what Archbishop Alban Goodier wrote of Modernism: "It was a juggling with words; it was an art of making words mean whatever men might please. Such a philosophy could bear only one fruit, whether in religion or in the lives of men; it was falsehood breeding falsehood, it was an intellectual and moral disease."[7] Loisy and Tyrrell, Fr. Schoof judges (p. 224), "found out how difficult it was for their real intentions to be given a fair hearing," as did Rahner and Schillebeeckx later. Or, as gallant von Hügel maintained, the Roman Hierarchy had interpreted Loisy's doctrine erroneously! In the following chapters, we shall find Dr. Schillebeeckx maintain that the criticism, in Pius XII's *Humani Generis*, of recent writing on the Eucharist is "probably based on a misunderstanding," and Thomas Sartory asserting that Pope Paul had missed the actual question in *Mysterium Fidei*. Rome must be uncannily fallible!

LAMENTABILI AND PASCENDI

The struggle continued, Loisy busily writing under eight different names, and, on July 2, 1907, the Holy Office issued the decree *Lamentabili*, a list of condemned propositions culled from Loisy's works. There followed, on September 6, the encyclical *Pascendi* which grappled with Modernism in its varying forms and caused a stir on more than one account. First, it was couched in terms that seemed unduly harsh, at least to Anglo-Saxon and American ears.[8] Next, many honest

[7] *The Dublin Review,* October, 1932.
[8] Dom Cuthbert Butler, in *The Vatican Council, 1869-1870,* tells how the Fathers had to tame the terminology of the early Roman drafts. When Pius IX denounced Gladstone as a viper attacking the bark of St. Peter, Gladstone's publisher "pointed out that the Pope's acquaintance with the language of the Billingsgate fishmarket proved that he could claim at least a nominal connection with St. Peter." Cf. Magnus, *Gladstone,* p. 235.

souls thought wrongly that it condemned Newman's theory of development of doctrine, since Modernists were taking over the great convert's terms to propagate views which he would have abhorred, and Fr. Tyrrell wrote explicitly in *The Times* that the encyclical condemned Newman. Loisy himself dismissed it as 'fantasy', and there could be only one end to the matter. He had not been unduly perturbed when his *celebret* was withdrawn. "My last Mass," he noted, "was celebrated on November 1st, 1906; the first was on June 30, 1879. This act had not lost for me all religious signification, but, during recent days, it had become a burden to me because it seemed to imply the profession of official Catholicism." He was excommunicated on March 7, 1908.

His story has been told here because it throws light on both the inner nature and the outer mask of Modernism, and because his ideas recur. It is a philosophic axiom that the same causes produce the same effects and, therefore, when a Catholic today loses his Faith but retains his ties of sentiment he will behave in much the same way as Loisy or Tyrrell, attempting to up-date dogma, looking to a holy, Catholic and Agnostic Church. Duchesne wounded the would-be Father of the Church by writing mordantly, "Your death will certainly be an irreparable loss to half a dozen people," but the real loss was occasioned by the death of his belief. His disbelief still cries out through other voices for repose. But it was not on Loisy, but on Tyrrell, that Cardinal Mercier picked as the articulate exponent of Modernism.

3

Father George Tyrrell

As he (Fr. Tyrrell) said in a letter to an intimate friend, he was 'as a dangerous man wandering forth he knows not whither.'

J. LEWIS MAY, Father Tyrrell and the Modernist Movement

A man who could write on the same day to two different friends—to one that his greatest longing was to say Mass again, to the other that the Roman collar choked him and that he much preferred to hear Mass as a layman—was surely swayed by moods to an almost unthinkable degree.

M. WARD, Insurrection versus Resurrection

Fr. Tyrrell's story is a tragic one and, in order that we should have a true picture of the man, I set at its head what was written by Ernest Dimnet and Archbishop Goodier who knew him well. I hope that we shall carry in our minds especially the moving picture which Dimnet painted, as we travel the road of this unhappy man's career. Dimnet first met Tyrrell in 1905 when the Irishman came over to Paris to see Bremond whom Dimnet describes as a strange migrant who flitted from flat to flat at intervals of only a few weeks. This is what Dimnet wrote of the Jesuit: "Tyrrell must have had enemies, but they must also have been people who never were in contact with him. It was impossible to see him without liking him and liking him instantaneously. Not that he was good-looking, for he was the reverse to such an extent

37

that I should consider it treason and a misrepresentation to describe his features. Nor was he particularly sociable, either. He lived so intently with his own thoughts that if you ceased to address him during a few minutes you found, on returning to him, that he was staring into space with, not infrequently, his lips moving in some inaudible conversation. . . . What made of Tyrrell a man whom you could not approach without loving was a capacity for human sympathy which you felt at once. . . . The painfully irregular features vanished as you took cognizance of the unique quality of the eyes, so unlike anything one generally sees in a very brainy person that what they suggested was the appeal of a beautiful child or that of a wounded creature . . . yet his manly dignity was unmistakable."

The wounded creature . . . the lips moving . . . it is no doubt the portrait of an eccentric, but it is of a very touching character. After his ordination, he spent a year on the mission at St. Helen's in Lancashire and there he earned deep love. "He never should have left St. Helens" his friends repeated later, and Maud Petre, who was devoted to him, wrote, "The poor at St. Helens were not slow—the poor never are slow—to recognise the true priest, the man of his people; he gave himself to them and they leaned on him. . . . This was the kind of affection that enslaved him, and well he knew it; he lost his independence to the weak and not to the strong. . . ." Tyrrell himself wrote of one of his superiors, "Had he for a moment taken a kind or affectionate line, I should have collapsed at once and lost all my independence," but J. Lewis May contributes in his biography: "The least touch of coldness, the least hint of superiority, or patronage, or arrogance, and all his hostility would be awakened, and with that awakening, his sense of humour, his generosity, his Christianity, all but vanished; the quality of his imagination sensibly declined."[1] Here, then, we have a man of admirable gentleness of heart when the temperature was warm, but a man ill-trained in obedience and humility.

[1] *Father Tyrrell and the Modernist Movement*, p. 131.

Archbishop Goodier, in his turn, when reviewing May's book, wrote: "Mr. May has used the illustration of Dr. Jekyll and Mr. Hyde; the reader of his work now sees, what at the time he did not see, that there were two Tyrrells, and in the end the evil genius in him got the better of the good. But he cannot forget the conversations on prayer and the insight into heaven which Fr. Tyrrell gave him; he cannot forget his 'I will say Mass for you tomorrow,' as if it were the one good thing he had to give. . . . Father Tyrrell's power lay in his heart rather than in his brain; when he wrote at the dictate of his heart, all the world went after him. But the day came when the brain began to dictate to the heart, and then followed disaster; all the more since, as we now can see, that brain was itself diseased."[2] This last is a reference to the Bright's disease which affected Tyrrell in his later years. One wonders what von Hügel would have made of the last sentences, since the Baron had written to him, "You are a German brain, an Irish heart," but he too admitted that his pupil was "a highly irascible, vindictive Celt." But we must not forget that, though Goodier admitted that Tyrrell could be "as abrupt and offensive as the most peevish," he stressed that he won the love of heart after heart. His fellow-Jesuits retained their personal affection for him even when they shook their heads over his incredible folly.

THE SETTING

Perhaps a General Council, by raising all sorts of expectations among the unbalanced, has for its immediate effect not purification and reform, but a rocking of the boat. It was so after Vatican II, and it seems that it was so after Vatican I also (1869-1870). Authority showed concern over current trains of thought. There was, for example, the matter of what has come to be called 'Americanism.' Isaac Hecker, an American, had left Methodism for the Catholic Church in 1844, and had been ordained priest in 1849. He joined, but had to leave, the Redemptorists, and founded the Paulists

[2] *The Dublin Review,* October, 1932.

for work in the United States. When he died, his biography
was written by W. Elliott, and then translated into French
by the Abbé Felix Klein (who died as late as 1953), a priest
in touch with Modernist circles. The book became the handbook of 'Americanism' in France.

The ethos of the movement as of Modernism was natural
as distinct from supernatural, and Leo XIII sent to Cardinal
Gibbons of Baltimore the apostolic letter *Testem Benevo-
lentiae* (January 22, 1899) in which he warned against it.
It is interesting to see the line that the 'Americanists' took,
for the particular reason that their outlook is alive again
today and debilitating religion. They held that the Church
should not be so concerned with orthodoxy of doctrine—
"dissidents should be helped into the Church by ignoring or
playing down certain elements of doctrine"—which recalls
the warnings which Pope Paul has had to utter. Human
welfare was the thing that mattered. There should be an
emphasis on natural, 'active' virtue, as distinct from passive,
supernatural virtue; indeed, such passive atitudes as humility
or obedience were a block to development. Needless to say,
the religious life of enclosed orders was quite out of keeping
with the needs of modern society.

This, again is the secularisation of the spirit in which
the second Modernist egg is incubating. As example, we have
the views expressed while in Scotland by Fr. Colm O'Grady,
M.S.C., Professor of the History of Modern Theology at
Louvain.[3] Fr. O'Grady held with Tillich that God is the
ground of our being and put in a good word for secularisation 'the trend towards greater attention to this world.' The
faith, he said, must be restated in modern terms. Monks,
nuns, monasteries, obedience and direct service of God?—
"They must view their existence to be the service of God
through a total dedication to the progress and development
of this world. In that sense they must understand their
existence to be totally secular . . . There should be no such
thing as a cloister . . . there should be no such thing as an
individual superior who makes decisions for all. Real consul-

[3] Cf. *Scottish Catholic Observer,* January 8 and 15, 1971.

tation by all the members should lead to a community decision. . . ." which will be a great improvement on the past when we regarded "every word of reverend mothers and fathers and bishops with some sort of sacred fear."

In such earthy soil Modernism grew and grows. The Catholic world, in Tyrrell's day, had its coteries of liberal Catholics as it has today, busy with criticism and with talk of renewal, and, when the Modernist word was spoken, so many of the liberals turned Modernist. Maisie Ward (*Op. cit.*, p. 191) tells how her mother disliked their meetings and "the criticism and irreverence that were constantly breaking out in conversation," and how neither her father nor mother "very much enjoyed the atmosphere of the Modernist group, which my mother especially felt to be a mutual admiration society living in a very small room. She wanted to throw open a few windows and let some air in to relieve a stuffy atmosphere." We hear of the same atmosphere in the *Memoirs* of Salvatore Minocchi, who was suspended from his priestly office, when he tells of meetings in the casa dei Missionari in Rome, attended by such people as von Hügel and Duchesne, in which "we laughed and sneered at the Roman court but no more than we did at the Jesuits."

And soon there was to be a combative Jesuit to help sneer.

LITTLE ANNE KELLY

It was a small maid-of-all-work who came to work for Tyrrell's mother, when he was eleven years old, who first put the idea into his head that there might be something in the Catholic religion. Ill-educated as she was, she knew her Faith and could stand up in argument to Tyrrell's mother. George Tyrrell liked a good argument and he never forgot this diminutive 'confessor to the faith,' though his interest was not as yet, he said, "an interest in religion as such, but simply in a paradox and novelty." Nevertheless, an interest developed, and he came under High Church influence. He left Ireland for England, and his first Sunday in London was Palm Sunday. He attended the blessing of palms in the

Anglican church of St. Alban in Holborn, and his visit marked a turning-point in his life. He wrote: "I cannot to this day lay my finger on any solid ground for the impression, for the service was as reverently and liturgically conducted as one could wish; but the sense of levity and unreality about the whole proceeding was to me so strong that I left the church in a few minutes with a feeling of sickness and anger and disappointment. I should say now that what I missed was that appeal to the historical sense which precisely the same ceremony would have made in a Catholic church, where it would have been the utterance of the great communion of the faithful, past and present, of all ages and nations, and not merely of a few irresponsible agents acting in defiance of the community to which they belonged."

Seeing a crowd of people pouring into St. Etheldreda's in Ely Place, he followed them into the crypt of the church. He relates: "in darkness and mid the smell of a dirty Irish crowd, the same service was being conducted in nasal tones, most unmusically, by three very typically Popish priests. Of course, it was mere emotion and sentiment, and I set no store by it either then or now; but oh! the sense of reality! Here was the old business being carried on by the old firm in the old way; here was continuity that took one back to the catacombs. . . ."

His judgment is curious. He was wrong in saying that it was *mere* emotion and sentiment, and wrong in saying that he set no store by it, for obviously he did. And it is arguable that emotion played too strong a part into bringing him into the Catholic Church which he joined in 1879, being then only eighteen. Is it only hindsight which makes one say that Tyrrell was received into the Church (and also admitted to the Jesuit Society) too quickly, that he never digested the Catholic Faith? It does not seem so, and this is the key to all his unhappiness, to the helpless way in which he thrashed about in the fisherman's net. Professor Percy Gardner, a non-Catholic, observed that "He never absorbed the Roman position." (It recalls Mr. T. S. Gregory's question, in his review of Charles Davis's apologia, "What misinformation induced 'the leading Roman Catholic theologian in Great Britain' [*sic*] to fancy that he was ever by conviction a Roman Catholic at all?")[4] Had he "absorbed" even the *Christian* position? He himself wrote in the introduction to *Christianity at the Cross-Roads*: "With all its accretions and perversions Catholicism is, for the Modernist, the only authentic Christianity. Whatever Jesus was, He was in no sense a Liberal Protestant. All that makes Catholicism most repugnant to present modes of thought derives from Him. The difficulty is not Catholicism, but Christ and Christianity. . . . If Rome dies, other churches may order their coffins." But was the man secure even in Christian theism? After taking his vows as a Jesuit, he read, and was deeply impressed by, Lacordaire's *Conferences on God*. It afforded him immense mental relief. "After all," he wrote, "my theistic doubts had never been quite slain. If I now believed in God without admitting my doubts to audience, it was not but I knew they were waiting outside the door. I had, by wilful and repeated practical assumption of the truth of theism, made it a habit of my mind, a necessity of my life. From a mere wish to believe I had passed to a will to believe, in defiance of felt doubts . . . at every step my practical grasp on theism was tightened; but in my mind there had been really no advance, only a smothering of ghosts that would arise again if ever my will should alter and my interest in Catholicism grow cold." This was his state of mind when he read Lacordaire— that he accepted theism because he first accepted the Catholic faith, which is hardly rational—and Lacordaire helped, but it does not look as if the great Frenchman supplied faith. Faith, the catechism tells us, is a supernatural gift which enables us to believe without doubting.

Here is, I am sure, the secret of all Tyrrell's torments and of his accusations of untruthfulness and dishonesty against those who did not agree with him. He did not have faith, which was the key to their belief and serenity.

[4] *The Tablet,* December 16, 1967.

THE JESUIT

The bare bones of the rest of the story are that he was admitted to the Jesuit Society the year after he was received into the Church. He came close to being dismissed before taking his vows, since his superior saw in him a "violent self-will that made him unfit for the Society." ("I might *go* away," the novice decided, "but I should not be *sent* away, come what might.") In the event, he was not sent away, and he was ordained priest in 1891. He was to say Mass for some fifteen years.

In 1897 came the second turning-point in his life. Articles which he had contributed to *The Month* had attracted the attention of von Hügel, and a meeting was arranged. The outcome was disastrous. The Baron talked this poor man, whose faith was so shaky, into learning German in order that he might dig into modern German philosophy, while, at the same time, putting him in touch with Loisy and nascent Biblical criticism. Troeltsch and Eucken, Harnack and Döllinger, were to be his authorities from now on. Archbishop Goodier recounted: "Once, at Richmond, in 1903, he came into the present writer's room with a German book in his hand. 'This is the first German book I have ever read,' he said. It was a volume of Eucken; and it would not be difficult to show how much of Eucken is reflected in his writing at that time and after. Indeed, this is almost certainly what he meant when he wrote to Baron von Hügel, a month or two before he died: 'I feel that my past work has been dominated by the Liberal-Protestant Christ, and doubt whether I am not bankrupt'."

From now on, his life as a Jesuit became increasingly distasteful to him, while his contempt for Rome and orthodoxy was fostered in the circles in which he chose to move. In 1902 he wrote to congratulate Loisy on *L'Évangile et L'Église*: "As being perhaps the only adequate reply to Harnack's *Wesen des Christentums*, your book may, I believe, escape the jealous attacks of those who guard the key of knowledge and who wish neither to enter themselves not to let others enter . . . You have many sincere admirers, though shackled and timid, in the Society. I do not think that the attitude even of this is entirely hostile, though, naturally, it is regulated by expediency and opportunism rather than by any interest in truth or religion." That same year, he wrote to the Baron that the "whole present spirit and policy" of his Society was odious to him.

This turning against his fellow-Jesuits had been accelerated by trouble with Rome and his Superiors over his "Perverted Devotion" article in the *Weekly Register* in 1899; the outcome was that he wrote what he termed "an absolutely fatuous and unmeaning letter" to the editor in explanation, and that he was moved from Farm St. to Richmond in Yorkshire. The English censors had seen nothing wrong in the article, but the General in Rome declared it "offensive to pious ears." Tyrrell wrote wittily to Bremond, "I wish Rome would either define pious ears or give a list of them so that one might know," but his fatal spiritual weakness showed elsewhere. He stopped saying Mass for several days.

There were moves on foot to arrange his 'resignation' from the Jesuit Society, but his own folly brought about expulsion, As Fr. Daly wrote (*art. cit.*, p. 266): "He circulated privately what he had been forbidden to publish, or else he published pseudonymously. He prevaricated when faced with direct questions about his authorship. He had no hesitation in employing, and was prepared to justify with vigour, the most blatant casuistry in defence of his guerilla warfare with the censors." So Fr. Michael Hurley, S.J., dubs him neatly "too jesuitical to be a true Jesuit." The final explosion came with the *Letter to a Professor*, which was really Tyrrell talking to his doubting self (1906); explosion and expulsion. An attempt was made to have Bishop Chisholm of Aberdeen take him into his diocese, but Tyrrell was unwilling to agree. He could now receive Communion but not say Mass. Finally, after his attacks on *Pascendi*, Bishop Amigo of Southwark deprived him of the Sacraments. He gave up going to Mass. When he died, the Baron and Miss Petre wrote a letter to *The Times*, to announce that he had not retracted his Modernist disbeliefs, and Bishop Amigo in consequence refused Catholic burial. Abbé Bremond came

over to pay his last respects to his friend, read some prayers
and preached at the graveside. The outcome for him was
that he was asked to take the anti-Modernist oath to clear
himself of suspicion; he did so, and brought down the Baron's
anger upon his head.

THE MODERNIST

I content myself with listing here Tyrrell's books before
giving an account of his doctrine. No attempt will be made
to trace the development of his ideas for coherent development there was little. Maud Petre wrote in her Journal in
1901: "I cannot get any unity in him—it seems as though
he might fall into pieces that could walk off different ways,
and I should not know which to follow." What was true of
the man was largely true also of his ideas. *Oil and Wine*
(written 1900, but not published until 1902); *The Faith of
Millions* (1901); *Lex Orandi* (1903), the last work to receive
an *imprimatur*; *Lex credendi* (1906); *Through Scylla and
Charybdis* (1907); *Medievalism* (1908), and, posthumously,
Christianity at the Cross-Roads (1909).

As a confirmed Christian, Tyrrell was a soldier of Christ,
and as a Jesuit, he had enrolled in a very special battalion,
but, as his writings continued to appear, the soldier had
panicked and run. We have already contrasted him with the
scholarly and tough Thurston who faced and solved problems.
Here is Tyrrell abdicating: "It is the irresistible facts concerning the origin and composition of the Old and New
Testaments; concerning the origin of the Christian Church,
of its hierarchy, its institutions, its dogmas; concerning the
gradual development of the Papacy; concerning the history
of religion in general—that create a difficulty against which
the synthesis of scholastic theology must be and is already
shattered to pieces. . . . My one preoccupation is to wind my
sinuous way between them so as to save all that is best in
my cargo of traditional dogmatic teaching."[5]

---

[5] *Medievalism*, Chapter X. "As to dogmatic theology," he rudely told
Cardinal Mercier, "it is no boast to assert that I have nothing to
learn from Rome or Louvain; for a man might say that and not say
much."

And how did he plan to save the cargo? In 1904, he wrote to Fr. Thurston, "The only hope now is quite a different understanding of the sense in which dogmas are 'true'." In 1905, he wrote to von Hügel, "It is not the articles of the Creed, but the word *Credo* that needs adjustment." There is something ridiculous about the direction to which he looked for a different understanding, when we remember Lady Blennerhassett's incontrovertible remark that Fr. Tyrrell's religion would never do for her washerwoman, and that such simple people form the great bulk of the Church's membership. The new understanding was to be found in "the collective subconsciousness of the People of God," as distinct from the magisterium of the Church. What did it matter to Tyrrell that the People of God were lustily singing "Faith of our Fathers" or its equivalent, and had no intention of budging from traditional belief? Tyrrell may have thought that he was saving the cargo, but most Christians would agree with the fifth annual report of the American Association for the Advancement of Atheism (c. 1937): the Liberals and Modernists "are heroically saving the ship of Christianity by throwing the cargo overboard! With what zeal the . . . whole crew of rescuers toss out the Virgin Birth, Atonement, and the Resurrection . . . how long will men sail the seas in an empty ship? They will go ashore and enjoy life with the Atheists. We welcome the aid of the Modernists and pledge them our fullest co-operation in ridding the world . . . of any serious acceptance of Christian theology." Tyrrell's "collective subconsciousness," however, like the "consensus of opinion" that we hear about today, had nothing to do with the great People of God as such but only with the hothouse groups within. Here the truth slips out: "difficulties have accumulated to a degree that makes the *ablest and most cultivated minds* to be those least capable of effecting a reconciliation between orthodox theology and the rest of the field of knowledge." One wonders: were the minds of Thurston, Lagrange or Grandmaison noticeably less able and cultivated than his or Loisy's?

We have seen Marcel Hébert profess a cagey belief in the "objective value" of God and of the resurrection. Tyrrell showed his hand more bravely—"I believe in the spiritual truth of what is not historical fact," he wrote in *Lex Orandi*, which, surprisingly, earned a Jesuit *Nihil obstat*. And, from early days, he insisted on the 'infinite inadequacy' of dogmatic expression and got himself into trouble accordingly. Speaking of Harnack, he said: "I suppose we agree as to the inadequacy of dogma . . . but he considers it an overstatement; I, an understatement." The claim of dogmatic inadequacy could, of course, be given an honest meaning, that it is impossible to state divine truth exhaustively in human terms; but what Tyrrell was saying was that it had not been stated *truly* by the Church. He is impatient with doctrinal definitions and orthodoxy and, rather than discuss fairly, raises Aunt Sallies. . . . "Faith is not theological orthodoxy"; "God will not examine us in theology or history or criticism. . . ."; "It is all but impossible to imagine the Christ of the synoptics . . . attaching the slightest religious value to the theologically correct formulation of the inscrutable mysteries prophetically symbolised by the Heavenly Father, the Son of Man, the kingdom of God, etc., or making salvation to depend on any point of mere intellectual exactitude." But, a simple soul would ask, did not Christ, the way, truth and life, set a value on truth? The truth of God's revelation cannot but be infinitely precious.

Obscurely, he made a distinction between dogma and its content. "The dogmas and definitions of popes and councils on their theological side are but the protective husks of revelation. . . . It is only the revealed kernel and not the theological husk to which they can bind our consciences. If they add a jot or title to the easy yoke and burden of Christ's teaching, let them be anathema."[6] Authority and uniformity were therefore out: "The lowest degree of truly spontaneous and independent spiritual unity, such as obtains in the Anglican Church, or even between the different Protestant sects, is infinitely more significant, strong and durable than the merely artificial and external uniformity to which you trust for the preservation of the Church and the Cath-

---

[6] *Medievalism.*

olic religion. In spite of all their religious heresies and division, the religious interest still lives and grows in Protestant countries, whereas it languishes and dies among Catholics under this modern craze for centralisation and military uniformity."[7] Smarting under Cardinal Mercier's criticism, this warm-hearted man has hot-headedly thrown truth to the winds for all his call for truthfulness. It was his disbelief that made him malign Catholic unity of belief as mere external uniformity. Again, if, as he maintained, dogma was subject to revision, what right had he to speak of Protestant doctrines as heresies? And, finally, there is an abyss of ignorance behind the notion that centralization, in the Catholic Church, is a "modern craze." Fr. Tyrrell had not done his home-work. As has been mentioned, the Modernists were blind to history.

AUTHORITY NO MORE

He has left little room for Pope or *magisterium* in his 'true' Christianity. In a letter of March 7, 1902, he wrote that the crying need of Catholicism was a "liberal infusion of Protestant ideas." If the Reformers of the 16th century, he said, had stayed in the Church, they would probably have brought about a healthier solution than Trent did of the problems.[8] "I entirely deny the Ecumenical authority of the exclusively Western Councils of Trent and the Vatican and the whole medieval development of the Papacy so far as claiming more than a primacy of honour for the Bishop of Rome. . . ."[9] Dr. Döllinger, who left the Church after Vatican I, is for Tyrrell "the great and staunchly Catholic Dr. Döllinger," "the greatest, the most learned, the most loyal Roman Catholic of the last century."[10] It should be obvious that what we are quoting now was penned in his last years, when Bright's disease was taking its toll, when even those who loved him were finding his outbursts impossible. Yet,

---

[7] *Medievalism.*
[8] Writing as 'Hilaire Bourdon', *The Church and the Future.*
[9] Cf. J. Lewis May, (*op. cit.,* p. 249).
[10] *Medievalism.*

as early as 1900, he had been behind Lord Halifax's attack, in *The Pilot*, on the Joint Pastoral of 1900 which defended the authority of pope and bishops, the *ecclesia docens*, over the *ecclesia discens*, and so left no room for ideas about collective subconsciousness determining doctrine. He took over, and made his own, the anti-Roman pugnacity of Robert Dell (who left the Church). "Today," he wrote in his reply to Mercier, "while the 'Modernism of the study' is not only unheeded but actively repressed by the Vatican bureaucracy, the modern spirit, felt rather than understood, idolised rather than criticised, has penetrated and inflamed with enthusiasm large numbers of the Catholic clergy and laity, and roused a spirit of revolt that may be ill to reckon with." Bliss should it have been in that dawn to be alive . . . but he was unhappy.

HUSK AND KERNEL

We can gauge the position into which he had drifted from a letter that he wrote to Loisy (October 12, 1903) after reading *Autour d'un petit livre*: "Though tiresome, the opposition of the bishops just now can serve only as an advertisement and a boost for your teaching. . . . A shrewd American publisher recently asked me to write a book for him *which would be condemned*; that proves the market value of such condemnations." It has been said of him that "He seemed to feel that the stained-glass windows of dogma are not vehicles of true light." The solution was to smash the windows. Let us see what was meant in practice by his distinction between the husk and the kernel. Writing to von Hügel, he speaks of "the legendary idealisation of the historical Jesus." He distinguishes between "the inward truth of history" and "historic truth." "That he was born of a Virgin and ascended into Heaven may be but a visibilising of the truth of his transcendence as divine."[11] Writing on July 13, 1907, he states: "All that interests us is to know that the resurrection was not fleshly. . . ." In *Christianity at the*

[11] Cf. J. Lewis May, *Op. cit.*, p. 219.

Cross-Roads, Chapter XII, we get: "the physical resurrection and ascension could, at most, be signs and symbols of Christ's spiritual transformation, of the fullness of His eternal and transcendent life. . . ." "At most" is eloquent. He denies the historic data of Christianity, and unhappily the Dutch catechism has followed his line and thrown doubt on our Lady's virginity. "What the book does," wrote Fr. Anthony Bullen in the *Catholic Pictorial* in late 1968, "is to leave aside the physical, medical fact of the virginity," leading the reader "into the realm of theology." But this is to lead the reader up the garden path, since the Catechism did *not* leave aside the physical fact; it discussed it and left the reader in doubt.

Tyrrell, Fr. Daly wrote (*art. cit.*, pp. 267-268), was convinced "that his opponents were censuring his views from a standpoint which identified Roman theology with Catholic orthodoxy and, worse still, with Christian revelation" which links him both to Loyson and to Küng and others today. He could never be made to see that what he wrote contradicted Catholic belief, savaged revelation; all that he could see was that he was challenging Roman theology. Again and again he⁻ speaks of theology when he should speak of doctrine, and, above all, he confuses Catholic doctrine with his *bête noire*, scholasticism. The whole burden of his two articles in *The Times*, in fierce reaction to the encyclical *Pascendi*, is that Rome is trying to pass off scholastic theology as Catholic belief; it is much the same line of attack as that taken by Fr. Schoof in *Breakthrough*: ". . . the fatal alliance between this (the Church's) teaching authority and neo-scholasticism . . .", as this system of thought has "become inextricably involved with the tradition of the Church in recent years, it has hardly been able to regard any other possible approaches to the reality of faith as anything other than heresies" (p. 148). Neither Tyrrell nor his modern counter-parts seemed to have stopped to ask themselves what relevance questions about scholasticism have to the facts of Christianity. Was Jesus born of a virgin? Was He God? Did he rise physically from the grave? Did He give us, literally, His Body to eat in the Eucharist? These are ques-

tions of fact, not of a school of philosophy, and they are
outside considerations of passing fashions of thought. "I
will not be a parasite to time, place, or opinion," Ben Jonson
said nobly. He would never have been dated enough to be
a Modernist.

Pascendi, Tyrrell asserted, is the work of "some subtle
scholastic theologian unusually well versed in the literature
of his subject, which, however, he criticizes in the light of
his own categories," and showed his scorn by adding immediately, "Were this not evident, one would sometimes be
tempted to think he might be a traitor in the orthodox camp.
For the picture he draws of modernism is so seductive to
an educated mind, and the counterpart he suggests so re-
pellent, as to make the Encyclical rather 'dangerous' reading
for the children of this world." Soon he was being rude to
the pope: "How far this subtle disquisition . . . emanates
from the mind of Pius X, or is even within his comprehension, is open to question." In the second article, he told
why the Modernist would neither accept the Church's teaching nor leave her: "Much as he may prize the sacramental
bread of life, he prizes still more the unleavened bread of
sincerity and truth. To secede would be to allow that his
calumniators were in the right; that Catholicism was bound
hand and foot to its scholastic interpretation. . . ."[12] Yet,
in a letter to Fr. Thurston (November 30, 1906), he gives
away that he is not concerned merely with philosophical or
theological interpretations but with hard facts: ". . . nothing
could persuade me that the old dogma of scriptural and
ecclesiastical inerrancy can be saved in any natural sense . . ."
Reinterpretation, then, was to save dogma by proposing unnatural senses, while the reinterpreter maintained that it
was "not the Church, but the theological school which
usurps her functions, that we have to fight against. If theologians quote authority against us, they beg the question,
for it is their whole *theory* of authority which is in question,

---

[12] "The twentieth century reformers are also determined to remain
within the Church and not to be separated from Rome . . . If there
is a threat of schism today it comes from the centre . . ." Mr. St.
John-Stevas, *Catholic Herald*, May 30, 1969.

far more than any detail of authoritative teaching." (Letter to von Hügel, January 27, 1904.)

Tyrrell was not an independent thinker and he derived his errors from northern Europe exactly as his counterparts do in the seventies. The tragedy was that he was not capable of understanding the great Englishman who could have saved his thinking. He read Newman's *Essay on Development* three times but it did not save him. "I feel that Newman is no longer in a position to help us. It is not the articles of the Creed that need to be readapted, but the word *Credo* itself . . ."[13] ". . . I believe faith will reappear, though I am not so sure that it will be Roman faith . . . How far away even Newman seems to one now! How little he seems to have penetrated the darkness of our day! His method and spirit are an everlasting possession; but of his premises and presuppositions hardly one has escaped alive."[14] And, writing to the Baron after the appearance of *L'Évangile et L'Église*, he described the book, incredibly, as "too indiscriminately conservative," adding, "it does not give us what Newman tried (vainly, I think) to give us, a criterion to distinguish false from true development." If he could not find that criterion in Newman, he could find it nowhere.

THE FRESH WINDS

Cardinal Mercier's Lenten pastoral, the year following *Pascendi*, was devoted to Modernism, and he concentrated his attention on "the most penetrating observer of the present Modernist movement—the one most alive to its tendencies, who has best divined its spirit, and is perhaps more deeply imbued with it than any other . . . the English priest Tyrrell." He went on to expose the fallacies of the movement and ended movingly with an appeal for loyalty to the Holy See: ". . . it is at this moment, when religious Protestants, harassed by Liberalism and tossed with doubt, are crying out in despair for the help of authority, and saying: 'Lord, save us! we perish!' that Modernists would rob us of that

---

[13] Letter to W. Ward, December 11, 1903.
[14] *Autobiography*, II, p. 144.

Head which the sectaries envy us, and would ask us to make again that experiment whose failure has been proved by four miserable centuries."

"No, my dearest brethren, let us not repeat that wretched experience. Let us gather more closely than ever round Peter, the Vicar of Jesus Christ."

Though Tyrrell knew that the pastoral had been specially commended by Pius X, he answered *Modernism* with a furious tirade, *Medievalism*, which established how accurate the Cardinal had been. Talking of his conversion as a youth, Tyrrell wrote: "Not one of the reasons on which I acted do I now acknowledge as of the slightest validity. They were those of the ordinary anti-Protestant apologetic of our proselytizers—tricks of exegesis and dialectical legerdemain. The present foundations of my Catholicism are far other . . . what I gradually learnt was . . . that the true and distinctive principle dividing Catholicism from Protestantism was that which barely escaped condemnation at the Vatican Council, and for adhesion to which Dr. Döllinger was excommunicated by Pius IX."

And there are some words which should interest every Catholic schoolboy who knows that the highly traditionalist Pope John threw open a window in the Church to let in a fresh wind, and every schoolmaster who has begun to wonder what kind of wind did in fact enter: "Your Eminence, will you never take heart of grace and boldly throw open the doors and windows of your great medieval cathedral, and let the light of a new day strike into its darkest corners and the fresh winds of Heaven blow through its mouldy cloisters?"

This was the sad man who, as Fr. Thurston said, came down in *Christianity at the Cross-Roads* "on the side of Nothing." "I doubt whether I am bankrupt!" And yet, I think, the belief in the divinity of Christ, which Loisy had lost, was still there. The Frenchman wrote something in his *Mémoires* which cannot fail to move: "In the last months of his life, Tyrrell's faith was like that of one clinging in desperation to the Christ of his soul." But 'clinging' is a feeble rendering of "qui se cramponne au Christ" . . . one sees the terror in the climber's eyes and the irons biting into the mountain face. It is no little thing to nail oneself to the God nailed on the Cross. May he rest in peace.

And now, with some insight into the nature of Modernism and Modernists, we turn to our own day. The Pope calls this moment in the Church's history "the grave hour," and it has become grave because authority has shrunk from tackling error. Charity has led authority to censure only in general terms, but these are blank cartridges and error declines to drop dead. Cardinal Heenan, in his article *The Authority of the Church* (*The Tablet, May* 18, 1968), wrote this of the Holy Father: "Constantly he returns to the theme of erroneous teaching of theology. Unfortunately, his condemnations are made in general terms. Since nobody knows which theologians are being condemned, it is impossible for bishops to take any action." This, of course, is not the whole story. *The Times* for October 1, 1907, printed an editorial, to march with Fr. Tyrrell's second article on *Pascendi*, which maintained: "the camp of the Modernists contains, as he hints, its 'Cardinals, Archbishops, Bishops,' . . . it has the spendid comfort of some great names. . . ." Equally, now, the Modernist has his mitred champions. I read today that Bishop Delargey of Auckland rushed to the defence of Fr. Hubert Richards' lectures "against the advice of senior priests of his diocese who disagreed with him. This was followed by a further attack by Bishop Ashby, of Christchurch. He suggested that Fr. Richards was in New Zealand as part of a grand catechetical design by the Bishops. This was not so. . . ."[15]

Apart from the fact that Modernism has spread upwards, I do not find the Cardinal's words wholly convincing, for reasons which will appear, but the truth in them was voiced in another troubled time by St. John Fisher: "We use bye-paths and circumlocutions in rebuking. We go nothing nigh to the matter. . . ." If that great realist were to pass judgement on our age, he would convict us, among other things, of Pelagianism, an over-optimistic view of hu-

---

[15] Letter of John Kennedy, editor of the *New Zealand Tablet, Catholic Herald,* October 27, 1972.

man nature. Strict discipline in the Church has vanished
since the recent Council because of an illusion that men have
grown mature, which is an assumption that the effects of
the Fall tapered off about 1962, when the truth is that,
thanks to surrounding paganism and scepticism, we are in
greater need of discipline than ever. We should heed the
wisdom of Herbert Butterfield, Professor of Modern History
at Cambridge, in *Christianity and History* (1949). He wrote:
"The plain truth is that if you were to remove certain subtle
safeguards in society many people who had been respectable
all their lives would be transformed by the discovery of
things which it was now possible to do with impunity . . .
some of the most inveterate talkers during my lifetime have
been the victims of precisely that optical illusion on the
subject of human nature . . . we have gambled very highly
on what was an over-optimistic view of the character of man."

In this book, I propose to deal with some of the attempts
at doctrine-substitution which can be justly classed as Modernist. Such are the erroneous views being circulated as to
transubstantiation, original sin, the truth of the Scriptures
and our code of morality (some early Modernists tended to
subordinate principles to practice, forming their own elastic
ethics).

The danger, of course, in suggesting that an error is
circulating in the Church is that people may assume that it
is to be found at all levels, and that the Church is near
collapse. Nothing could be further from the truth. Lady
Blennerhassett's washerwoman sings 'Faith of our Fathers'
through the centuries; a machine has probably replaced her
in our time but, whatever she works at, she holds her Faith
firm . . . and she has never heard of Loisy, Tyrrell, Küng,
Davis or Schillebeeckx. If she has heard, she still couldn't
spell most of their names. The fallacies are epidemic only
in the ranks of the clergy, religious and more academic lay-
people. Nevertheless, Mr. Frank Sheed wrote in *Is it the
Same Church?*—"And to strengthen the feeling that the
teaching Church is divided, every week brings news of some
revolutionary-sounding denial by some theologian somewhere
—and not a sound out of their own hierarchy! . . . There is

hardly a doctrine or practice of the Church that I have not heard attacked by a priest." Therefore, it stands to reason that authority must wake up to its duty.

And this recalls that there are many things which do not stand to reason, in the sense that their truth or falsehood cannot be settled by rational exercise. Such are the mysteries of religion and even of human nature. If any innocent, then, opens this book, looking to find the truth of transubstantiation, of original sin, of Christ's consciousness, or even of sex, neatly tied up in incontrovertible syllogisms, he is in for a disappointment, and this is where the intellectuals are bogged down, if they think that brains are the only truth-diviners. The Church has defended reason against Luther and others, but within reason. Many truths can be reached only by revelation, and this revelation is kept unadulterated by a divinely-guarded Church and not by a Brains Trust; and so the final word has to come from authority. An early part of the book will therefore be devoted to clarification of the nature of the *magisterium*, that is, teaching office, of the Church.

I hope it is agreed that errors can be attacked in charity, but it may be replied that to show assurance is to show pride. However, the man who upholds the ancient teaching is not propped on the reed of his own opinion as he echoes popes and Councils. He draws his assurance from both autocracy and democracy. From autocracy—because he is rooted to the rock which holds the Church, and thus ultimately, in von Hügel's phrase, is sustained by "the transcendent God who backs and needs the autocratic Pope." From democracy —in two ways. First, the body of ordinary Catholics is with him. Blame this on their ignorance or credit it to sound faith—but they are with him. He remembers what St. Hilary wrote at the time of the Arian attack: "The ears of the people are holier than the hearts of the priests." Secondly, he cries with Thomas More, "Let me go now to those that are dead and that are, I trust, in heaven." He counts the votes of the dead, and this is the vote-casting of tradition which can give a man humble certainty. Chesterton asserted in *Orthodoxy*: "Democracy tells us not to neglect a good man's opinion, even if he is our groom; tradition asks us not to neglect a good man's opinion, even if he is our father . . . We will have the dead at our councils."

If there is a cry, then, for more democracy in the Church, let us have it, and the dead, the Church Triumphant, will carry the election. *Securus iudicat orbis terrarum* is the rule of St. Augustine which a friend imparted to Newman before his conversion. "He repeated these words again and again, and, when he was gone, they kept ringing in my ears . . . For a mere sentence, the words of St. Augustine struck me with a power which I never had felt from any words before. To take a familiar instance, they were like the 'Turn again Whittington' of the chime; or, to take a more serious one, they were like the 'Tolle, lege,—Tolle,lege,' of the child, which converted St. Augustine himself. 'Securus judicat orbis terrarum!' " (*Apologia*, Chapter III.)

4

The Teaching Authority

*We define that the Holy and Apostolic See and
the Roman Pontiff holds the primacy of the Church
throughout the whole world; and that the same
Roman Pontiff is the successor of St. Peter, the
Prince of the Apostles, and the true Vicar of Christ,
the head of the whole Church, and the father and
teacher of all Christians and that full power was
given to him, in Blessed Peter, by our Lord Jesus
Christ to feed, to rule, and to govern the universal
Church.*

The General Council of Florence (1438-1445).

We shall call upon our dead, the saints and doctors of
the Church, to teach the true nature of the authority which
the Son of God gave to Peter and his successors at Rome,
and of the corresponding duty on our part of accepting and
obeying. It is vital that we form an honest picture of that
key-authority before proceeding with other matters, and for
two reasons. First, it is because much of our argument will
rest on the basis of papal authority and there is no point in
building on it if it is largely human clay and not rock. One
remembers that Thomas More told his friend Bonvisi that
he thought papal supremacy a human ordinance, and then,
a few days later, reproached himself, saying, "that opinion
alone was enough to make me fall from the rest, *for that
holdeth up all.*" It is futile, for example, to cite an encyclical
to determine some point of dogma or morality, if a Catholic
may reply that the Pope is expressing 'his opinion' and that,
though we must respect it, the discussion may go on as be-

fore.[1] Secondly, some who are utterly sincere in reprobating anything which smacks of 'legalism' still betray a juridical approach towards papal authority because of a hypnosis induced by the first Vatican Council's definition of papal infallibility. They have discarded their son-to-father, or flock-to-shepherd, relationship in a way undreamed of by the Council Fathers, a way against which tradition cries out, as we shall see.

Human beings being frail, this imbalance has naturally been rife mainly among those who were already deviating from Catholic doctrine even if only by a minor angle of deflection. To them, papal decisions have been disagreeable, and they have received them, not with "Peter has spoken through the mouth of Paul," but with the words, "Is he speaking infallibly? If not, I need not accept." Such an attitude is out of touch with the realities of life. It is as if people would agree to travel by train only if guaranteed that the driver was incapable of error; rather, as if the flock refused to follow God's appointed shepherd without a written guarantee ruling out any possible slip. Those who limit security to infallible utterances must study how rarely such utterances have been made, though constant guidance was required. Butler in *The Vatican Council*, 1869-1870, wrote "Dublanchy in the Dictionnaire gives a list of papal . . . utterances, which by common consent are looked upon as certainly infallible. . . . There are just twelve such in the whole range of Church history . . ." (p. 472). Since then, there has been the definition of the Assumption.

Now we summon the dead, remembering that none of those whom we quote spoke of *ex cathedra* pronouncements. Each bears witness to the tradition stemming from apostolic

---

[1] An article in *Scottish Catholic Herald*, August 16, 1968. *Herder Correspondence*, September, 1968, said of *Humanae Vitae,* "What in fact we have to deal with would seem to be nothing other than the private theological opinion of the Bishop of Rome." Tyrrell, in *The Times* for October 1, 1907, wrote off *Pascendi* as "a catena of the personal opinions of Pius X and his immediate entourage . . . the 'Roma locuta est' of the journalists falls flat."

times regarding the duty of accepting the teaching of Rome.[2]
We begin with near-apostolic times, calling St. Irenaeus of
Lyons (c. 130-c. 200) who heard the Faith taught by Polycarp who in turn had listened to St. John the Evangelist.
"It is a matter of necessity," he taught, "that every church
should agree with this church (Rome), on account of its
pre-eminent authority, that is, the faithful everywhere."
(Mr. John Lawson, a non-Catholic writer, comments in *The
Biblical Theology of Saint Irenaeus*, "To St. Irenaeus Rome
was most certainly an authority none must question, as she
cannot be imagined as ever in error.")

We move a few years in time to St. Cyprian (+258),
though one must bear in mind Fr. M. Bévenot's cautions in
his introduction to Cyprian's works—see also the article by
N. Afanassieff in *The Primacy of Peter in the Orthodox
Church.*—"Heresies and schisms have no other origin than
that obedience is refused to the priest of God, and that men
lose sight of the fact that there is one judge in the place
of Christ in this world." "It (the see of Rome) is the root
and mother of the Catholic Church, the Chair of Peter, and
the principal Church whence sacerdotal unity has its source."
"To be in communion with (Pope) Cornelius is to be in
communion with the Catholic Church." "If a man does not
hold fast to the oneness of Peter, does he imagine that he
still holds the faith? If he deserts the Chair of Peter upon
whom the Church was built, has he still confidence that he
is in the Church?" "He built the Church (on Peter) . . .
in whom he made unity originate and be visible." ". . . that
faith of the Romans which perfidy cannot approach."

The reader is asked to note how repeatedly it is insisted
that unity is to be found only in agreement with papal teach-

---

[2] The references will be found mainly in *The Church and the Papacy*
by T. G. Jalland, D.D., *The Church and Infallibility* and *The Idea
of the Church* by Bishop B. C. Butler, *The Celtic Church and the
See of Peter* by Rev. J. C. McNaught, *The End of Religious Controversy* by Bishop John Milner, *A Chain of Error in Scottish History*
by Major M. V. Hay, Leo XIII's *Satis Cognitum* (1896), *Studies on
the Early Papacy* by Dom John Chapman, and *St. Peter: His Name
and His Office* by T. W. Allies. Of these, the Rev. J. C. McNaught
and Dr. Jalland are non-Catholic.

ing, and obedience to 'Peter'. So we hear St. Basil (c. 330-
379): "(The Church's) ruler is none else but one who represents the person of the Saviour, and offers up to God the
salvation of those who obey him, and this we learn from
Christ Himself in that He appointed Peter to be the shepherd of his Church after Himself." In that same century
resounds the voice of St. Ambrose (c. 339-397), famed for
his saying "Ubi Petrus, ibi Ecclesia"—"The Church is where
Peter is." He writes to the Emperor Gratian: "Your clem-
ency was to be entreated not to suffer the Roman Church,
the head of the whole Roman world, to be thrown into dis-
turbance. For thence, as from a fountain-head, the rights
of venerable communion flow unto all." He tells, too, how
a cautious man makes sure that the bishop he is addressing
is an orthodox Catholic, asking him "if he is in communion
with the Catholic bishops, that is, with the Roman Church."

The witness of St. Jerome, in that same troubled century, is famous, St. Jerome whose authority was in such
esteem among the Celts of the West that St. Columbanus
said that anyone who came contesting his teaching would
be rejected as heretical. Jerome wrote to Pope Damasus
(376 A.D.): "Since the East . . . is tearing piecemeal the
undivided tunic of Christ . . . I have considered that I ought
to consult the Chair of Peter and the faith praised by the
mouth of the Apostle (Romans 1,8), asking now the food
of my soul where of old I received the garment of Christ. . . .
It is but with the successor of the fisherman and the disciple
of the cross that I speak. Following none in the first place
but Christ, I am in communion with your beatitude, that is,
with the Chair of Peter. On that rock I know the Church
is built. Whosoever shall eat the Lamb outside that house
is profane. If any be not with Noah in the ark, he shall
perish. . . . Whoso gathereth not with thee scattereth; that
is to say, whoso is not with Christ is of Antichrist." Again:
"On the one side storm the raging Arians, supported by the
powers of the world. On the other, a Church torn in three
parts tries to seize me. . . . Meantime I cry aloud: "If any
is joined to the Chair of Peter, he is my man!" Then, against
Rufinus: "What does he call his faith? That which the

Roman Church possesses? Or that which is contained in the volumes of Origen? If he answers, 'the Roman,' it follows that he and I are Catholics . . ." And, against Jovinian: "For this reason out of the twelve one is selected, that by the appointment of a Head the occasion of schism may be taken away." There it is—the whole *raison d'être* of the papacy!

The witnesses crowd thickly in the fourth century precisely because it was a time of attack on traditional doctrine. We summon next St. John Chrysostom (c. 347-407). . . . "Christ made Peter the teacher not of that see (Jerusalem) but of the world. . . ." His favourite name for Peter and his successors is "coryphaeus," a conductor or choirmaster, and he names Peter "the foundation of the Church . . . the man without education who closed the mouth of philosophers, who destroyed the philosophy of the Greeks as though it were a spider's web. . . ." "Peter, the base, the pillar." Again he writes: "For what is proper to God alone, that is, to forgive sins, and to make the Church immovable in so great an onset of waves, and to cause a fisherman to be stronger than any rock, when the whole world wars against him, this He Himself promises to give; as the Father said, speaking to Jeremias, that He would set him as a column of brass and as a wall; but Jeremias to a single nation, Peter to the whole world. . . ." "God allowed him to fall, because He meant to make him ruler of the whole world. . . ."

St. Augustine (354-430) belongs also to both the fourth and fifth centuries. One of his most famous sentences, phrased in three crisp words 'Causa finita est', occurs in this passage: "On this matter (the Pelagian dispute), the findings of two Councils have been sent to the Apostolic See, and answers have been received thence. *That matter is ended*". He said trenchantly, "You are not to be looked upon as holding the true Catholic faith if you do not teach that the faith of Rome is to be held," and, listing the ties which bound him to the true Church, he claimed: "I am held in the Catholic Church . . . by the succession of bishops down to the present episcopate from the very See of Peter the Apostle, to whom the Lord after His resurrection entrusted His sheep to be fed. Lastly, I am held by the very name of Catholic."

For the Church to have unity, one man must be the teacher and the judge whose decision is final. Here now is St. Optatus of Milevis, a contemporary of St. Augustine, writing to a Donatist opponent: "You cannot be unaware that in the city of Rome the episcopal chair was bestowed upon Peter first . . . in which single chair unity was to be preserved by all . . . lest the other apostles should maintain each his several chair; so that he who established another chair over against the unique chair would be a schismatic and a sinner.": Even a heretic like Nestorius, it should be noted, coined his own version of *Causa finita est* when he said of Eutyches: "He had received judgment. What other judgment was required beyond that which the Bishop of Rome had made?"

Ubi Petrus, ibi Ecclesia, St. Ambrose had said. Not many years later, the saying was echoed by St. Patrick (389-c. 461). In the Book of Armagh, his version is set down: "As ye are Christians, so be ye Romans," and the rule of St. Patrick is preserved in the *Hibernensis*, the eighth-century collections of canons: "If any questions arise in this island, let them be referred to the Apostolic See.

St. Peter Chrysologus (c. 400-450) is another giant of Patrick's day, and he also linked faith with obedience to Rome: "We exhort you in all things . . . to pay obedience to what is written by the most blessed Pope of the Roman city; for St. Peter, who both lives and rules in his own see, grants to those who ask for it the truth of faith."

Next we call witnesses from the sixth century. We have already mentioned that St. Columbanus stressed how tightly the Celts held to the beliefs of St. Jerome. Now St. Columbanus gives his own testimony, writing to Pope Boniface IV (608-615): "I have pledged myself on your behalf that the Roman Church will never defend a heretic against the Catholic faith . . . the purity of the stream is not to be ascribed to the channel but to the source . . . We indeed . . . are bound to the Chair of Peter . . . I believe that the column of the Church is always solid in Rome . . . O King of Kings, do thou follow Peter, and let the whole Church follow thee."

A Catholic is one who holds the same teaching as does the Apostolic See . . . so St. Irenaeus; so Cyprian; so Jerome; so Augustine. And so also St. Maximus (c. 580-662): "If a man does not want to be, or be called, a heretic . . . hasten before all things to be in communion with the Roman See. If he is in communion with it, he should be acknowledged by all and everywhere as faithful and orthodox. He speaks in vain who tries to persuade me of the orthodoxy of those who . . . refuse obedience to His Holiness the Pope of the most holy Church of Rome: that is, to the Apostolic See."

Thus the test of Catholicism is handed down. The identical teaching is given by St. Bernard (1090-1153) in the early Middle Ages: "The solicitude of all Churches rests on that one Apostolic See, so that all may be united under it and in it, and it may be careful for the sake of all to preserve the unity of the Spirit in the bond of peace." It is heard again from the mouth of St. Thomas Aquinas (c. 1225-1274): "The drawing-up of a creed is the prerogative of him to whom it falls to say the final word as to what things are of faith, so that all may hold them with unshaken faith. This, however, is the right of the Supreme Pontiff, to whom the graver and more difficult questions, which arise in the Church, are referred, as is laid down in the Decretals. For which reason the Lord said to Peter when he made him supreme pontiff: *I have prayed for thee, Peter, that thy faith may not fail, and thou, being once converted, strengthen thy brethren.* And the reason for this is, that there must be only one faith shared by the whole Church . . . which cannot be secured, unless any question of faith which arises is settled by him who rules the whole Church, with the result that his sentence is firmly accepted by the whole Church. And in this way a new drawing-up of the creed is the prerogative of the supreme pontiff, as are all other matters which concern the whole Church. . . ."[3] Again, in his *Contra errores Graecorum*, chapter XXXII, under the sub-heading "That it is the pope's prerogative to settle matters of faith," St. Thomas writes: "We also demonstrate that it is for the aforesaid pontiff to settle matters of faith. For Cyril states in the *Thesaurus*, 'Let us remain members attached to our head, our apostolic throne of the Roman Pontiffs, from whom we must learn what we should believe and hold.' Again, Maximus in his letter to the Eastern Christians says, 'All the ends of the earth which have sincerely believed in the Lord and Catholics everywhere who profess the true Faith, look to the Roman Church as to the sun and receive from it the light of the catholic and apostolic Faith; and rightly so . . .' It is clear, too, that he is set over the Patriarchs since Cyril says that it is for it, i.e., for the apostolic throne of the Roman Pontiffs, 'alone to rebuke, correct, lay down, loose, arrange, and bind in the place of Him Who appointed him.' " St. Thomas's authority is not diminished by the fact that the passage attributed to St. Cyril is actually the work of some other earlier Christian. (Cf. Otto Bardenhewer, *Patrology*, p. 367.) We shall return to the *Contra Errores Graecorum* on a later page. St. Thomas firmly upholds the teaching authority of the Church which resides especially in the pope. Against such authority, he states, "neither Jerome nor Augustine nor any other of the sacred doctors upheld his own opinion," and he refers to St. Jerome's appeal to the faith of Peter in the see of Peter.[4]

Four voices call from England in harmony with the saints and doctors who have testified. The first is St. Anselm (c. 1033-1109): "It is certain that he who does not obey the Roman Pontiff is disobedient to the Apostle Peter, nor is he of that flock given to Peter by God." The second is St. Thomas Becket (+1170): "Who doubts that the Roman

---

[3] *Summa Theologica*, Secunda Secundae, Q.I, Art. X. Compare with St. Thomas's words those of Dr. Küng: "In the papal *Credo* (1968) the Pope in typical Roman fashion identified himself with the Church without consulting it . . . and put questionable theologumena of the Roman tradition on a par with the central statements of the Christian faith." (*Infallible?* Foreword, p. 21.)

[4] *Ibidem,* Secunda Secundae, Q.XI, Art. II.

Church is the head of all churches and the source of doctrine?" And here is the other Thomas, More, who died under the other King Henry: "I am moved to obedience to that See, not only by what learned and holy men have written, but by this fact especially, that we see so often that, on the one hand, every enemy of the Christian faith makes war on that See, and that, on the other hand, no one has ever declared himself an enemy of that See who has not also shortly after shown most evidently that he was the enemy of Christ and of the Christian religion. . . . God will not forsake His own Vicar."[5]

The fourth voice is, surprisingly, the voice of the king who killed More. Mgr. Philip Hughes, in *The Reformation in England*, gives points from the king's *Assertio VII Sacramentorum* against Luther (Part III, Chapter I): 'Luther, in fact, "cannot deny but that all the faithful honour and acknowledge the sacred Roman see for their mother and supreme". . . . What punishment is too great for the man who "will not obey the Chief Priest and Supreme Judge upon earth?". . . . It is vain, says Henry, to imagine distinctions between Christ's church and the Pope's church . . . "the whole church, not only is subject to Christ, but for Christ's sake, to Christ's only vicar the pope of Rome." As for the Church itself, it "has from God not only the power of discerning betwixt divine and human senses of scripture . . . but also . . . betwixt divine institutions and the traditions of men . . . Christ's care being that His Church may not err in any manner whatsoever." '

A point which must be faced is: if the pope is to be the source of unity, then, as St. Thomas Aquinas maintained, it falls to him "to say the final word as to what things *are* of faith." The pope cannot be God's bar to disunity if a Catholic is free to contest as against the pope: "But I do not hold that this matter is of divine revelation. Therefore I deny your competence to teach it." Those who maintain this line have not grasped the *raison d'être* of the papacy. . . . "that by the appointment of a Head the occasion of schism

---

[5] *Blessed John Fisher,* by Rev. T. E. Bridgett, p. 139.

may be taken away." This point is of importance as, since the publication of *Humanae Vitae*, voices have claimed that Scripture is silent or ambiguous on the matter of contraception, and have denied the pope the right to echo the Church's tradition as distinct from Scripture texs, or to pronounce with authority on the natural law since this, they are convinced, lies outside the boundary of revelation. (Yet Vatican II, in the *Declaration of Religious Freedom*, laid down that it is the Church's duty to "declare and confirm by her authority those principles of the moral order which have their origin in human nature itself." It is accordingly the pope's duty, and a Catholic cannot appoint himself arbiter of the scope of tradition.)

Cardinal Newman wrote in his *Letter to the Duke of Norfolk*: "Another limitation is given in Pope Pius's own conditions set down in the *Pastor Aeternus*, for the exercise of infallibility: viz., the proposition defined will be without any claims to be considered binding on the belief of Catholics, unless it is referable to the Apostolic *depositum*, through the channel either of Scripture or Tradition: and, though *the Pope is the judge whether it is so referable or not*, yet the necessity of his professing to abide by this reference is in itself a certain limitation to his dogmatic action." What Newman wrote there regarding infallible teaching— and he seemed, as we shall establish later, to extend infallibility to encyclicals—is applicable to all authoritative papal teaching, and it is worth recalling that Newman pointed out that the error involved in the statement "Papal judgments and decrees may, without sin, be disobeyed or differed from" is a denial of the principle of the teaching of the great Anglican, Hooker. "It is plain to common sense," he emphasized, "that no society can stand if its rules are disobeyed. What club or union would not expel members who refused to be so bound?"

PAPAL CLAIMS AND THEIR ACCEPTANCE

We go on now to indicate how the Holy See asserted its claims in early days without challenge except from heretical and schismatic forces which even most modern dissidents would recognise as such. Precisely because the claims harmonised with the belief of the faithful, because the Pope's claims were what *he* had been taught to accept in his own youth, there was no general challenge. We remind the reader that we are not treating here of a claim to teach only in a defined area of infallibility, but of a claim that papal teaching in general, given to the Church, must be accepted, whether it concerns doctrine or morals. Catholicism, after all, is not a bare handbook of dogma but also a way of life, and, indeed, the Scriptures tell us that the early Christians spoke of their religion as "The Way".

About 96 A.D., Pope Clement wrote to the Church at Corinth, and Harnack has commented on the letter that it proves "that already at the end of the first century the Roman Church . . . kept watch with maternal care for the distant churches, and . . . knew how to utter the word that is an expression of duty, of love and of authority at the same time." This was the word: "If some do not obey what God has said by us, let them know that they will be involved in no small sin and danger."

When St. Ambrose urged that the decrees of a local council must be sent to Rome for scrutiny, he was expressing age-old custom. Pope Innocent I wrote in 416 to a Council which sought ratification of its statutes: "You decided that it was proper to refer to our judgment, knowing what is due to the Apostolic See, since all we who are set in this place desire to follow the Apostle from whom the very episcopate and whole authority of this name is derived. . . . You have . . . preserved the customs of the Fathers and have not spurned that which they decreed by a divine and not human sentence, that whatsoever is done, even though it be in distant provinces, should not be ended without being brought to the knowledge of this See, that by its authority the whole just pronouncement should be strengthened, and that from it all other churches (like waters flowing from their natural source and flowing through the different regions of the world, the pure streams of one incorrupt head), should receive what they should enjoin. . . ."

Boniface I (418-422) wrote: "None has ever been so rash as to oppose the apostolic primacy, the judgment of which may not be revised; none rebels against it, unless he would be judged in his turn." "It is clear that this church (Rome) is to all the churches throughout the world as the head is to its members, and that whoever separates himself from it becomes an exile from the Christian religion, since he ceases to belong to its fellowship."

Pope Leo the Great (+461) taught the same lesson: ". . . the direction of the universal Church should converge to the one See of Peter, and nothing anywhere disagree from its head." It is the authentic teaching which we have already learned from the pen of St. Irenaeus. Pope Leo wrote also: "The Lord takes care of Peter in a special way and prays especially for Peter, as if the perseverance of the others would be more safely ensured if the soul of their leader should stand unconquered. It is in Peter, then, that the strength of the others is safeguarded. . . ." Again: "He (our Lord) originally assigned it (the responsibility of the episcopate) to the most blessed Peter, the head of all the apostles; and intends that from him, as from the head, His gifts shall be conveyed to the whole body, so that whoever dares to secede from the foundation of Peter may know that he is excluded from communion with God."

The evidence is repetitive and to that extent tiring but its very repetition is its strength and proof of the folly of those who cry 'Creeping infallibility!' when told that they must accept papal teaching. History, be it said, is silent about creeping infallibility but loquacious about galloping insubordination.

At the Council of Ephesus (431 A.D.), the papal legate asserted: "It is he (Peter) who unto this day and without intermission both lives and judges in his successor." Sixtus III (432-440) wrote to John of Antioch: "The blessed Apostle Peter handed down in his successors that which he received. Who would wish to be parted from the doctrine of that Apostle, whom the Master Himself instructed before the rest? . . . he received the original and direct faith which can admit of no dispute."

Twice at least appeal was made to the *fact* of unblemished continuity of teaching at Rome. We read in the formula of Hormisdas, signed in 519 by 250 Eastern bishops: "We cannot ignore the declaration of our Lord Jesus Christ when He said: Thou art Peter, etc. Moreover, the truth of His words is borne out by the facts, since in the Apostolic See the Catholic religion has always been preserved without spot . . . Wherefore I hope that I may deserve to be with you in one communion, such as is defined by the Apostolic See, where the permanence of the Christian religion is intact and genuine. . . ."

Pope Agatho (678-681), a Greek who is said to have given privileges to some English monasteries and to St. Paul's cathedral in London, wrote to the sixth ecumenical Council at Constantinople: "The holy Church of God . . . must confess with us the formula of truth and apostolic tradition, the evangelical and apostolic rule of faith, which is founded upon the firm Rock of blessed Peter, the Prince of the Apostles, which by His favour remains free from all error." The bishops acclaimed his words with, "It is Peter who speaks through Agatho!"—as, at Chalcedon, they had cried out, "Peter has spoken thus by Leo!" It is of value, too, to record what the writers of the 28th canon, at Chalcedon, wrote to Leo of Dioscorus: "He had in his folly confronted him to whom the Saviour entrusted the custody of the Vine, that is, your holiness, and had chosen to excommunicate him who was zealous to make one the body of the Church." It recalls the words which St. Optatus (c. 370) addressed to the Donatists: "Whence is it therefore that you strive to obtain for yourselves the keys of the kingdom of heaven, you who fight against the chair of Peter?"

The rights, and duties, of Rome are shown again in the Middle Ages in the formula of faith professed by the Emperor Michael Paleologus, through his legate, at the second Council of Lyons in 1274: "As it (the See of Rome) is bound to defend the truth of faith beyond all others, so also if any question should arise concerning the faith it must be determined by its judgment." The Middle Ages have also set down, in the decree of the General Council of Florence which is printed at the head of this chapter, that the Roman Pontiff is "the father and teacher of all Christians . . . full power was given to him, in Blessed Peter, by our Lord Jesus Christ to feed, to rule, and to govern the universal Church". Again and again this identical teaching recurs in the official decrees of the Church. The right of the pope to withdraw some serious matter from discussion in the Church and reserve it for his own judgment is clearly recognised as part of his authority as teacher of the whole Church. "Rightly can the popes, because of the supreme power given them over the whole Church, reserve for their adjudication any specially grave matters." (Trent, Session XIV, cap. 7.) An example of this was the way in which Paul VI reserved to himself the final judgment on contraception, and the way in which Fr. Bernard Häring expressed, at the time, the Catholic attitude: "Of course every theologian and every Catholic will humbly accept a decision by the teaching authority of the Church on this subject . . . *even if it runs counter to his own previous opinion.*"[6]

Pius XII was not, then, 'creeping infallibly' when he laid down in *Humani Generis*: "Nor is it to be supposed that a position advanced in an encyclical does not, *ipso facto*, claim assent . . . Such teachings come under the day-to-day teaching of the Church, which is covered by the promise, 'He who listens to you, listens to me' (Luke X, 16). For the most part the positions advanced, the duties inculcated . . . are already bound up . . . with the general body of Catholic teaching. And when the Roman Pontiffs go out of their way to pronounce on some subject which has hitherto been controverted . . . this subject can no longer be regarded as a matter of free debate."

In the light of the evidence of the centuries, the reader can now spot the falsity of the Modernist, whether it is Tyrrell going on about "the new-fangled dictatorial conception of the papacy—i.e., of a privileged private judgement" (*Medievalism*) or Fr. Richard P. McBrien writing in *Do We Need the Church?* (p. 182): ". . . it is one of the great

[6] *Catholic Herald,* May 29, 1964.

theological and pastoral tragedies of our time that the average Christian attitude towards the papacy and papal authority should be formed almost exclusively within the context
of the birth-control issue. . . . Both extremes have accepted . . . the post-Vatican I ecclesiology which exalted the
Pope to a kind of supertheologian." The attitude of traditional Catholics was formed through the centuries and they
received *Humanae Vitae* in the light of tradition; the phrase
Roma Locuta est did not originate in 1870. "Progressive"
Catholics, however, abandoned tradition when papal teaching
hurt, precisely as Henry VIII quietly relegated the *Assertio*
when the Pope would not give a verdict in his favour. Nor
did Vatican I make the pope any more a supertheologian
than he was to Jerome or Aquinas; he is something far
greater, the Rock. Once again, the Modernist has ignored
the facts of history.

THE SECOND VATICAN COUNCIL

The recent Council takes up our theme, teaching that
God's people clings to the faith and penetrates it more deeply "under the lead of a sacred teaching authority to which
it loyally defers." (*Lumen Gentium*). Now we look at what
the same constitution affirms about papal power, and let
each word be carefully weighed on reading as it was at
writing. . . . "In virtue of his office, that is, as Vicar of
Christ and pastor of the whole Church, the Roman Pontiff
has

> full,
> supreme,
> and universal
> power
> over the Church. And he can
> always
> exercise this power
> freely."

The Council continues: "Together with its head, the
Roman Pontiff, and never without this head, the episcopal
order is the subject of supreme and full power over the uni-

versal Church. But this power can be exercised only with
the consent of the Roman Pontiff. For our Lord made Simon
Peter alone the rock and key-bearer of the Church, and
appointed him shepherd of the whole flock." Again: "The
Roman Pontiff, as the successor of Peter, is the perpetual
and visible source and foundation of the unity of the bishops
and of the multitude of the faithful." "Bishops, teaching
in communion with the Roman Pontiff, are to be respected
by all as witnesses to divine truth." (By implication, a
bishop rejecting papal teaching, is to be considered as a false
witness, or, as Bishop Butler reminded us in *The Idea of the
Church*, p. 43, "a schismatic is one who refuses to be subject
to the Roman See.") "In matters of faith and morals, the
bishops speak in the name of Christ and the faithful are to
accept their teaching and adhere to it with a religious assent
of soul.

> This religious submission
> of will
> and of mind

must be shown in a special way to the authentic teaching
of the Roman Pontiff even when he is not speaking *ex
cathedra* . . . in such a way that his supreme magisterium

> is acknowledged with reverence,
> and the judgments made by him are sincerely adhered to
> according to his manifest mind and will."

Since 1968, we have seen agonised attempts by some
to maintain that they were still giving assent when they were
dissenting. Men who were by conviction opposed to anything
smacking of legalism tied themselves into legalistic knots
attempting to be papists while being anti-papal, but the
Council decrees are addressed not to lawyers but to open
Christian hearts. In addition, attempts to corrode the terms
'assent' or 'submission' collapse before the command that
the papal magisterium is to be acknowledged with reverence,
and the Pope's judgments are to be sincerely adhered to.
This involves three points: (1) the pope is our supreme
teacher, not adviser or colleague; (2) we must meet his

authority with reverence, not debate; and (3), in consequence, give credence to his teaching, our obligation being not merely to be silent but to accept.

THE COUNCIL OBSCURED

To see how a Catholic can obscure this, we turn to Dr. John Marshall's *You and the Church*. (The staff at Corpus Christi College of Catechetics, London, resigned because Cardinal Heenan objected to five of their visiting lecturers. Dr. Marshall, Fr. Gregory Baum and Fr. Enda McDonagh were the only three named.) Dr. Marshall is happy with Vatican II until he comes to the passage which we have just quoted. He then prints (p. 63) the first sentence regarding religious submission down to and including "not speaking *ex cathedra*," and he proposes as the Council's teaching: "Because the pope is supreme pastor of the church his word must be listened to with attention and respect . . . statements like 'the pope has spoken—discussions must cease' are nonsensical." (Alas, poor Augustine!) He jealously guards from the reader that the Council drives the point home with: submission "must be shown in such a way that his supreme magisterium is acknowledged with reverence, the judgments made by him *are sincerely adhered to . . .*" Thus readers are misled by the writing, tailored to fit a case, which has sprung up since *Humanae Vitae*. Dr. Marshall has 'spiked' the Council, and he himself admits (p. 79): "It is the wresting of quotations out of context which enables current distortions to be presented as if they were the true picture." The terms 'assent', 'submission of will and of mind' are strong enough alone, but 'sincerely adhered to' destroys any facade of doubt and must not be evaded. One notes that Dr. Marshall states (p. 63): "The Pope has no special access to truth either in his statements which are infallible or in those which are not." He has side-stepped the issue, since Truth has promised unique access from the other direction—*to* the Pope. "I have prayed for thee, that thy faith may not fail . . . it is for thee to be the support of thy brethren."

Guided by Vatican II and St. Thomas Aquinas' teaching that it is the pope's prerogative to formulate the creed and bind all Catholics to his teaching, we see how far people can drift when we read Fr. Richard P. McBrien's *Credo Presents One View* in the *Dubuque Witness*, July 18, 1968, referring to Pope Paul's *Creed of the People of God*: "In so far as this document allows the views of one particular school of theology (a minority view, let it be added, that was clearly rejected at Vatican II) to intrude itself upon the ground of authentic Christian tradition, the *Credo* has transformed itself from an expression of common faith binding the whole Church together, into a personal brief of one party in the current theological debate." There are several points to note here. First, there is the appeal either to a nonexistent decree of the Council or to an imaginary spirit set over against the letter of the decrees. Next, there is the obliteration of the supreme magisterium of the Pope. And, lastly, there is the substitution of a bogus majority vote, springing from a secularised outlook. I say 'bogus' because Fr. McBrien has given no evidence that the majority of theologians differ from the Pope, and, if he had, his majority would confront the great mass of the faithful. And I write "springing from a secularised outlook" since the approach derives from politics. When "the whole world groaned to find itself Arian," it was, we repeat, loyalty to God to be in the apparent minority. Lastly, Christ has picked out a 'minority' of one to cement the majority in truth, and, if we challenge papal teaching, we betray—as Cardinal Gilroy of Sydney put it—a mentality that is "radically uncatholic, radically unorthodox. Plainly it is a rejection of the authentic ordinary magisterium of the Vicar of Christ."[7]

The claim to authority today is met at times with a cry that authority is 'out' and service 'in.' The dilemma is a false one. It is true that the Pope's ancient title is *servus servorum Dei*, but what kind of a servant must he be? Cardinal O'Boyle gave us the answer: "The Pope is set over us by Christ to serve us—yes. But not to serve us as a waiter serves us in a restaurant, according to our desires. Rather to serve us as Christ served us, as one sent by the Father

[7] *L'Osservatore Romano,* April 4, 1968.

to feed men a better food than they asked for."[8] The Pope serves the bread of the Gospel even when we clamour for a stone.

Again, it is easy to view the right to cry 'causa finita est' as intellectual repression, but, in fact, the Holy See speaks with authority on a question only after it has been discussed in theological circles, and *in* circles, with the inconclusiveness known to all who have attended seminars. It is because men will talk for years and never agree, and because majority votes are no sure criterion of truth, that there has to be a voice with the final say. Because of this Erasmus wrote wearily in Reformation days: "It is not that the words of Christ are not enough for me; but surely it is not strange if I take as their interpreter that Church by whose authority I believe in the canonical Scriptures. Others, perhaps, may be cleverer or stronger; as for me, I rest safely in nothing so much as in the certain judgments of the Church. Of reasons and arguments there is never an end." There is never an end, especially as old errors are tricked out in new costumes every few centuries. As Chesterton wrote in *The Catholic Church and Conversion*: "Nine out of ten of what we call new ideas are simply old mistakes. The Catholic Church has for one of her chief duties that of preventing people from making these old mistakes; from making them over and over again for ever, as people always do if they are left to themselves. . . . She does dogmatically defend humanity from its worst foes, those hoary and horrible and devouring monsters of the old mistakes."

We are, then, bound to accept papal teaching given to the universal Church. Such obedience is of the essence of Catholicism and, remembering the parable of the Good Shepherd, we can see an unintended truth in Professor Rogier's dictum that "Obedience is the virtue of sheep."[9] Newman wrote in the *Essay on the Development of Christian Doctrine* that, while the supremacy of conscience was basic to natural religion, the supremacy of the magisterium (Apostle, Pope,

---

[8] A lecture delivered in New York, March 2, 1969.
[9] See *Herder Correspondence*, August, 1964.

Church, Bishop) was the essence of revealed religion; the inward guide has been supplemented by, and, to that extent, subordinated to, an outer guide, and it is important to remember this key teaching, when the natural light is so often today set up against supernatural light, revelation preserved and expounded by the Church's teachers. Cardinal Heenan has lamented that "An article in . . . *Concilium* is at least as likely to win their (Catholic theologians') respect as a papal encyclical,"[10] which is to put mere human cleverness in the scales against the charism given to Peter. Neither Jerome nor Augustine, said St. Thomas, upheld his own view against Rome.

A PRIDE OF BISHOPS?

It will have been noticed that, when we cited the Council's decree as to the duty of giving assent to the teaching of bishops, we set in italics the qualifying phrase—"teaching in communion with the Roman Pontiff." That is, bishops delete their own authority if they go maverick and teach in opposition to Rome, "the perpetual and visible source of the unity of the bishops." The Council's outlook had been expressed in advance by Leo XIII in *Satis Cognitum* (1896): "Above all things the need of union between the bishops and the successors of Peter is clear and undeniable. This bond once broken, Christians would be separated and scattered, and would in no wise form one body and one flock. 'The safety of the Church depends on the dignity of the chief-priest, to whom if an extraordinary and supreme power is not given, there are as many schisms to be expected in the Church as there are priests.' (St. Jerome, *Dialog. Contra Luciferianos*, n.9). . . . But the episcopal order is rightly judged to be in communion with Peter, as Christ commanded it, if it be subject to and obeys Peter; *otherwise it necessarily becomes a lawless and disorderly crowd.* It is not sufficient for the due preservation of the unity of the faith that the head should merely have been charged with the office of superintendent, or should have been invested solely with a

---

[10] *The Tablet,* May 18, 1968.

power of direction. But it is absolutely necessary that he should have received real and sovereign authority which the whole community is bound to obey."

We have in our time glimpsed "a lawless and disorderly crowd", as some bishops are disregarding Rome, and traditional doctrine and morals as a concomitant, and we looked suddenly on the face of anarchy and schism when some hierarchies accepted *Humanae Vitae* and others "qualified" it. If we are willing to face up honestly to what such lawlessness can encompass, and be warned, we have to turn to the fourth century. St. Gregory Nazianzen wrote bitterly in 382 A.D.: "If I must speak the truth, I feel disposed to shun every conference of bishops; for never did I see a synod brought to a happy issue, and remedying, and not rather aggravating, existing evils," while St. Hilary wrote in 364 A.D.: "Up to date, the only reason why Christ's people is not murdered by the priests of anti-Christ, with this deceit of impiety, is that they take the words which the heretics use, to denote the faith which they themselves hold. The ears of the people are holier than the hearts of the priests." "Since the Nicene Council," he lamented, "we have done nothing but write the creed. . . . We impose creeds by the year or by the month; we change our minds about our impositions; then we prohibit our changes; then we anathematize our prohibitions."[11] No doubt the good man, in holy indignation, was laying it on a bit thick, and yet—this is collegiality minus Peter, the weathervane of the majority vote, and thus history teaches us why von Hügel spoke of the transcendent God Who needs and backs the autocratic Pope, and why Newman, as Mr. John Coulson indicated, "saw the Pope as a ruler, not a philosopher—'he strangles whilst we prate'— in whose person the Church addressed the wild intellect of man with blows not words. . . ."[12]

Not only the Fathers rebut, but history dismisses, *one* possible interpretation of a speech made at the National Mission Study Week at Cavan in September, 1968. I quote

[11] Cf. Newman, *On Consulting the Faithful in Matters of Doctrine.*
[12] *Introduction* to above.

from *The Irish Times* (September 6): "The Rev. James O'Connell, S.M.A. . . . outlined developments in the Church in which the Papacy would become more merged with local churches and while retaining a certain primacy would lose its absoluteness of control. In the future Church, he said, the Pope would not be burdened with the claim to the supreme monopoly of theological wisdom or with the system of pervasive control which had produced a centralising and career-ridden Curia." There is not a word there which could not be given an orthodox interpretation, but spoken today, by a priest who suggested that we might allow polygamy to native converts, it rings subversive. The Pope must retain 'absolute' control even if he devolves, and arguably should devolve, many matters to local bishops. He does not claim, nor has anyone claimed for him, a monopoly of theological wisdom, and, something which is not honestly faced up to so often, central control has been imposed because of local failings. It may be legitimately advanced that papal control of some matters is unnecessary, exactly as we grumble at Whitehall or Washington, but it cannot be denied that central control in general rose from provincial abuses. Central control has been almost abolished as far as Holland is concerned, and the Dutch Church is in shards.

The Bishop of Cork, Dr. Lucey, rose to comment on Fr. O'Connell's speech, and did so in a sad vein: "The winds of change seem to blow ahead much further than I anticipated." He explained: "The Pope has not a monopoly of theological wisdom but he has, and the Church have, the promise of Christ that He would be with them—not with the theologians." It was an answer to the wits who think it original to cry that "the pope does not have a hot-line to the Holy Ghost," ignorant that the gibe is seventy years old, Tyrrell having got in first with his "special telegraph between Heaven and the Pope." Because there *is* a link between heaven and the papacy, from God's direction in both senses, even the 14th century conciliarist, Pierre d'Ailly, taught: "It is the privilege of the Roman Church, which no other individual church possesses, to be able to represent the universal Church."

With respect, Bishop Lucey was inexact in his first re-mark. The winds are whistling back to the dismal Siberia of the 4th century when the Church was split by the dissension of bishops, with the papacy largely unheeded, for over sixty years. Newman wrote in his *Letter to the Duke of Norfolk*: "Say that the Christian policy remained, as history represents it to us in the fourth century . . . there would be a legion of ecclesiastics, each bishop with his following. . . . each with his own views . . . all over Christendom. It would be the Anglican theory, made real." "It couldn't happen today," one mutters, and then finds Mr. St. John-Stevas writing that "The situation of the Roman Catholic Church in England can only be described as Anglican."[13] Again, we who live in democracies, know that, for all the drawbacks, democracy can work, and we know that, if bishops are in accord with the Holy See, they can be effective. And yet . . . the Press reports are not encouraging when they tell us of international synods. "Disastrous end to chaotic, frustrating Synod" was the *Catholic Herald's* banner (November 12, 1971), referring to the Third Synod of Bishops. "An unsatisfactory and often disheartening assembly," said the report of Fr. John F. X. Harriott, S.J. (*ibidem*). It was a repeat of the report of the symposium of European bishops at Chur two years previously. . . . "Cardinal Heenan said that, so far as he was concerned, it was all a waste of time" (*Catholic Herald*, July 18, 1969). Hence our need of the pope!

Bishop Butler cannot have realised how pessimistic he sounded when he said in an interview:[14] "We (progressives) are thus certain of the Council. I am not sure that we are certain of the Pope . . . I think the emphasis has been on a Papal Monarchy over the last 100 years. For the next 100 it will be on the democratic rule of bishops."

LIGHT FROM VATICAN I

Vatican II complemented Vatican I, and, inverting that, Vatican I complemented Vatican II. Let us see therefore,

[13] *The Sunday Times Magazine,* December 29, 1968.
[14] *The Sunday Times,* December 5, 1965.

to make our picture more complete, what was the infallible teaching of the first Vatican Council. It laid down: "For the Holy Spirit is not promised to the successors of Peter so that, through His revelation, they may bring new doctrine to light, but that, with His help, they may keep inviolate and faithfully expound the revelation handed down through the Apostles, the deposit of faith. And indeed all the venerable Fathers have adhered to the apostolic doctrine of Peter's successors, and all the holy orthodox Doctors have revered and kept to it, in the full knowledge that the See of Holy Peter remains always unstained by error in keeping with the divine promise. . . ."

"This charism, therefore, of unfailing truth and faith was divinely bestowed on Peter and his successors in this See, that they might devote this wonderful gift to the salvation of all, so that the whole flock of Christ, guarded by them from the poisonous food of error, might feed on heavenly doctrine that, the occasion of schism removed, the whole Church might remain one and, set on its foundation, stand firm against the gates of hell." (Denzinger 1836, 1837.)

There followed the famous definition of papal infallibility when defining, *ex cathedra*, a doctrine of faith or morals. Preceding these passages came a warning that it was error to imagine that one could appeal over the Pope's head to a General Council, and, following them, the Council taught that the Pope's definitions were final of themselves and did not require the consent of the Church.

As we gather from the reference given above to the Fathers and Doctors, to most of whom a technically infallible pronouncement of the Pope was unknown, the assistance given to the Pope is not limited to the rare occasions when he solemnly defines, and the statement about the Holy See's remaining always unstained by error is not confined to 'infallible' utterances. It states a historic fact about the Pope's teaching *qua* Pope to the Church, in spite of occasional private error on his part. The exercise of the papal extraordinary magisterium, when, if we may use the phrase, he "fires the big guns," is exceedingly rare. Often, too, his function is exercised in a negative kind of way. "Indeed," wrote Newman, in the *Apologia*, "it is one of the reproaches against the Roman Church, that it has originated nothing, and has served as a sort of *remora* or brake in the development of doctrine. And it is an objection which I really embrace as a truth; for such I conceive to be the main purpose of its extraordinary gift." Both steering and braking are, however, involved in the charism. The Holy Spirit guides the papacy down the straight road of doctrinal development or at least exposition, and radio and press nowadays broadcast a stream of teaching from the Holy Father. It is not without significance that it is only after stressing the normal, the assistance given constantly to the Pope as he carries out his task, that the first Vatican Council went on to speak of the abnormal or rare, the exercise of his full authority in defining doctrine.

Here we may dispose of an error which has cropped up in Dr. Küng's *The Living Church*. Vatican I, he claims, "clearly stated the limits of papal infallibility," but in fact it did no such thing. It said carefully that the Pope taught infallibly when certain conditions were verified, but it did not say that he taught infallibly only then. It was a careful commitment and we must not make the Council affirm more than it intended. Another Council may go further than Vatican I, as doctrine develops, and it might be a great pity if it does since people can be so awed by infallibility that they forget our 'daily bread', which is *authority* in teaching.

FOR INFALLIBILITY, READ INDEFECTIBILITY?

It will have been remarked that, though this chapter is headed *The Teaching Authority*, attention has been paid almost exclusively to the teaching office of Rome and to what is called the ordinary magisterium of the Pope as distinct from the solemn magisterium which defined the doctrines, for instance, of the Immaculate Conception and the Assumption. The latter exercise of office has been taken for granted since it is not in general called into question today. Even there the statement has had to be a careful one, as a call to abandon the doctrine of papal infallibility has been made by Bishop Francis Simons, S.V.D., a Dutchman, in his book *Infallibility and the Evidence.* Bishop Simons felt that he "had no choice but to publish his case" but it is not a Catholic case. As Bishop Butler wrote: "To admit the possibility of development is not the same as conceding the possibility of jettisoning the very principle of infallibility. To do the latter would not merely be to part company with the Church of Vatican I and II or the Church of the Council of Trent. It would be to part company with the Middle Ages, with the great Church of the first four Councils, with the pre-Nicene Church and the Church of the New Testament."[15]

FR. TYRRELL RIDES AGAIN

What the Bishop has said does not only disqualify Bishop Simons as a Catholic spokesman, but indicates also the folly of the position adopted, as we saw, by Tyrrell. Because Rome would have none of his doctrine-substitution, he disowned the Councils of Trent and Vatican I, thinking that he could stop there, not seeing that he was disowning all Catholicism. And this is the position into which a Modernist is forced by the rigours of logic—that, as he is sure that he is right, and the Church wrong, he must either deny, or try to reinterpret, infallibility. Probably he will do each at a different stage, beginning, one assumes, by substituting some version of final indefectibility for true infallibility. We listen to Tyrrell writing to his imaginary University professor (p. 56): ". . . we feel sure of some men that though they may go wrong for a while they will come right again . . . we have faith in the man . . . Analogously, it seems to me that a man might have great faith in the Church, in the people of God, in the unformulated ideas . . . at work in the great body of the faithful . . . and yet regard the Church's consciously formulated ideas . . . about herself as more or less untrue to her deepest nature, that he might refuse to believe her own account of herself as against his

[15] *The Tablet,* November 25, 1967.

instinctive conviction of her true character; that he might say to her: . . . 'You know not your own essential spirit.' " But what, one asks, if her essential Spirit is the Holy Ghost Who guards her from all error in doctrine?

Tyrrell, of course, wavered uncertainly. At one stage, supreme authority belonged to the *consensus fidelium*—in practice, his intellectual sympathisers—and therefore "To say that the pope is infallible is only to make him official interpreter of the faith of the faithful."[16] This flows again from the pen of Fr. McBrien (*op. cit.*, pp. 187-188): "The conclusion must be, therefore, that infallibility applies only to the Church as a community, and to the Pope as spokesman of the community. . . . Personal papal infallibility, as understood by post-Vatican I theologians, is a theological fiction. . . ." Just before these words, Fr. McBrien has shown the usual Modernist disregard for what ordinary Catholics hold: "The more conventional Catholic understanding of papal infallibility makes of it a meaningless and useless enterprise." Has it not occurred to him that, if this is what the 'community' hold and held, and the pope has echoed it as their spokesman, then, by his own rules, his views are nonsense?

Writing of Tyrrell, Ranchetti remarked (*op. cit.*, p. 52): "One thing only was never in doubt: the error of Rome, an error obstinately maintained and restated, consisting in refusal to take account of a changed situation, *to recognize the need to introduce into the concept of infallibility modifications* . . . and to maintain the distinction between the *Ecclesia docens* and the *ecclesia discens*. . . ."

This brings us to Dr. Küng who has taken up, perhaps without knowing it, Tyrrell's thesis of the wandering spirit of truth. Rebelliousness has its own momentum, and a rebel ends up by holding positions which were quite alien to him when the process of criticism and insubordination began. The career of Luther is a prime example—as Catholic dogma is an integrated system, one denial was found to lead to another. "How did I get here?" the dazed rebel may be pic-

[16] Cf. Jean Rivière, *op. cit.*, p. 202.

tured as wondering as he reaches the unplanned *terminus
ad quem*.

To reach an accurate reading of Dr. Küng's position
now, we do not go to the conservative critics, who might
be biased in their estimate, but to observers 'outside the
walls.' His friend, Charles Davis, in an interview published
in *The Month* (January, 1971), passed the verdict: "He has
denied the doctrine of infallibility in the sense in which it
was defined." Dr. Mascall, of the Church of England, sees
him in the same quandary as 16th century Reformers and
corrects Hugh Montefiore's "Anglicanism" to "Lutheranism",[17] while Harvey Cox, the Baptist theologian, came out
breezily with: "He is a straight Protestant theologian who
wears a Roman collar. I'm more Catholic than Hans Küng
is."[18]

This is no idle gossip but is relevant to the point under
consideration which is the attempt to reinterpret infallibility.
Davis remarked in the interview mentioned: "Because of
their paradoxical position, people who hold more or less the
same views as I do and yet remain within the Church seem
to suffer distorting effects on their thinking. I get an impression of . . . an uneasy subtlety or ingenuity in arguing."

This uneasy ingenuity is patent in Küng's thesis. He
is no longer at one with the Church in belief—over the
teaching of *Humanae Vitae*, for one thing, and, with the
blunt honesty and courage which accompany his rebellion,
he has conceded that the teaching in that encyclical "meets
all the requirements of infallibility, although it is not issued
in solemn form." There is his quandary: he is convinced
that his opinions are right, and yet the 'infallible' Church
teaches otherwise . . . then, if he is to remain in the Church,
the doctrine of infallibility must be adjusted.

"If," he said, "we have a lot of errors in the Church
we have to consider this. . . . I think we could express the
word 'infallible' by a much better word that is also very
traditional . . . 'the indefectibility of the Church in truth

[17] See page 148.
[18] Cf. *The Tablet,* August 8, 1970.

or the indestructibility of the Church in truth.' " He locates this infallibility or indestructibility in the way in which countless good people, in spite of the Church's doctrinal errors, have lived by the light of the Gospel. It requires, however, only a moment to spot what Davis calls the "uneasy ingenuity." Where Bishop Simons seems to reject our doctrine with little ado, Dr. Küng is trying to switch the doctrine. He indicates steadfastness in love of our Lord, for which, thank God, so many of our non-Catholic brethren have been renowned, and pleads, "Think of infallibility *that* way!" But this is not infallibility, freedom from error, and his formulation means little more than devout continuance in error through the centuries. Even if he adds that the Holy Spirit will finally come to the rescue and lead the Church out of error again, that is no excuse for eviscerating the doctrine of infallibility, which is that God does not permit error in the Church's teaching even for the second required for a gasp of horror. It is quite another thing, of course, to say; "I simply do not accept defined doctrine," but consistency should then demand a move to the separated brethren. It is not to be wondered at that the Italian Hierarchy warned Catholics that "a Catholic expressing the opinions Professor Küng holds could not call himself a member of the Church in the full sense of the word," but it is disturbing that his Liverpool lecture was organised by the Liverpool Catechetical Centre.

In July, 1973, the Sacred Congregation for the Doctrine of the Faith issued a document entitled *Mysterium Ecclesiae* which rejected the Tyrrell-Küng belief-substitute. It was laid down that "the faithful are in no way permitted to see in the Church merely a fundamental permanence in truth which, as some assert, could be reconciled with errors contained here and there in the propositions that the Church's Magisterium teaches to be held irrevocably. . . ." Dr. Küng's reaction has been to assert that "the Congregation for the Doctrine of the Faith is not capable of making a contribution which will help us to answer the questions on Church, ministry

and infallibility. . . ." (*Catholic Herald,* July 13, 1973), which
sounds like the chime of 'Mad Martin's bell.' (How quickly
a man drifts when his anchor slips! When Luther submitted
his *Resolutions* to Leo X in 1518, he had professed: 'Approve
or disapprove; for me your voice will be that of Christ!")
Dr. Küng has felt compelled to explain "Why I am staying
in the Church" (*Catholic Herald,* August 17, 1973), and the
one ground which he does *not* adduce is the only ground for
staying—belief in the Church's divine foundation and sta-
bility under God's protection. His grounds are the grounds
also for remaining Anglican or Lutheran. He is staying in
the Church as "here all the great questions are asked: the
where and whence, the why and how of man and his world."
But those questions are asked everywhere; the glory of the
Catholic Church is that God has given her the answers,
though, as we have seen in his reaction to *Mysterium Ecclesiae,* he will not accept them. Dr. Küng may still be unaware of it, but his *apologia* shows that he has lost his Faith.
The prophet who set out to cry in the wilderness is still
crying, but now the message is "I am lost!"

If a Catholic wishes to remain Catholic, he cannot attribute error to the Church's infallible teaching. This is
what St. John Fisher stressed, with a spice of irony thrown
in: "If, then, anyone will attentively consider the solicitude
of Christ for us—if he believes without hesitation that the
Holy Ghost does not reside in the Church to no purpose . . .
if, lastly, he views the unanimous consent of so many churches
during so many centuries . . . it will surely be impossible for
him to believe that now only at last has risen upon Luther
alone the light of truth, never so much suspected by any of
the ancient fathers, and the exact contrary of what they all
maintained. For if truth has so long lain hid in darkness,
waiting through so many centuries for its deliverance by
Luther, it was to no purpose that Christ bestowed such care
upon our forefathers. It was to no purpose that the Spirit
of Christ was sent to teach them all truth. . . ."[19]

[19] Cf. Fr. T. E. Bridgett, *Blessed John Fisher,* pp. 132-133.

SAME DOCTRINE, SAME MEANING

Fr. Edward Kelly, S.J., writing in *The Tablet* (December 2, 1967) put forward this view: "While it may be true . . . that no one should be included in the visible limits of the Catholic communion who refuses to accept what the Church has infallibly guaranteed, it should also be noted that no one is required to accept a particular person's understanding of the Church's infallible dogmas as infallibly guaranteed." He did not see that a man accepts "what the Church has infallibly guaranteed" only if he accepts what is *meant* by the definition, and it recalls the passage from *Through the Looking Glass* which Cardinal Heenan produced in *L'Osservatore Romano* (May 23, 1968):

" 'When I use a word,' Humpty Dumpty said . . . 'it means just what I choose it to mean—neither more nor less.'

'The question is,' said Alice, 'whether you can make words mean so many different things.'

'The question is,' said Humpty Dumpty, 'which is to be the master—that's all.' " The Cardinal added, "Yes, that's all. That's the whole question. Who is to be the master? That's what we mean by magisterium. The teacher must be restored to authority."

Substitution of content, hand-in-hand with continuity of label, is basic to modernism. However, Vatican I defined: "That meaning of the sacred dogmas must always be retained which Holy Mother Church has once taught, nor may it ever be departed from under the guise, or in the name, of deeper insight," and decreed: "If anyone shall say that, because of scientific progress, it may be possible at some time to interpret the Church's dogmas in a different sense from that which the Church understood and understands, let him be anathema!" (Denzinger 1800 and 1818. This teaching must be borne in mind when we treat of attempts to reinterpret transubstantiation and original sin.)

For many years, in the wake of the first wave of modernism, priests had to affirm on oath: "I sincerely receive the doctrine of faith which the orthodox Fathers have transmitted to us from the Apostles, *always in the same sense and meaning.* And therefore I reject absolutely the false and heretical view of the evolution of dogmas, according to which they may change meaning so as to receive a different sense." *Pace* Fr. Kelly, there is one infallibly guaranteed sense to each infallible dogma, which is why the Commission of Cardinals found fault with the Dutch catechism and stressed: "It should be clearly stated in the catechism that the infallibility of the Church does not give her only a safe course in a continual research, but the truth in maintaining the doctrine of the faith *and in explaining it always in the same sense* (cf. Vat. I, Const. *Dei Filius*, ch. 4, and Vat. II, Const. *Dei Verbum*, ch. 2). 'Faith is not only a seeking of the truth, but is above all certain possession of it.' (Paul VI . . .) Nor should the readers of the catechism be allowed to think that the human intellect arrives only at verbal and conceptual expressions of the revealed mystery. . . ."

Mysterium Ecclesiae, the document issued by the Congregation for the Doctrine of the Faith in July, 1973, carries this emphatic teaching: "As for the *meaning* of dogmatic formulae, this remains ever true and constant in the Church, even when it is expressed with greater clarity or is more developed. The faithful must shun the opinion, first, that dogmatic formulas . . . cannot signify truth in a determinate way, but can only offer changeable approximations to it, which to a certain extent distort or alter it. . . . Those who hold such an opinion do not avoid dogmatic relativism and they corrupt the concept of the Church's infallibility relative to the truth to be taught or held in a determinate way."

If the sense of a doctrine is challenged, it is for the magisterium to indicate it. Vatican II taught in *Dei Verbum*: "The task of authentically interpreting the word of God, whether written or handed on, has been entrusted exclusively to the living teaching office of the Church, whose authority is exercised in the name of Jesus Christ." As Councils can be held only rarely, the task of judging *will* normally fall on a "particular person", the one mentioned in the profession of faith of Paleologus—"so also if any question should arise concerning the Faith it must be determined by its (Rome's) judgment." One notes there the repetition of the phrase used in the *Hibernensis:* "If any questions arise in this island. . . ."

The Church, then, uses meaningful words and teaches truth, a true meaning. She is blessed in that the language in which she enshrines her truth is beyond the attrition of change, for, as Chesterton put it, the choice between Latin and a modern language is not between a dead language and a living one, but between an immortal language and a dying one.

BISHOPS & THE ORDINARY MAGISTERIUM

We have written at some length of the teaching authority—'the Board of Governors and Teachers'—with barely a mention of the college of bishops, and this could be construed as showing a serious imbalance. It would do so if this book were not aimed at correcting existing imbalances— "Trimming the Ark"—and the fact is that there has been a mounting attack on papal authority and very little sniping at episcopal teaching authority, one reason being that the bishops (outside Council) seldom exercise it. Cardinal Heenan wrote in the article already referred to: "No matter how novel or brash the theory, it is most unlikely to be condemned by a local bishop or hierarchy . . . it is true that the Pope does regularly draw attention to the dangers of theological innovations. Nobody else in authority follows his example. . . . Magisterium, like hierarchy, has become a dirty word. That may be why so few bishops are willing to risk unpopularity by exercising it. . . . Today outside Rome it has become so unsure of itself that it rarely attempts even to guide." There it is, the abdication of the bishops in face of the microphone-seizers, and this is why attack has been concentrated upon Rome. Indeed, the bishops have been cheered on with cries of "Collegiality!" in the hope that they might muffle the voice of Peter, while, at the same time, their collegial teaching in Vatican II, regarding the Pope's supreme authority, has been tidied away in the sacristy cupboard. Only the courageous individual bishop has been picked out for pelting, while the mass of bishops have been true pontiffs, 'bridge-builders', facing both ways.

"It is now an urgent task," declared the *Catholic Herald* of August 2, 1968, "to clarify the meaning of the 'ordinary' but infallible magisterium. . . . At present, nobody knows (it)." Clarification was there, however, for the seeking in the texts of Vatican I and II. Vatican I, Session 3: "All those doctrines are to be held with divine and Catholic faith which are preserved in God's word, whether written or handed down, and which are put forward for belief, as divinely revealed, by the Church, either by solemn definition or by means of her ordinary and universal teaching authority." What this last is appears in Vatican II's *Lumen Gentium*: "Although the individual bishops do not enjoy the prerogative of infallibility, they can nevertheless proclaim Christ's doctrine infallibly . . . provided that while maintaining the bond of unity among themselves and with Peter's successor, and while teaching authentically on a matter of faith or morals, they concur in a single viewpoint as the one that must be held conclusively." And, when the bishops give such teaching—teaching conclusively on faith or morals in harmony with Rome and one another—we learn from Canon 1325 of the Code of Church Law: "Any baptised person, still claiming the name of Christian, who pertinaciously rejects or doubts any of the truths to be held by divine and Catholic faith, is a heretic."

It should not be necessary to say so, but the reader must realise that the last passage above does not refer to the 'extraordinary' magisterium of bishops met in ecumenical council, but to their teaching in their own dioceses as they hand on traditional doctrine. Another thing which should be evident is that the Pope and bishops are teachers armed with authority; they are not our pupils. Authority does not well up from below, and the Commission of Cardinals was disturbed by another failing in the Dutch catechism. They asked "that the new Catechism clearly recognise that the teaching authority and the power of ruling in the Church is given directly to the Holy Father and to the bishops joined with him . . . and . . . not given in the first place to the people of God to be communicated to others. The office of Bishops, therefore, is not a mandate given them by the people of God, but is a mandate received from God Himself. . . ."

"It is to be brought out more clearly that the Holy Father and the bishops in their teaching office do not only assemble and approve what the whole community . . . believes . . . the people of God . . . cling indefectibly to the word of God under the leadership of the magisterium, to whom it belongs authentically to guard, explain and defend the deposit of faith."

This should help to crush a 'Jacobin' error in circulation at the moment, an error phrased to supplant hierarchy with democracy ('Jacobin', as it happens, originally meant a Dominican!) and ultimately aimed at deposing accepted doctrine. The error is cropping up in all sorts of forms, some fairly innocuous, some deadly. The reader will now be in a position to see what qualifications are required in, for instance, the following passage: "The truth in this world is only acquired by the strenuous effort of the community. The revealed truth was therefore entrusted to the Church as a whole, and has to be found through corporate efforts of the whole ecclesiastical body."[20]

The shortcomings of this statement become apparent if we compare with it the teaching of the outstanding pastoral letter, *The Church in our Day*, issued by the North American Hierarchy in January, 1969: "Infallibility is thus always subordinate to revelation and somehow includes the witness of all the Church's people. Infallible teaching . . . however, receives its clear expression and definition only in that magisterium which speaks when the bishops exercise their office in harmony with Peter or when Peter defines . . . infallibility involves the entire believing community, but not as if it were the result of a community consensus or dependent upon some explicit community acceptance of apostolic teaching."

[20] From *Intelligent Theology*, Vol. 3, p. 143, by Piet Fransen, S.J.

CONSENSUS VERSUS MAGISTERIUM?

Pope Paul spoke in the same vein and nailed the modernism of the opposing view in 1968: "See! the Apostle is the teacher. He is not merely the echo of the religious conscience of the community. He is not merely the expression of the opinion of the faithful . . . as the modernists said . . . and as some theologians dare to assert today." On January 11th of that same year, he gently corrected these who "would like to recognise in this magisterium more than anything else the task of confirming the 'infallible belief of the communion of the faithful.' "

It brings to mind how, later that year when the Holy Father had given his children bread when some begged for a stone, tragic appeals were made to an imagined 'opinion of the faithful'. When, in England, Canon Drinkwater reacted to *Humanae Vitae* by asking, "Is there not a sort of consensus conscience, gathered from the wisest and best minds that an individual can discover?",[21] Dom David Knowles replied that, on many moral issues, "the Church stands firm against what is now a majority of educated opinion in many of the most civilised countries of the world." The moral was that "the wisest and best minds" are in reality those promised guidance by the Holy Spirit.

The appeal to a consensus against the magisterium was discredited long ago. A condemned error of the 17th century Gallicans is that a papal judgment is final only if a consensus of the Church agrees (Dz. 1325), and Vatican I and II use the same terms to teach that papal definitions are irreformable "of themselves, and not from the consent of the Church" (Dz. 1839 and *Lumen Gentium*).

Lastly, it has to be squarely faced that, if the Pope is the source and centre of unity, a true *consensus fidelium* can be secured only by accepting his doctrine *because* it is his. The consensus to which Canon Drinkwater appealed could never exist except in imagination. It has, however, been suggested that past consensus of belief arose from fear

---

[21] *The Tablet,* October 2, 1968.

and was not genuine. . . . "people were afraid to speak out!" It is an ill-considered argument, since there is no doctrine that some heretic has not impugned, winning for himself a band of followers and ending up expatriated, with the consensus of orthodox Catholics unshaken. The solidarity and continuity spring instead from the guidance of the Holy Spirit. . . . "I will ask the Father, and he will give you another to befriend you, one who is to dwell continually with you for ever. It is the truth-giving Spirit . . . he will be continually at your side. . . . It will be for him, the truth-giving Spirit, when he comes, to guide you into all truth." (St. John 14: 16-17 & 16:13)

WHEN BISHOPS DISAGREE

The passages given above from Vatican I and II maintained that bishops teach infallibly when, in union with the Holy See, they teach unanimously on a matter of faith or morals. If, then, the the college of bishops, with Peter at its head, taught for the first three centuries that Jesus is truly God, that teaching is infallibly true, even though, at the dawn of the fourth century, Arius arose to contest it and won support from bishops. Later disbelief does not invalidate infallible teaching. The point is not an academic one but of pressing importance. Fr. John McHugh of Ushaw College, in a series of three articles contributed to *The Clergy Review* (August, September & October, 1969), admitted that pope and bishops had concurred in a single viewpoint as the one which must be held as regards contraception. . . . "The Catholic world in general, and the bishops in particular, appear to have accepted without demur Pius XI's judgment at that time (the time of *Casti Connubii*): and therefore we say that in 1930-1 there was moral unanimity within the Church about the sinfulness of artificial contraception." (There was, of course, unanimity long before Pius XI and *Casti Connubii*; they reaffirmed tradition in the face of developments in the Anglican Church.) But Fr. McHugh went on: "By 1960 . . . this moral unanimity was no longer to be found," and the reader is left with the impression that

later dispute cancels the force of age-old unanimity. This it
no more does than "the whole world groaning to find itself
Arian" negated the true doctrine of Christ's divinity. The
Church says, with better reason than Pilate, "What I have
written, I have written!" and this adherence to the unchanging truth points to the error of Dr. Schoonenberg, who, while
admitting that the ordinary magisterium taught that our
Lady remained bodily a virgin, gives weight to the lack of
universal consent today. *Veritas manet*.

IS TRUST COMPATIBLE WITH FALLIBILITY?

Some Catholics, it was said, demand of an item of teaching, usually papal teaching, "Is it infallible?" when they
should be concerned with its authority. It is legalistic to
be obsessed with infallibility, for, if the Pope is speaking
with authority to the whole Church on faith or morals, we
are bound to accept his teaching as Vatican II was insistent.
We remind the reader of the way in which *Humani Generis*
held that the teaching advanced in an encyclical demands
assent, not just respect, and closes a debate. Here a perfectly
reasonable, a necessary, objection suggests itself: "If he is
not teaching infallibly, then he may be wrong. How can
assent be demanded to possible error?" The answer is given
in *Humani Generis*: "Such statements come under the day-
to-day teaching of the Church, which is covered by the
promise, 'He who listens to you, listens to me' (Luke X, 16)"
coupled with the additional argument, which is no light-
weight one, that "For the most part the positions advanced,
the duties inculcated . . . are already bound up . . . with the
general body of Catholic teaching." This underlines that
the Pope does not pull answers out of a bran tub, but draws
from the well of tradition; one marks that the Popes, in their
encyclicals, are at pains to advertise their sources, to clinch
that their teaching is traditional. (*Humanae Vitae*, for instance, lists part of its ancestral tree: the catechism of the
Council of Trent, Leo XIII, Pius XI, Pius XII, John XXIII,
Vatican II.)

Yet I think that the first part of Pius XII's explanation is as crucial as the second, and it could be expressed in the following way: "The question that you are asking is a perfectly natural one, but you are asking it in a supernatural context where it does not apply. You are reacting as if this were a dilemma of man's making, demanding a human solution, whereas there is only the problem of trusting God, and we cannot trust God if we do not trust His Vicar." "Is one not perhaps doing an outright disservice to the papal primacy by transferring Christological terms to the Pope?" asks Dr. Küng in *The Living Church*, but it was our Lord Who made him head-on-earth; it was the cornerstone who named Simon 'Rock', and the Good Shepherd Who handed over the crozier, entrusting him with the charge of guarding the sheep. Then . . . we must leave it to God!

But, someone will ask, what about past papal errors? The late Dr. Hilda Graef outlined this type of objection: "I think the difficulty many of us sometimes 'dissenting' Catholics have is that quite a few—non-infallible—decisions emanating from Rome in the past have turned out to have been mistaken," and she evidenced Boniface VIII's *Unam Sanctam* and Galileo, together with the *Syllabus of Errors*. Another Catholic gloomily predicted that the argument that "the faith consists of any jottings which any Pope may at any time have committed to paper, is likely to be widely used in the near future."[22]

What, then, is the truth in these matters? Has the Pope taught error to the Church? Is the jotting as solid as the encyclical, the private remark as weighty as an address given to a 'sounding-board' audience (e.g., doctors or midwives) and intended to resound throughout the world? To clarify, we quote first from Dom John Chapman's *The Condemnation of Pope Honorius* (p. 111): "The more solemn the utterances of the Apostolic See, the more we can be certain of their truth. When they reach the maximum of solemnity, that is, when they are strictly *ex cathedra*, the possibility of error is wholly eliminated. The authority of a

[22] *The Scotsman,* August 5, 1968.

Pope, even on those occasions when he is not actually in-fallible, is to be implicitly followed and reverenced. That it should be on the wrong side is a contingency shown by faith and history to be possible, but by history as well as faith to be so remote that it is not usually to be taken into con-sideration. There are three or four examples in history."

The Pope has, then, been wrong, *but in not one of those rare cases was it a matter of his trying to foist error in faith or morals on the whole Church.* And thus (Professor) Dom David Knowles wrote in his *Peter has Spoken* when some tried to discredit *Humanae Vitae* by appealing to historical cases: "Attempts have been made to draw parallels between the Encyclical and previous declarations of popes that have either been reversed . . . or have passed into desuetude. . . . Some of them are indeed 'motes to trouble the mind's eye'. . . . But I have not seen in any documents alleged by any writer on the Encyclical a single example that could by any stretch of wording be called a parallel to the occasion and solemn enunciation of *Humanae Vitae*."

It emerges that the solemnity surrounding a papal utter-ance, its occasion, matter, the audience (large or small) to whom it is addressed, all have a bearing on our certainty of its secure truth. Dom Paul Nau, in his article *The Authority of Ordinary Teachings of the Pope* (*Theology Digest*, Vol. VII, No. 1, 1959), gives three tests for measuring the force of a papal utterance: (1) the Pope's intention to engage his teaching authority; (a) The 'resonance' of his teaching in the Church; and (3) the continuity of his doctrine with past teaching. In judging the authority of any individual pro-nouncement, therefore, we must go by these three gauges and stifle personal inclination. *Humanae Vitae* has, of course, been a test-case in our day. One notes, as an example, that Canon H. F. Drinkwater wrote of Pope Paul's *Credo of the People of God*, which was 'sprung' upon the Church: "Short of what is technically called infallibility, its immediate ex-trinsic authority could not easily be over-stated,"[23] and yet, though the Church had waited with bated breath for the

---

[23] *Catholic Herald,* January 3, 1969.

answer given with such solemnity in *Humanae Vitae*, he questioned its binding authority and made his appeal to a "sort of consensus conscience," though Dom David Knowles wrote: "I . . . consider that *Humanae Vitae*, the deliberate prayed-for, pronouncement of a pope to the whole world on a grave and disputed moral issue, given with Petrine authority as the teaching of the Church, stands apart from almost all encyclicals of the past hundred years."

I quote again from Dom Chapman (*op. cit.*, p. 112): "It is a matter of history that no Pope has ever involved the whole Church in error . . . that Rome has always retained the true faith. If this was wonderful in the 7th century, it is more wonderful after thirteen more centuries have passed." It could be objected that this is a Catholic parallel to the Whig interpretation of history which saw the growth of Parliament's powers as a thing that was somehow intrinsically right and inevitable; what happened must be right! And yet a great mind, outside the Church at the time, saw this precise truth. Newman tells us, in chapter IV of the *Apologia*, how, in his latter days as an Anglican, he wrote to Archdeacon Wilberforce "expressing my difficulty as derived from the Arian and Monophysite history . . . as being in fact an admission of Bishop Bull's: viz. that in the controversies of the early centuries the Roman Church was ever on the right side . . ." and got the answer: "I don't think that I ever was so shocked by any communication . . . as by your letter of this morning. It has quite unnerved me. . . ."

Papal errors are museum pieces, of some interest to the antiquarian but of minimal effect on the life of the Church. This should be established if we devote some time to a brief study of the historical objections which are being raised by those in difficulties over papal teaching, even if there is some ghostly laughter from the direction of Hyde Park Corner since these are the very cases which 'stout Protestants' once brought up. H. M. Carson, for example, in his anti-Catholic *Roman Catholicism Today*, published in 1964, whistled up the shades of Liberius, Honorius and Galileo in an attempt to discredit the papacy; today Catholics practise the same necromancy. Newman had to explain patiently, for the benefit of Gladstone's England, the truth about Honorius, *Unam Sanctam*, Gregory XVI and Pius IX's *Syllabus of Errors*; now patience, like charity, must begin at home.

The facts of these historical cases will be indicated here as briefly as the matter will allow, and it should emerge in each case that the objection raised makes no impact upon the authority of papal teaching as given in an encyclical or other solemn form. In fact, papal authority is confirmed. . . . "Is that the best the devil's advocate can do," one asks, "with nearly twenty centuries to draw upon?"

Pope Liberius (353-366). Liberius, coming to the chair of Peter when semi-Arianism had succeeded Arianism as the main threat to orthodoxy, was put under extreme pressure by Constantius II to force him to condemn St. Athanasius and sign semi-Arian formulas. The facts are disputed but, as Bishop Butler noted (*op. cit.*, p. 167), it cannot be shown that Liberius signed anything positively erroneous. Dr. Jalland, of the Church of England, affirms that the pope signed "a colourless dogmatic formula." (*The Church and the Papacy*, p. 231.) Far from backing false doctrine, Liberius stressed in a letter to the emperor: "After the custom and *paradosis* of my predecessors, I have permitted no enlargement, no diminution of the episcopate of the city of Rome. Keeping safe that faith, which has been passed on through a succession of many great bishops, among whom there have been numerous martyrs, my constant hope is that it will be preserved unimpaired."

Pope Honorius I (625-638). England has reason to be grateful to Honorius, who encouraged King Edwin of Northumbria, sent St. Birinus to preach in Wessex and sent the pallium to St. Paulinus as first metropolitan of the northern province. He was a good man and pope but, incredibly, was classed as a heretic by the Sixth Ecumenical Council, and a look at Denzinger helps to explain why. Denzinger 251, under the title 'Honorius I', carries a headline "Concerning the two natures and operations in Christ," but, when we read the papal letter under this heading, we meet: "We confess *one* will in our Lord Jesus Christ," which seems, *prima facie*,

Monothelite heresy, the denial to our Lord of a human will.

The background of the letter is as follows. . . . Sergius, Patriarch of Constantinople, wrote to the Pope, asking whether it was correct to speak of one operation, or two operations (one divine, one human), in Christ. Honorius replied in two letters, the first of these being the one which occasioned scandal, and we observe right away what Newman pointed out in his *Letter to the Duke of Norfolk*—the measureless difference between these letters, "written almost as private instructions," and an encyclical addressed to "All the Venerable Brothers, etc." with all the apparatus of a formal pronouncement.

Next, one could not do better than quote the Reverend H. K. Mann, *The Lives of the Popes in the Early Middle Ages*, Vol. 1, Part 1, p. 342: "For on the matter of the controversy, Honorius formulated no decision. On the question of 'one or two wills,' all that he really insisted on was *silence* on the part of those already engaged in disputing on the subject brought before him. Whatever that subject was, and whatever the Pope may have thought or written upon it, all he wanted was *not* to instruct the Catholic world upon it, but to avoid (as he hoped) worse trouble, and that the Catholic world should not be stirred up on the matter, through the disputes which he wished his letter to end."

As implied in this passage, Honorius stated explicitly in his letter that he was not trying to teach the Church dogma. It remains to explain why the Church historian should speak of Honorius as formulating no decision, when the letter speaks of one will in Christ, and why he should write as if the subject of the Pope's letter is questionable. The explanation is to be found in the fact that it *can* be heretical (and normally would be) to speak of only one will in Christ, but it is also possible to do so in an orthodox sense. Thus—has Christ a divine will and a human will, i.e., two wills? The answer has to be 'Yes'. But . . . can there be two 'wills' in Christ, His human will clashing with His divine will, as our lower nature rebels against our better self in sin? The answer is 'No', and thus we read in Scripture, "Not my

will but thine be done." Now it seems undeniable that
Sergius and Honorius were not on the same wavelength.[24]
So Dr. Jalland writes (*op. cit.*, p. 363) that Honorius, or
his secretary, was "quite unaware of the true nature of the
problem which faced the Emperor and his patriarch, and
was concerned only to emphasise the absolute sinlessness of
our Lord's human life. . . . A little reflection might have
shown the Easterns that Honorius (or rather his secretary)
had touched upon a far more subtle aspect of the problem
than those which they themselves appear to have considered.
All that mattered to them was that a doctrine of 'one power
of volition' in Christ could now be published to the Empire
as possessing the *imprimatur* of the Roman See. Even if
they observed that the Pope was actually discussing a psychological problem, while they themselves were concerned with
metaphysics, they preferred to ignore the difference."

We quote from Fr. Mann once more (p. 338): ". . . there
is not a single *heretical* sentence in his letter. There is indeed a sentence which is not wise—the sentence in which he
doubts whether the new terms 'one or two operations' are
useful or desirable. Subsequent adoption of the term 'two
operations' showed its usefulness. And there is a sentence in
his letter which, at first sight, seems heterodox, viz., where
he agrees with Sergius that there is only 'one will in Our
Lord.' But the very reason that he gives for his statement
shows that he was referring to the *resultant* will of Our Lord,
i.e., to the will of Our Lord when reduced to action, and not
to the number of wills in the second person of the Blessed
Trinity after His incarnation. He says that Our Lord had
one will, viz., one will in agreement with the divine will,
because He assumed a *perfect* human nature, not one in
which the 'law of the flesh' warred against 'the law of the
spirit' (Romans VII, 25)."

That this is the true interpretation of what Honorius
wrote is established by other evidence. Dr. Jalland, we saw,
spoke of "Honorius or his secretary. . . . Honorius (or rather

[24] "Obviously Sergius and Honorius are at cross purposes."—Mgr.
Philip Hughes, *History of the Church,* Vol. I, p. 361.

his secretary). . . ." Who was the mysterious secretary? St. Maximus provides the answer.

Some years after the death of Honorius, Maximus was engaged in controversy with Pyrrhus, the successor of Sergius, and Pyrrhus had played what seemed a trump card in advancing Honorius as upholding only one will in Christ. Maximus demanded, "Who is the more worthy interpreter of the Pope's letter, the one who wrote it in the Pope's name, and who is still alive . . . or those at Constantinople who say what they wish?" Pyrrhus accepted the loaded question, replying, "Certainly the one who composed the letter." Maximus then revealed that the letter had been penned by the man who now occupied the papal throne, John IV, and that John had written to the Emperor Constantine insisting that Honorius (or he himself) had taught no heresy. The 'apologia' of Pope John is printed as Denzinger 253, and he writes that the letter to Sergius taught that "in our Saviour there can by no means be two contrary wills, that is in his members, since He was free of those weaknesses which result from Adam's fall. . . . My aforesaid predecessor, therefore, teaching on this mystery of Christ's incarnation, declared that there were not in Him what is found in us who are sinners . . . conflicting wills of the spirit and of the flesh. This teaching some have twisted to suit their own ends, alleging Honorius to have taught that there is but one will to His divinity and humanity which is indeed contrary to truth."

Elsewhere, St. Maximus voiced his indignation at the brassy impertinence of Pyrrhus in daring to suggest that the Holy See would uphold heresy, and, writing to Marinus, he repeats that Honorius did not deny the two wills that go with the two natures, but denied only two opposing wills. He had talked the matter over, he said, with the abbot Anastasius who had just come back from Rome where he had taken up the matter specifically with high ecclesiastics and the 'Abbot John' who had drawn up the letter, and Rome had been horrified at the construction which was being put upon the letter in the East. Maximus was eloquent about the deceitful tactics of those who misconstrued and so cast a slur on (his words) "the Roman See, that is, the Catholic Church."

But good and truth are oft interred with a man's bones, and when, at the Sixth Ecumenical Council in 680, the two letters of Honorius were produced, nobody present had heard of them before and nobody remembered the explanation of John IV and the apologetic of St. Maximus. Honorius was lumped with intransigent heretics. "And in addition to these we decide that Honorius also, who was Pope of elder Rome, be with them cast out of the holy Church of God, and be anathematized with them, because we have found by his letter to Sergius that he followed his opinion in all things and confirmed his wicked dogmas." The Seventh Ecumenical Council rubbed it in by including him in its list of heretics, though Leo II came nearer the mark with, "So far from quenching the flames of heretical doctrine, as befitted apostolic authority, he actually fed them by sheer negligence."

Poor Honorius! His name has been hard dealt with, and it would be more fitting if those, who attempt to make capital out of him, were to show him the sympathy which they lavish on Galileo. The story does illustrate, however, as Bishop Butler wrote, that "the Church has always been acutely sensitive to doctrinal inaccuracies which may have baneful effects far outside the purview of the theologians who originate them, effects in the spiritual and moral efforts of the faithful." (*Op. cit.*, p. 199). In addition it shows the shock felt by Catholics at apparent error in a letter from the pope's hand, even though the letter was addressed to an individual and insisted that it did not wish to crystalize dogma. It is curious, at a time when 'progressives' throw up the story that Honorious taught heresy, holding that there was only one will in Christ, to read in *that* issue of *The Sower* (p. 75), that pupils reading the old catechism (now, it is suggested, discredited) "have the impression of . . . two wills within a single individual—a bybrid person."

It may be added that there is considerable naiveté in an attempt to raise the case of Honorius in objection to papal infallibility, as the case was thoroughly ventilated at the first Vatican Council, Hefele the historian producing a brochure

for the occasion. The Council defined with the facts before
its eyes . . . and one of the lighter passages of the debates
is too good to pass over. Archbishop McHale of Tuam
claimed that the simple Irish did not want definitions; "they
held the doctrine practically, having sucked it with their
mother's milk." Bishop Verot of St. Augustine, Florida,
countered: "it is true that the Irish believe in the Pope's
infallibility; but they also believe in their priests' infallibility—and not only do they believe it, but they beat with
sticks any who deny it."

UNAM SANCTAM (1302 A.D.)

A Welshman, looking at the date of *Unam Sanctam*
(also 'gone over' at Vatican I) notes it as a year after the
creation of the first Prince of Wales, following on the defeat
of Llewelyn, and a Scotsman records it as four years after
Falkirk, and three years before Wallace was subjected to the
butchery invented for 'traitors' by Edward I and left as an
inheritance for the Catholic martyrs. This sets the bull in
its historical background of emergent nations. The struggle
between *imperium* and *sacerdotium* was over, and the papacy
now had to deal with kings. Two of them, Edward and Philip
the Fair of France, were at each other's throat, and it was
for the pope to separate them if he could.

First came the bull *Clericis Laicos*, an attempt to stop
the war by cutting off the warriors' supplies of money. Then,
as a reaction largely to the outrageous behaviour of Philip
the Fair, there followed the statement of the Church's
uniqueness, of papal authority, and of the superiority of the
spiritual power over the temporal, known as *Unam Sanctam*.
The Latin text is in Denzinger (468 & 469), though four
passages are omitted, and it can be read in English in E. F.
Henderson's *Select Historical Documents of the Middle Ages*,
pp. 432ff.

A study of the bull must prove disappointing to those
seeking sling-shot. H. Daniel-Rops comments, in *Cathedral
and Crusade* (p. 570): "It made no reference to direct papal
intervention in temporal affairs; it did not even condemn the

thesis of a state founded upon natural law. In short, its
terms were so restrained . . . that modern theologians find
no difficulty in reconciling it with their own teaching, and
it continues to bind Catholics even in the altered climate of
today." "So restrained" would seem to be debatable since
the bull has occasioned such animus, and yet Sir Maurice
Powicke writes: ". . . *Unam Sanctam* is one of the most
carefully drafted documents which have emerged from the
papal chancery. Two of its main theses are derived, through
Giles (of Rome) and other writers, from a famous passage
in Hugh of St. Victor and the equally famous . . . treatment
by St. Bernard of the doctrine of the two swords. In the
same year, 1302, in which the bull was issued, the same high
claims were admitted in formal terms by the chancellor of
Albert of Austria, the emperor-elect."[25] Professor George H.
Sabine seems at first to adopt a radically different position,
saying that the bull "took the most advanced ground on
papal imperialism that was ever written into an official document,"[26] and yet he concedes, "The difference between this
theory and that held by Gregory VII lay not so much in a
claim to greater power. Perhaps it would have been difficult
to formulate a more august conception than was held by
Gregory. The difference is essentially legal; it consists in a
greater precision in the conception of the pope's authority. . . ." (*op. cit.*, p. 236).

The bull begins by teaching that there is no salvation
outside the Catholic Church, "a dogma," as Newman wrote
in the *Letter* referred to, "which no Catholic can ever think
of disputing. . . . Not to go to the Scripture, it is the doctrine
of St. Ignatius, St. Irenaeus, St. Cyprian, in the first three
centuries, as of St. Augustine and his contemporaries in the
fourth and fifth. It can never be other than an elementary
truth of Christendom; and the present Pope (Pius IX) has
proclaimed it as all Popes, doctors, and bishops before him."
Those puzzled by the doctrine should read Newman's exposi-

[25] Sir Maurice Powicke, *The Christian Life in the Middle Ages,* Chapter 3, p. 54.
[26] *A History of Political Theory,* p. 238.

tion, and note that he found it harmonising with one of the Anglican Articles.[27]

There is one Church, the bull teaches, and one Head, Christ, Who has committed His whole flock to the care of Peter. Then, following St. Bernard, we have mention of the two domains, spiritual and temporal, typified by two swords, and "Both swords, the spiritual and material . . . are in the power of the church; the one, indeed, to be wielded for the church, the other by the church; the one by the hand of the priest, the other by the hand of kings and knights, but at the will and sufferance of the priest. One sword, moreover, ought to be under the other, and the temporal authority to be subjected to the spiritual. . . ."

King Philip alleged that the pope was claiming direct temporal rule in France, but the allegation was hotly denied by Boniface. . . . "For forty years now, we have been versed in law, and we know that there are two powers ordained by God. Who on earth, then, would believe, or *could* believe, that such absurdity, such nonsense, could enter our head? We state that we intend in no way to usurp the jurisdiction of the king. . . . What the king, and every other Catholic, cannot deny is that he is subject to us *by reason of sin*." (Denzinger 468, footnote.)

"By reason of sin"—there is the key to the claim to the right of control over the way in which civil power is exercised ("at the will and sufferance of the priest"), to the ultimate subordination of temporal power to spiritual. The Church rejects the divine right of kings or führers, in its absolute sense, and the totalitarian state. It will not con-

[27] See also Karl Rahner, *Theological Investigations,* Vol. II, pp. 36-88. I draw attention to Pope Paul's explanation in his *Credo of the People of God:* "We believe that the Church is necessary for salvation, because Christ, who is the sole Mediator and Way of salvation, renders Himself present for us in His Body which is the Church. But the divine design of salvation embraces all men; and those who without fault on their part do not know the Gospel of Christ and His Church, but seek God sincerely, and under the influence of grace endeavour to do His will as recognized through the promptings of their conscience, they, in a number known only to God, can obtain salvation." Cf. also, Fr. H. de Lubac, *Catholicism, VII, Salvation Through the Church.*

cede the right of a Philip to treat his subjects intolerably,
nor of a Stalin to liquidate millions in the interests of state
planning; it is Robin Hood who is the Catholic hero and
not the grasping Sheriff of Nottingham. St. Ambrose barred
the Emperor Theodosius from entering the church when he
had ordered a massacre; this was not a claim to interfere in
politics as such, but to pass judgment on the morality of
political action and the use of the temporal sword. Though
Europe is no longer uniformly Catholic, few today would
dispute that political action must be subjected to the scrutiny
of moralists and not allowed to infringe human rights . . .
this is the ground of a thousand demonstrations and marches,
and it is interesting to note the swing-round in attitude that
history has enforced. In the seventies of last century, the
German Emperor was the darling of the English Whigs and
Bismarck's *Kulturkampf* almost a crusade in their eyes.
("The cause of the German Emperor," declared Lord John
Russell, "is the cause of liberty, and the cause of the Pope
the cause of slavery.") Gladstone launched an attack on the
way in which, he thought, Catholic faith weakened the allegiance of citizens to the civil power. In our day, however, the
complaint has been the opposite—that Catholics are uncritical in their obedience to their government, that German
Catholics should have risen, after hearing *Mit Brennender
Sorge* read on Palm Sunday, 1937, and made short work of
the Nazi system of the new "Emperor" Hitler which was
the "cause of slavery." We have all heard the current questions which involve a demand that the spiritual sword should
be considered over the temporal—Why did the Church not
excommunicate Hitler and release Catholics from obedience
to him? Why did Pius XII not denounce the pograms against
the Jews? All these are implicit admissions that politics
must be harnessed under the rules of morality. Modern man,
if he has any Christian philosophy left in him, is very certain
that there must be a limit to the State's claims and actions.

Sir Maurice Powicke illustrates this in his own inimitable
way. He takes a manifesto, written by H. G. Wells on behalf
of an international liberal party, and replaces the name of
the party throughout by the word "Church", pointing out

that the manifesto then becomes much what Boniface VIII would have written, though he adds, "I am inclined to think that these sentences would have seemed rather crude to the medieval canonist. They lack precision and balance, although they show the right spirit." (*Op. cit.*, p. 55) It suffices to cite, by way of sample, one or two sentences from the amended version: "The Church acknowledges no more than a conditional loyalty to any established government or authority. . . . The support of the government is subject to the condition that the acts of government be themselves reasonable and legal and that the law respects the prior claims of the common welfare of humanity. This denial to government of any absolute rights is a fundamental article with the Church."

However, it would seem that the item judged to be most 'vulnerable' today is not the mid-section, of which Jean Rivière states in *Le Problème de l'église et de l'état au temps de Philippe le Bel* that not only its origins but its very phraseology are to be found in the most ancient writers, drawing attention also to the influence of St. Bernard, Hugh of St. Victor and Alexander of Hales, but the concluding sentence. Admitting that, from a theological standpoint, the bull raises no serious problems, Rivière treats of the final clause "which alone has the weight of a definition." Even this, he says, affirms only a general duty of submission to the Pope, and he mentions that the dogmatic definition at the tail of the document is only a formula taken from St. Thomas. The definition runs "We . . . define . . . that it is absolutely necessary for a human being's salvation that he be subject to the Roman Pontiff"—an affirmation which links up logically with the dogmatic teaching at the beginning of the bull; if it is necessary for salvation to 'belong' to the Church, then it is vital to submit to him whom Christ appointed its head on earth.

Bishop Butler, rejecting the suggestion that the Church had abandoned, in Vatican II, the claim to be the unique Church of Christ, wrote in his article *The Church and the Churches* (*The Tablet*, May 4, 1969): "The Council did not, and could not, make such a surrender. The claim to unicity is absolutely basic to Catholicism, and is implied in a statement of Boniface VIII which is held to be infallible: "We declare, pronounce, define that it is altogether necessary for salvation that every human creature should be subject to the Roman Pontiff' " and he added: "I apologise to our separated brethren for the crudeness of this affirmation. A modern pope or council would have found a better way of saying the same thing. Nevertheless, the underlying conviction is something about which we cannot bargain; and nobody . . . should be required to surrender his profoundest articles of faith in the interests of dialogue."

St. Thomas' thesis—"We show also that it is necessary for salvation for every human creature to be subject to the Roman Pontiff"—is recalled in Boniface's definition, and is to be found in *Contra Errores Graecorum* on the heels of the passage reproduced on page 66. St. Thomas wrote: "And Chrysostom, writing on the Acts of the Apostles, says that 'Peter is the most holy head of the blessed apostolic throne, the good shepherd.' . . . . We show also that it is necessary for salvation to be subject to the Roman Pontiff. For St. Cyril says in the *Thesaurus*: 'And, brethren, let us so imitate Christ that we, His sheep, may hear His voice, remaining within the church of St. Peter; and do not let us be puffed up with pride, or the cunning serpent may perchance extrude us because of our dissension. . . .' And Maximus, in his letter to the Eastern Christians, says: 'We say that the universal Church is founded and held firm on the rock of Peter's confession . . . and in this Church it is necessary for the salvation of our souls that we should remain, and we have the duty of obeying him, loyal to his faith and confession.' "

Once again, the saint has supported his view by drawing upon St. Maximus, the confessor who, after being flogged, had his tongue cut out and his right hand cut off because he would not embrace error, and he has found support again in the pseudo-Cyril. Neither he nor Boniface can be credited with some monstrous innovation; they teach that there is one Church, necessary for salvation, and that her head is the Pope, to whom all who seek salvation must make submission.

Boniface, a man with a streak of paranoia, made many enemies and—as enemies will—they put a false interpretation on innocent statements. When, for example, Admiral Roger Loria went on at length about the joys which indubitably awaited him in heaven, the Pope dourly commented, "Maybe, maybe not!" The remark was used to prove that Boniface, who had disbelieved only in Loria, did not believe in heaven. It was not the first or last time that papal words were seized upon as a handy weapon, but let it be admitted that here was a man who certainly earned enmity.

Galileo (1564-1642)

Twenty-seven years ago I was engaged in answering, in the daily Press, a non-Catholic who insisted that Galileo was tortured by the Inquisition for teaching that the earth went round the sun. I see that I quoted then what T. H. Huxley wrote to Mivart in 1885: "I looked into the matter when I was in Italy and I arrived at the conclusion that the Pope and the College of Cardinals had rather the best of it"—and I consider the words still worth quoting today even if the verdict calls for amplification. Galileo was not physically tortured. Arthur Koestler in *The Sleepwalkers* holds that Robert Bellarmine realized the true nature of scientific thought better than did Galileo; Galileo in a magnificent letter to his friend Castelli wrote more wisely on the interpretation of Scripture than did Bellarmine or any other scholar of the time; the Pope and Holy Office came out of the affair looking shabby . . . and yet Sherwood F. Taylor, who wrote his *Galileo and the Freedom of Thought* for the benefit of the Rationalist cause, was led by his investigation to enter the Church.[28]

The story goes back to a priest, Nicholas Copernicus, who, urged on by Cardinal Schoenberg and Bishop Giese,

---

[28] See Fr. James Brodrick's *Galileo: The Man, his Work, his Misfortunes,* p. 148.

published in 1543 his great work *De Revolutionibus orbium coelestium*, which rejected the Ptolemaic view of the universe and the doctrines of the Aristotelians and taught that the sun, not the earth, was the centre of the solar system. There was no outcry and the Council of Trent (1545-1563), which dealt with current hersy, had no complaint to lodge against the view.

Yet, when Galileo taught his heliocentric view of the world, bitter controversy arose. Why? The answer is found largely in the character of the man. Fr. Brodrick, who confesses himself a fervent admirer of Galileo and who lays it on rather thick about the "proud, rancorous pope" or the "proud, implacable pope" indulging in the "blackest thoughts of revenge" on "one of the brightest spirits in human history," nevertheless admits that 'Galileo loved to score off people and to make them look silly," (*Op. cit.*, p. 63), and he quotes another admirer, Rudolf Thiel, as saying, "By nature this great scientist and scholar was bellicose, passionate, spiteful, ruthlessly determined and unscrupulous in his choice of methods." (p. 14). Koestler (*Op. cit.*, p. 363) is even more outspoken: "Vanity, jealousy and self-righteousness combined into a demoniac force which drove him to the brink of self-destruction. . . ." Dons or scholars being touchy, his relations with them degenerated rapidly between 1611 and 1616.

Up to 1616, however, the authorities—Pope and Cardinals—actually encouraged discussion of the Copernican system as long as it kept to the language of science and did not cross the frontier of theology. Cardinal Dini was explicit in a letter to Galileo in 1615: "One may write freely as long as one keeps out of the sacristy." The conflict broke out when the sacristy was invaded. Not Galileo but his opponents dragged the argument 'into the sacristy' by alleging that the heliocentric viewpoint flouted Scriptural truth. Unhappily, Galileo played into their hands by advancing his teaching not as hypothesis but as established fact.

What was the position at that time when a writer advanced a theory which seemed at variance with Scripture? It depended on whether he put it forward as hypothesis or fact. The Copernican system, for all Galileo's dogmatism, was not demonstrated—"he had no proof" (Koestler, *Op. cit.*, p. 436)—"he was wrong at a critical point—mistaken in his science and premature in his dogmatism" (Professor Butterfield, *Christianity and History*, p. 10)—and, if he had been content to claim only 'working hypothesis,' there would have been no *furore*. It would have been a matter of "We will discuss this further when you bring proof, and, if necessary, adjust our interpretation of Scripture." But, to Galileo, his teaching *was* gospel truth. Professor Butterfield sees, on both sides of this quarrel, "that intellectual arrogance, or mental rigidity, or stiff-necked self-assurance which manages to interpolate itself into all forms of scholarship and science." (*Ibidem*) Rejecting the Ptolemaic astronomy, Galileo assumed that his hypothesis was the only alternative, though, as Pierre Duhem noted, "To justify that conclusion, one would first have to prove that there was no other imaginable combination of hypotheses which could cover the facts."

There were two main events in the unfolding of the Greek tragedy. In February, 1616, the eleven 'periti' of the Holy Office returned to the cardinals a verdict that the Copernican view was heretical and contradicted Scripture. Galileo, however, was allowed to teach the very same views as *hypothesis*. This he failed to do, publishing some years later his famous *Dialogue Concerning the Two Great World Systems*, in which he taught Copernicanism openly as established fact, and, with incredible tactlessness, put an anti-Copernican argument sacred to the pope himself into the mouth of a simpleton, while dubbing his opponents "dumb idiots" and "mental pygmies, hardly deserving to be called human." The upshot was his famous appearance before the Holy Office, in which he abjectly perjured himself, insulting his own intelligence and the intelligence of his audience by swearing that the book was intended to discredit, not defend, Copernicanism. It is scandalous that the Holy Office should have been instrumental in reducing a great, if turbulent, man to such degrading falsehood.

It is not, however, to be held against the Inquisitors, as we saw, that they failed to accept Galileo's word for his views. When the old scientist was blind, he was visited by another great man, also destined to blindness, John Milton, who was fascinated by the debates of the day, and Milton listened with interest to his arguments but came away unconvinced. Readers of *Paradise Lost* may remember that, in Book VII, Adam raised these questions with the archangel Raphael, only to be told:

> "Solicit not thy thoughts with matters hid;
> Leave them to God above; him serve and fear."

Finally, how does this case affect the authority of Rome? Did the Pope teach infallibly that the Copernican view contradicted Scripture? The answer is that he did not teach it at all and was not convinced of a contradiction. He wrote to Cardinal di Zoller stating that "Holy Church had not condemned the opinion of Copernicus nor was it condemned as heretical, but only as rash; and, moreover, if anyone could demonstrate it to be necessarily true, it would no longer be rash." (Sherwood F. Taylor, *op. cit.*, p. 109) It was not an unreasonable attitude, and the Pope neither signed nor ratified the Holy Office's condemnation, which shows him to have been more balanced than his *periti*. Galileo, according to Koestler, had thought himself capable of outwitting all and making a fool of the Pope and so brought upon his head the misfortunes which had never befallen Copernicus. One moral of the story is that scholars must not overestimate their own intelligence. And the teaching authority of the Pope? The wretched facts are as irrelevant to that as were the victory celebrations in the Vatican after the Boyne.

MIRARI VOS (1832)

The encyclical *Mirari Vos* of Gregory XVI has been used by more than one Catholic in recent attempts to curtail papal prestige, the ground for contempt being, in Mr. Peter de Rosa's words, that Gregory XVI, followed by Pius IX and Leo XIII, taught that "the right to freedom of conscience in religious matters is 'sheer madness.'" But it depends on what one means by 'freedom of conscience' and modern dissidents should first have pondered what Newman wrote in his *Letter*, defending Pius IX's *Quanta Cura* of 1864 which referred back to Gregory XVI and his term 'madness' (*deliramentum*). If we are to be fair, he pointed out, words must be given the meaning they bear in their context. He instanced: "In like manner, if the Pope condemned 'the Reformation,' it would be utterly sophisticated to say in consequence that he had declared himself against all reforms; yet this is how Mr. Gladstone treats him, when he speaks of (so-called) liberty of conscience."

Newman stressed that Gregory and Pius were not attacking true freedom of conscience, but 'so-called liberty,' 'the most foul fount of indifferentism,'—"There is no scoffing of any Pope . . . at that most serious doctrine, the right and the duty of following that Divine Authority, the voice of conscience, on which in truth the Church herself is built. So indeed it is, did the Pope speak against Conscience in the true sense of the word, he would commit a suicidal act. . . . His mission is to proclaim the moral law. . . . On the law of conscience and its sacredness are founded both his authority in theory and his power in fact. . . . The championship of the Moral Law and of conscience is his *raison d'être*."

We hope to return to Newman's teaching on conscience in a later chapter. Meanwhile, we urge those who wish to see *Mirari Vos* in its true light both to read the whole encyclical and to study Professor Roger Aubert's *L'enseignement du magistère ecclésiastique au XIXe siècle sur le liberalisme* in *Tolérance et communauté humaine* (pp. 77-82). This is now out of print, but Professor Aubert gave an account of his argument and conclusions in *Concilium* (September, 1965), under the heading of *Religious Liberty from 'Mirari Vos' to the 'Syllabus'*. In addition, reference may been made to *Roman Catholicism and Religious Liberty* by Dr. A. F. Carrillo de Albornoz.

One or two quotations will demonstrate that there was no attack on true freedom of conscience. "Liberty of conscience," Gregory wrote to the Czar Nicholas 1, "must not be confused with liberty not to have a conscience," and

Aubert comments (*Concilium*, p. 51): "The latter expression is much more important for understanding the real meaning of the encyclical . . . what the document condemns is, above all, an apologia for liberty and liberties that seem to stem from a naturalistic concept of man. Rome unmasked in the concrete liberalism of the period a clear statement of man's emancipation from God and a deliberate rejection of the primacy of the supernatural."

Aubert had already pointed out (p. 50): ". . . there was no intention at Rome of closing the doors in practice on every instance of 'modern liberty', including freedom of worship and of the press. Proof of this is to be found in the fact that at the very moment when . . . . *Mirari vos* was being written, Gregory XVI not only refrained from disavowing—as some people urged him to do—the Belgian Constitution of 1831, based on these liberties and on the principle of separation of Church and State, but he went further: in spite of certain denunciations he named the vicar-general Sterckx as archbishop of Malines. This was the man who had undertaken to justify these principles. . . ."

Gregory used precise phrases, in *Mirari vos*, to show that he was rapping totally unrestricted freedom—"plena illa atque immoderata libertas opinionum . . . freno quippe omni adempto." It is hard to see how a sensible man could fault his viewpoint. "All that the Pope has done," Newman wrote in his *Letter, à propos* of Pius IX though it applies equally to Gregory, "is to deny a universal, and what a universal! a universal liberty to all men to say out whatever doctrines they may hold by preaching, or by the press, uncurbed by church or civil power. Does this not bear out what I said . . . of the sense in which Pope Gregory denied a 'liberty of conscience'? . . . . What if a man's conscience embraces the duty of regicide? or infanticide? or free love? You may say that in England the good sense of the nation would stifle . . . such atrocities. True, but the proposition says that it is the very right of every one, by nature, in every well-constituted society." Then he quickly deflated English championship of unrestricted freedom: "If so, why have we gagged the Press in Ireland on the ground of its being seditious? . . . . It seems a light epithet for the Pope to use, when he calls such a doctrine of conscience *deliramentum*: of all conceivable absurdities it is the wildest and most stupid." He added a query which we should ponder: "Has Mr. Gladstone really no better complaint to make against the Pope's condemnations than this?"

We may append another query: was it fair to be so belligerent when an Italian qualified liberty and never to turn a hair when someone as totally English as Dr. Johnson taught, as we know from Boswell, that every man is entitled to liberty of conscience in religion, but that the magistrate may rightly interfere if he teaches a doctrine contrary to what the society holds to be true, that "people confound liberty of thinking . . . with a liberty of preaching"?

As Mr. de Rosa added the name of Leo XIII to the names of Gregory and Pius, let us see what he had to say. If Professor H. J. Laski could write of Newman's *Letter*, "It remains with some remarks of Sir Henry Maine and a few brilliant dicta of F. W. Maitland as perhaps the profoundest discussion of sovereignty in the English language,"[29] Leo's *Libertas praestantissimum* might qualify for comparable superlatives. He taught: ". . . it is unlawful to demand, to defend or to concede an *indiscriminate* liberty of writing or teaching or of religious opinion as if these were so many rights inherent in human nature. For if they were conferred by nature it would follow that *there would be a right to disparage and defy God's authority. . . .*" (Denzinger, 1932.)

After laying down that freedom of conscience does not involve the right to trample on the first commandment, refusing worship to God, he says that "it may also be taken in the sense that the individual has in the state the right to obey the will of God in accordance with his own conception of his duty and to follow His precepts without let or hindrance. This freedom, the freedom worthy of the children of God . . . has always been the subject of the Church's prayers and her special attention." (Quoted from Albornoz,

---

[29] *Studies in the Problem of Sovereignty,* p. 202. See also *The Political Thought of John Henry Newman,* by Terence Kenny.

Op. cit., p. 72. *Libertas praestantissimum* may be read in its entirety in *The Pope and the People*, edited by A. Keogh, S.J.)

Catholics who ridicule *Mirari vos* must pause to consider how Vatican II insisted that its teaching left "untouched traditional Catholic doctrine on the moral duty of men and societies towards the true religion and towards the one Church of Christ," pinning the qualifying phrase "within due limits" to its vindication of a man's right to act according to his beliefs, and driving it home with "provided that the just requirements of public order are observed" (*Dignitatis Humanae*).

"The eternal law of God is the only rule which human liberty must follow," Leo taught. Such a principle condemned the unrestricted liberty of the Indian thugs who, following the tenets of their sect, and conscience, strangled wayfarers. And we today are not in a position to contradict when he speaks of the evils which "are the offspring in great part of the false liberty which is so much extolled, and in which the germs of safety and glory were supposed to be contained." London has been hailed in a newspaper headline as "Abortion capital of the world" and the press gives every few months new statistics in connection with the execution squads. . . . "Abortions for under-12's in first year of Act" (May 7, 1971); "Abortion ends one in seven pregnancies" (January 11, 1972); "Abortion on demand as figures leap. . . . Abortions in 1971 showed an increase of 42,925, to 126,774, on the 1970 total of 83,849"; "10,000 came to England for abortion in 1970"; and a corollary: "Health chiefs are so shocked by the latest figures for venereal disease in Hertfordshire that they have decided to keep them secret. . . . Latest national figures reveal that Britain's VD clinics dealt with 250,000 cases in 1970—an increase of 120,000 over the previous year." (Dec. 21, 1971) The abortionist has been granted full 'freedom of conscience' to out-Herod Herod; it has indeed proved *deliramentum*.

Catholics are fortunately not the only people left who can spot the folly of unrestricted freedom. The descendants of those who cried out in horror when Pius XI exchoed Gregory XVI—have the wisest of them—acquired a distaste for total liberty. I quote from the review by Kathleen Nott, a humanist, of *The Permissive Morality* by C. H. and Winifred Whiteley: "Indeed, it is hard to deny that in about two generations we have changed over from a strict . . . social ethic which conceived life as a task to be accomplished by responsible people, to the more permissive view that the aim of life is happiness or satisfaction. As examples, the authors list: sexual freedom, both in deed and word; the collapse of parental domination. . . . Morality, they think, must be an objective rule, dogmaticallly taught. . . . It is lack of these moral braces which has given us our society. . . . I think, too, more often than I used to, that we are, if not totally 'worm-eaten,' at least nibbled by excessive liberalism."[30]

Miss Nott estimates the decline to have taken place in two generations or so, but Newman's *Letter* shows that the decline, the *deliramentum*, was there in his time as England ridiculed the objective standards which the Popes upheld. "Men of the present generation," he wrote, ". . . are shocked to witness in the abiding Papal system the words, ways and works of their grandfathers. In my own lifetime has that old world been alive, and has gone its way. Who will say that the plea of conscience was as effectual, sixty years ago, as it is now in England, for the toleration of every sort of fancy religion? Had the Press always that wonderful elbow-room which it has now? . . . Could *savants* in that day insinuate what their hearers mistook for atheism in scientific assemblies, and artisans practise it in the centres of political action? Could public prints day after day, or week after week, carry on a war against religion, natural and revealed, as is now the case? No; law or public opinion would not suffer it; we may be wiser or better now, but we were then in the wake of the Holy Roman Church, and had been so from the time of the Reformation. We were faithful to the tradition of fifteen hundred years. All this was called

---

[30] *The Observer,* December 6, 1964.

Toryism, and men gloried in the name; now it is called Popery and reviled."

THE SYLLABUS OF ERRORS, 1864

Sixty-four years after the Syllabus was published, Noel Vesper, a Protestant philosopher who was also a pastor of the Reformed Church, published *Les Protestants, la Patrie, l'Église* and in it he lauded the Syllabus for having put an unerring finger on spiritual error and unmasked the anti-Christian forces of the era. He judged: "It is not beyond the bounds of possibility that the Syllabus, which so shocked public opinion, may appear in the course of time to have been the last and greatest bulwark by which the West tried to defeat resurgent barbarism." That is the view of a man who carefully read the document and, in all likelihood, followed up its references to contexts, and it paints a very different picture from that put forward, for example, in E. L. Woodward's *Three Studies in European Conservatism*. The author of the latter book, an Oxford Don, lamented: "The ideas upon which the best minds of modern Europe were attempting to build up a new society were 'monstrosa opinionum portenta' . . . . Outside the morbid atmosphere of the curia no man could take this miserable catalogue with any seriousness; within the curia the words were scarcely understood."

This is magnificent stuff for the hustings, but the last statement gives it away. It is not reasoned comment, but rhetoric resounding in a vacuum from which reality and careful consideration have been excluded. The 'liberalism' which the Syllabus confronted—"the ideas of the best minds of modern Europe"— was the synthesis of the philosophy of the *Encyclopaedia*, whose editor, Diderot, was credited with the ambition to "strangle the last king with the bowels of the last priest," and it had received its baptism of blood round the guillotine. Further fruits were soon to appear. Karl Marx's *Das Kapital* appeared a year after the *Syllabus*; seven years after it, the Communists shot Archbishop Darboy of Paris as he blessed his executioners; they massacred thousands. It was the era of Cavour who divorced politics from morality ("What rascals we would be if we did in our private life what we do in our public!"), of Garibaldi who hated the Church, of the rising star of Bismarck who contested her rights. Nine years after the *Syllabus*, Renan published his *La Vie de Jésus*. If Pius IX, after his early support of liberal causes, came to oppose liberalism, the fault lay in the liberals.

There is a telling picture of nineteenth-century liberalism in its reality in J. E. C. Bodley's *France* (pp. 117ff): "The intolerant system under the Third Republic differs from all persecutions known to history, in that it is not only practised in the name of Liberty, but it aims at laying official disability on an established religion. . . . No one has any idea what a noxious . . . creature is the anti-clerical in the province. . . . Under the mask of free-thought he would like to prevent his neighbours from thinking differently from himself . . . he is an aggressive persecutor. . . . The café is the meeting-place of these guardians of liberty. . . ." It brings back the dreary talk of the mini-Zolas in Werfel's *The Song of Bernadette*, and goes to explain why Dr. T. S. Eliot, in a lecture given in Cambridge, declared that a Christian had more in common with an African savage than with an European liberal. "Get rich!" was the famous counsel of the French liberal Guizot, and Mr. Michael Oakeshott, in *The Social and Political Doctrines of Contemporary Europe*, ranks Liberalism with Communism as a materialist doctrine.

This may seem rather general, but it is relevant not only to the *Syllabus* as a whole but especially to the last condemnation (No. 80), which rejects the suggestion that the papacy "can and ought to come to terms with Progress, Liberalism, and the New Civilization." Dom Damian McElrath, in the preface to *The Syllabus of Errors of Pius IX— Some Reactions in England*,[31] writes of the document, "It was a declaration of war against the *evils* of modern society. Modern society failed to see the distinction—it viewed the document as a damnation of itself." And No. 80 seemed to be the most sweeping damnation of all. *Punch* expressed

[31] Bibliothèque de la Revue D'Histoire Ecclésiastique, Louvain, 1964.

the average Englishman's reaction with a cartoon, entitled *The Pope's Mad Bull*, which depicted a bull banging its head in vain against a wall inscribed 'Science—Common Sense—Toleration—Civil and Religious Liberty—Progress."

Gladstone made easy capital out of 'No. 80' and Newman devoted Section 7 of his *Letter* to his arguments . . . though Acton (God forgive him!) judged that he supported his case with "enormous lies." Newman turned to the relevant Allocution of March 18, 1861: "The Allocution is a long argument . . . that the moving parties in that Progress, Liberalism, and New Civilization make use of it so seriously to the injury of the Faith and the Church, that it is both out of the power, and contrary to the duty of, the Pope to come to terms with them. Nor would these prime movers themselves differ from him here; certainly in this country it is the common cry that Liberalism is and will be the Pope's destruction and they wish and mean it to be so."

As the Allocution showed, however, and No. 80 must be read in its light, it was the ideas of Cavour and the Piedmontese Government in particular to which the Pope refused to adapt. "Every Italian," wrote Mr. E. E. Y. Hales in *Pio Nono* (p. 259), "knew that 'Progress, Liberalism, and Recent Civilisation' meant the closure of the convents and monasteries, and the imposition of secular education. . . . In England, however, Progress and Recent Civilisation meant primarily the Great Exhibition of 1851, while Liberalism meant conservatives like Peel or Mr. Gladstone. . . ." The adverbial clause falls short of the full truth, since liberals had passed legislation hostile to the Church whenever power got into their hands. This would be known in Britain, and Newman's words about the common cry in England that Liberalism would be the end of the Pope proves that the English were not so innocent of the facts. It is not to be wondered at, then, that the papal lamb begged to be excused from couching with the liberal lion; the lion was rampant. We see this if we follow up the reference attached to proposition 80. It relates to the allocution *Iamdudum cernimus* of March 18, 1861, in which the Pope protested that oppression of convents and monasteries masqueraded under the titles of 'modern civilization and liberalism' and declared, "If, by the term *civilization* must be understood a system invented on purpose to weaken, and perhaps to overthrow, the Church, never can the Holy See and the Roman Pontiff be allied with such a civilization!"

Apart from the anti-Catholic aggressiveness of the New Society, there was its sheer materialism. Pius IX asked in *Quanta Cura*, "Is there any one who does not see . . . that a society of men which has broken all bonds of religion and true justice, can have no other object before it save that of planning for and amassing wealth and in its actions can follow no other law save the unbridled greed of a mind which is a slave to its pleasures and desires?" He was writing in the era of *Oliver Twist,* and the year of the Syllabus was the year of the abortive chimney-sweepers' Act which came in large measure as a result of Kingsley's *Water Babies,* describing the relations of little Tom to his master Grimes. Whoever talked of modern society or new civilization in a euphoric vacuum, it was not the Pope. The Great Exhibition of 1851 which gloried in the prosperity of the middle classes marked no moral advance. The "advance of modern civilization" which he sought to stem was the spread of unbridled capitalism—the Exhibition came only five years after the Great Hunger in Ireland, when, thanks to English indifference, 3000 died each week in the workhouses alone—and he took his stand also against atheism, communism, indifferentism and pseudo-free-thought which was often bigotry in disguise. Before describing the provenance of the *Syllabus,* I think it of value to print part of a letter to *The Times* (July 5, 1970) from Mr. Ronald Chamberlain, a former M.P. In it he gives his opinion as to why the party in power lost the 1970 election: "We needed someone who would roundly condemn the grasping selfishness on both sides of industry . . . who would expose . . . the 'permissive society,' with its rash of abortions and drugs . . . in short, anyone who would guide us towards the standards of conduct and behaviour and responsibility that we all know in our hearts to be right." Basically, that is an Englishman's cry, from the wreckage that 'liberalism' has caused, for Pius IX or Leo XIII. Cardinal Manning, trying to calm down Gladstone, suggested to him that, even in their lifetime, Wisdom might be justified in her children, Pius IX be proved right in his pessimism. Pius has certainly been vindicated by now.

ORIGIN

The origin of the *Syllabus* . . . Odo Russell in a dispatch to his uncle 'Finality Jack' at the Foreign Office traced the *Syllabus* to a request made for such a catalogue by the bishops who met in Rome in 1862 for the canonisation of the Japanese martyrs. In this he seems to have been in error. Cardinal Pecci, the future Leo XIII, persuaded a Provincial Council to write to Pius IX, appealing for a guiding list of errors then circulating, and it was this which resulted in the *Syllabus* as we know it.[32] It is not what one might call a "free-standing" pronouncement, but an *aide-mémoire*, dependent on contexts, comparable to the index at the end of a book, the condemnations finding their true sense when one followed up the references appended. There are eighty errors catalogued, each with its reference leading back to one of the thirty-two allocutions, etc., listed. The errors are grouped under ten headings according as they deal with (1) pantheism, etc; (2) qualified rationalism; (3) indifferentism, etc.; (4) communism, etc.;[33] (5) the Church and its rights; (6) civil society and Church-state relations; (7) ethics; (8) Christian marriage; (9) the temporal sovereignty of the pope; and (10) the liberalism of the day.

Many of the 'condemnations', even without benefit of context, are immediately acceptable to a thinking Catholic, but I have qualified 'condemnations' since, in spite of the title of the *Syllabus* (or 'catalogue of modern errors') and Cardinal Antonelli's introductory letter, the latter individual sent to Mgr. Dupanloup the message that the Pope wishes the propositions to be "regarded rather as warnings than as actual condemnations." (One condemns unmitigated error,

---

[32] See C. G. Rinaldi, *Il Valore del Sillabo,* Rome, 1888.
[33] Strictly speaking, this is not one of the eighty, but the references are given for past censure.

but warns against a proposition which lacks a vital distinction. The proposition may contain a strong element of truth but require 'weeding'.) A Catholic could not quarrel, for example, with No. 40) and concede that the Church's doctrine is contrary to the well-being of society—at least, not unless (like Tyrrell) he had lost faith in her doctrine—and he would be unlikely to contest, as against No. 56, that human laws are free to ignore God.

A reasonable Catholic could see the truth of every single point taken in its context; so could an open-minded non-Catholic; so *did* an unbeliever. Emile Ollivier, a lawyer of liberal tendencies and an unbeliever, who became Napoleon III's Prime Minister during the first Vatican Council, wrote a two-volume work *L'Église et L'État au Concile du Vatican*, of which Dom Cuthbert Butler in *The Vatican Council*, Chapter VI, said: "I have to say that of all books of history I have read, this one comes perhaps the nearest to the ideal of historical objectivity and impartiality . . . he scouted as chimerical the fears entertained on the score of the *Syllabus*: his explanation and defence of the *Syllabus* is the best— better than Dupanloup's, better than Newman's."

What, then occasioned such a furious reaction in Victorian times, a reaction which still has tired echoes today? The answer is, in part, exposed in this excerpt from H. J. and Hugh Massingham's introduction to *The Great Victorians*: "The very novelty of their (the Victorians') revolt against established canons of knowledge and philosophy caused them to assume and assert the infallibility of their discoveries. In most fields they really thought they had said the last word. . . . The era consequently tended to become one of capital dogmas in capital letters. Unlike the great thinkers, they do not strike one as having their noses close to the ground . . . the slightest red herring of emotion, of vanity, a passing scent of ephemeral interest, and the eager dogs suddenly disappear, wagging their tails and barking importantly, presently to return with a tremendous air of discovery. Indeed, there was obviously something impure in Victorian thought, and it is this which accounts for the tragic waste of talent and genius." This was the crude infallibility which barked so furiously at papal correction, seeing it as both an impertinence and an anachronism, a *deliramentum*. ("Whom the gods have doomed to perish, they first make mad" was the reaction of the *Morning Advertiser*.) The Victorians with no true philosophy of man, far less prophetic vision, could not be expected to trace a line in advance from Bismarck to Hitler and Belsen, from Cavour to Fascism, or to read in the condemnation of communism a prophecy of the millions to die in Stalin's slave-camps; or to know that contempt for the link between God and behaviour that was demanded by proposition 56 of the *Syllabus* would bring the nightmares of Dresden, Nagasaki and Hiroshima. If twentieth-century man is so quick to sneer at 'prophets of doom', what could one expect of nineteenth?

Newman, tackling in his *Letter* the question of why the Syllabus was received with such an outcry in Britain, judged: "So large and elaborate a work struck the public mind as a new law, moral, social and ecclesiastical, which was to be the foundation of a European code, and the beginning of a new world, in opposition to the social principles of the 19th century. When this belief was once received, it became the interpretation of the whole *Syllabus* . . . as if it had for its object in all its portions one great scheme of aggression. Then, when the public mind was definitely directed to the examination of these erroneous *Theses*, they were sure to be misunderstood, from their being read apart from the context, occasion and drift of each. They had been noted as errors in the Pope's Encyclicals and Allocutions in the course of the preceding eighteen years, and no one had taken any notice of them; but now, when they were all brought together, they made a great sensation."

". . . they were sure," Newman said, "to be misunderstood. . . ." It is, I think, undeniable that the publication of the *Syllabus* did far more harm than good, as did St. Pius V's *Regnans in Excelsis* of 1570. The necessary warnings had already been made in the allocutions and encyclicals which preceded. But this is no excuse for attacking the eighty propositions on the basis of a reading unrelated to the contexts supplied, nor is it ground for representing that the teaching conveyed was untrue or unimportant. The *Syllabus* had not the authority of an encyclical, since it was only an *aide-mémoire* and did not bear the papal signature, but, as Newman wrote, it was "to be received with profound submission, as having been sent by the Pope's authority to the Bishops of the world." This is all the more impressive in that he himself had heard of the document with dismay, knowing how it would be turned against the Church. The respect which he bore towards papal authority emerges from his writing that the Pope might personally "issue a fresh list of propositions in addition, and pronounce them to be Errors, and I should take that condemnation to be of dogmatic authority, because I believe him appointed by his Divine Master to determine in the detail of faith and morals what is true and what is false."

Newman, Aubert, Albornoz—all force attention to the need of reading each 'condemnation' in the context of its encyclical etc. Terence Kenny wrote in *The Political Thought of John Henry Newman*, "It is amusing that even today this obvious and necessary step is often missed." If, for example, we look at propositions 15,55 and 77, which were advanced in the *Scottish Catholic Observer* correspondence columns as "plainly unequivocal strictures," we find that it is the strictures which are qualified and the liberal catchwords of that time which were sweeping and general. Once again, we find shady practice trying to pass under the cover of a fair-sounding principle.

Proposition 15 runs: "Every man is free to . . . profess the religion he should believe true, judged by the light of reason." Why should the Church, the champion of reason, object? We turn to the two references supplied. The first is *Multiplices inter* of June 10, 1851, a condemnation of F. de Paula G. Vigil's *Defence of the authority of the Government and Bishops against the claims of the Court of Rome*. Vigil, we discover, denied the Church's claim to be founded by the Son of God, rejecting the ideas of divine commission and guidance. And *therefore*, he held, every man should follow his own reason; for him, it was reason *versus* revelation. The second reference concerns the allocution *Maxima quidem* of June 9, 1862, which condemns those rationalists who "deny any influence of God in the world and among men, and rashly argue that human reason, without any reference to God, is the sole judge of truth and falsehood, right and wrong. . . ." Deriving truth from reason bereft of supernatural revelation, "they accord to every man a kind of primordial right" in religion. The Pope has censured reason for closing its ears to the Word of God.

Proposition 55 runs: "The Church ought to be separated from the State, and the State from the Church." Why, when Gregory XVI appointed as Archbishop of Malines the champion of separated Church and State, should Pius IX fault this principle? We turn to the context, the allocution *Acerbissimum* of September 27, 1852, and find that the reservation refers to the Republic of New Grenada where separation was being demanded, not on its own merits, but as part of a general attack on the Church to try to strip her of legal defence. It was merely an item in a pattern of assault. Curiously, the only mention lies in the melancholy words, "We say nothing of the demand that the Church be separated. . . ." But he had made clear that the liberals' intention was to hamstring.

Proposition 77 reads: "In the present day it is no longer expedient that the Catholic religion shall be held as the only religion of the State to the exclusion of all other modes of worship." Aubert has it that the error lies in "declaring without any qualification that there was no longer any case, in the middle of the Nineteenth Century, in which the maintenance of Catholicism as the religion of the State was still justified"—and this is sensible enough, but the matter leaps into focus when we thumb the relevant allocution, *Nemo vestrum*, of July 26, 1855. It refers to Spain, recalls the pact made in 1851 to ensure the Church's freedom and the teaching of religion in schools, and indicts the way in which anti-religious forces were now flouting the concordat, refusing to allow bishops to ordain or convents to admit novices. The warning, then, narrows down to a rejection of what is trying to hide under the umbrella of proposition 77 in that one country at that point of history.

Thus, if one wishes to speak truthfully about the *Syllabus*, one does not embark on the topic until one has looked up the "why, where and how far" in a collection like the *Recueil des Allocutions etc citées dans L'Encyclique et Le Syllabus du 8 Decembre 1864*. No. 79, for example, nailed the error that unrestricted liberty to say and write what one liked would not lead to moral corruption and indifferentism. The allocution locates the proposition in its true background—Mexico. The vindication was the brutal persecution of religion by Calles this century. No. 17 rejects the suggestion that those who are *in no way* linked to the Church can be saved. Many an indignant non-Catholic has overlooked 'in no way', ignorant of the background of doctrine, unaware, too, that the Pope of the *Syllabus* was on the best of terms with the Protestant Odo Russell, told him that non-Catholics could be saved, and then pulled his leg by adding, "For those who, like yourself, have lived in Rome at the very Fountain of Truth and have not recognized and accepted it, there can be no salvation!"

Let us end this section by reading what Pius IX had to say on this particular point and what Leo XIII, who 'sparked' the Syllabus, had to say about toleration. First, Pius IX in *Singulari quaedam* of 1854 (context of proposition 17): ". . . we wish to rouse your episcopal . . . vigilance to combat the opinion that *for a certainty* the way of salvation can be found in any kind of religion. Nevertheless, you will . . . show your flocks that this dogma of the Catholic faith conflicts in no way with the divine mercy and justice. It must be held as certain that those who labour under ignorance of the true religion will not on this account, if the ignorance is invincible, be held guilty of any fault in the sight of God. And who would dare to take upon himself to define the limits of such ignorance in view of the difference in people and places, in mental capacities and disposition, and many other things that must be taken into consideration?"

Leo XIII, *Immortale Dei*, 1865: "No one has any legitimate ground for accusing the Church of being an enemy of either just tolerance or healthy and justifiable liberty. While the Church considers that it is not right to put the various forms of worship on the same footing as the true religion, it does not follow that she condemns heads of states who, with a view to achieving good or preventing evil, in practice allow these various creeds each to have their own place in the state."

These are the true views of the men responsible for the *Syllabus*.

5

Transubstantiation

. . . that fictitious transubstantiation for which they fight more fiercely at the present day than for all the other articles of their faith.

> JOHN CALVIN,
> Institutes of the Christian Religion.

I . . . do solemnly and sincerely, in the presence of God, profess, testify, and declare that I do believe that in the Sacrament of the Lord's Supper there is not any transubstantiation . . .

> Declaration which barred Catholics from Parliament before 1829.

Whosoever you be who assert new dogmas, I beg you to spare Roman ears, spare that faith which was praised by the mouth of the Apostle. Why after four hundred years do you try to teach us what we knew till now? Why do you produce doctrines which Peter and Paul did not think fit to proclaim? Up to this day the world has been Christian without your doctrine. I will hold to that faith in my old age in which I was regenerated as a boy.

> ST. JEROME, Ep. 84.

Now, with a sense of relief, we climb back out of the dark vaults of history into our own century. We had to brave the dust and cobwebs and lift the lids and look upon

Liberius and Honorius, Boniface, Galileo, Gregory and Pius, but we are glad that the task is done and we are back in the light of day. But not quite of today; it is 1908, the year of the Eucharistic Congress, and a tremendous spectacle greets our eyes. A great procession of the Blessed Sacrament is winding through the streets; it seems as if the whole Catholic Church is involved, priests and people. Every Catholic who can walk must surely be here in the procession, his heart on flame as the Bride of Christ bears witness to her love of the holy Eucharist! But no—the men who are absent are those who spoke most often of 'the People of God.' Von Hügel's *Letters* reveal the group of Modernists "watching critically and aloof from a housetop." Not for them the simple pieties of the multitude!

And one remembers that gloriously open man, David, bringing the ark of the Lord from the house of Obededom into his own city and, almost like a clown in a circus parade, dancing "with all his might before the Lord", and Michol looking down from a window and curling her lip and despising him, and later telling him that he had made an exhibition of himself in front of the serving-maids. She received a wonderful answer from the unselfconscious fighting-man: "I will both play and make myself meaner than I have done. And I will be little in my own eyes: and with the handmaids of whom thou speakest, I shall appear more glorious." "Therefore", the Scripture adds laconically, Michol remained barren to the day of her death—she had been barren first in mind; she was a pre-figure.

We remember her when Modernism comes swirling greyly like a fog round traditional belief in the Eucharist and therefore round traditional devotion to and joy in the Blessed Sacrament. For this is the God, the God in the tabernacle, who truly "gave joy to our youth," to us sleepy-eyed altar-boys who dragged ourselves out of our beds at half-past six or seven to serve Mass and, content perhaps with *Vidi aquam* instead of a real wash, hurried through the dark streets to Mass. Love for our Lord has fed on the Eucharist, grown round It, become articulate over It, and the great hunger for God has grown in the feeding. It is before the tabernacle that

> "The holy time is quiet as a nun
> Breathless with adoration,"

and the spiritual appetite of belief is infectious. I remember preaching about the Real Presence, and spiritual hunger for the Bread of life, and translating for the congregation St. Bonaventure's breathless, tumultuous prayer. . . . "O gentlest Lord Jesus, pierce the very marrow of my soul with the most sweet and health-giving wound of Thy love, with a true, serene, apostolic and most holy love, that my soul may languish and melt with love and desire for Thee, may long for Thee and faint in Thy court, may yearn to be dissolved and to be with Thee. Grant that my soul may hunger for Thee, the Bread of angels, the refreshment of holy souls, our daily super-substantial bread, having all delight and relish and all pleasant sweetness. Let my heart ever hunger for, and feed upon, Thee Whom the angels delight to gaze upon, and may the very core of my heart be filled with Thy delightful savour. May it ever thirst for the fountain of life, the fount of wisdom and knowledge, the spring of eternal light, the torrent of happiness, the abundance of the house of God. . . ." (I took the prayer from the *Veni Mecum* given to my uncle on his ordination in Rome in 1906, the year of 'last Mass' for both Loisy and Tyrrell.) As it happened, there was a non-Catholic farm-labourer, aged seventeen, in the church when St. Bonaventure's faith and love cried out again after seven centuries, and, a few days later, he sent me a message through a third party. In all his life, the good lad said, he had never heard anything so beautiful as that prayer. Could he please have a copy? Not long afterwards, a second message came: would I instruct him and receive him into the Church?

And now the Modernists have come back to explain away the Real Presence with transignification 'signifying nothing.' If Belloc 'rose' when the remote and ineffectual Don dared attack his Chesterton, what is the horror of a Catholic when the Don attacks the real presence?

Not very long ago, a young priest wrote to me, after I had published an article on *The Real Presence*: "How on earth can Christ be physically present in the Holy Eucharist? Surely his physical presence refers to the Body in Heaven. . . . The physical stuff of bread certainly remains . . . even after the words of consecration. . . . I may not be in agreement with Pope Paul, but I feel sure I am with Charles Davis. Finally, I consider that the Dutch theologians' 'transignification' is a much better term than 'transubstantiation'—because the vast majority of Catholics have only one concept of 'substance'—the vulgar sense ('stuff')."

I could have replied that the faith of the vast majority of Catholics is not to be lightly dismissed, that I had avoided saying that our Lord was physically present in the Eucharist (for reasons which will appear later), though I had been emphatic about His being present in His physical reality, and I might well have answered his opening question, after rephrasing it, with the words of two cardinals. First, from the *Apologia*: "It is difficult, impossible, to imagine, I grant;—but how is it difficult to believe? . . . What do I know of substance or matter? just as much as the greatest philosophers, and that is nothing at all." And, from Cardinal Gibbons' *The Faith of our Fathers*: "You tell me it is a mystery above your comprehension. A mystery, indeed. A religion that rejects a revealed truth because it is incomprehensible, contains in itself the seeds of dissolution, and will end in rationalism." They, of course, were addressing non-Catholics, whereas I was dealing with a Catholic priest. . . . I recommended Francis Clark's excellent pamphlet *A 'New Theology' of the Real Presence?*

But what has happened that a priest can write in such an unhappy vein and that, when the encyclical *Mysterium Fidei* was mentioned to a young Belgian priest by the assistant in a British bookshop, this judgment was returned: "Oh, *that?* It's a lot of rubbish. We heard about it in Belgium before it appeared, and we didn't bother reading it"? What has happened is that neo-modernism is switching the content of doctrine, partly under the influence of scientific views and modern philosophy and partly spurred by an

ecumenical desire to bridge the gulf of conflicting Eucharistic
doctrines. The movement takes its origin in northern Europe
as history would lead us to expect.

Here, at the risk of sounding John Bullish, I suggest
that, when we have to wrestle with some of the theology
which is churned out in northern Europe, it does well to
remember Beachcomber's Dr. Strabismus of Utrecht (whom
God preserve!). Strabismus was a joke, but the joke had a
point and too many have forgotten the point. The English-
speaking peoples can be as stupid as the next man, but we
are prosaically stupid and it is only when we are beguiled
by the lorelei of the Rhine that we tend to spout nonsense.
As a concrete example of what an American can do under
foreign influence, here is a passage from *Eucharistic Theology*
by Fr. Joseph Powers, S.J.: "A colleague has remarked that
it takes a greater act of faith to believe that what is present
on the altar before the consecration is bread than to believe
it is Christ after the consecration. This is probably true. . . ."
If we are going to keep our balance, it is imperative that we
remember the ephemeral scholarship of the early years of
this century. Professor Butterfield wrote (*op. cit.*, p. 9):
"It was often noted in the earlier decades of the present
century how greatly it had become the habit of Protestants
to hold some German scholar up their sleeves—a different
one every few years but always preferably the latest one . . .
the German scholar having decided in a final manner whatever point might have been at issue . . . Acton was warned
not to play this game of waving German professors at his
fellow Catholics . . . he not only failed to take the advice,
but added the weight of his influence to a tendency that was
making historical scholarship perhaps over arrogant and
certainly too pontifical." His voice is echoed by the bitter
cry of the Jesuit theologian, Fr. Kleutgen, directed at his
Fatherland: 'I want to have nothing more to do with that
country or with its confused, yet so inflated, minds." (Cf.
Fr. R. M. Wiltgen, S.V.D., *The Rhine Flows into the Tiber*.)

There is a saying of Voltaire which must also be taken
into consideration: "In France every man is either an anvil
or a hammer; he either beats or is beaten." It ties in with

the dictum that every eve in France is St. Bartholomew's
Eve, and they hint that another northern race may be short
of calm common-sense, and warn us to be critical of theology
imported from the Common Market. Fr. Schoof writes in
Breakthrough: ". . . there are only two countries . . . where
the Catholic revival seems to be able to take root . . . France
and Germany. . . . After the Second World War, Dutch
theology also became internationally known on the fringe of
the French and German linguistic zones." It triggers unhappy memories of 'revivals' inspired by Luther and Calvin,
especially when Fr. Schoof speaks of Dr. Schillebeeckx's
'striking' idea of "development through demolition." (Cf. pp.
17 and 220.)

THE SIMPLE, NAKED TRUTH

Fr. P. O'Neil, in his *St. Thomas in the Blessed Sacrament and Mass* (1935), wrote well: "No one can equal St.
Thomas in clearness and simplicity, because he thoroughly
understood what he was writing about; and above all *because
he believed.*" This deserves meditation. First, one can write
clearly of profound matters; fog does not arise from the subject matter. Secondly, disbelief will result in obscurity often,
though the latter can spring from mental sluggishness. The
man who has lost his faith may try to lose, not deny, doctrine,
if he wishes to stay in his niche. Speaking to the cardinals
on April 17, 1907, St. Pius X took Modernist writing to
task: ". . . there is charity without faith, which is tender
towards unbelievers, and throws open the way to eternal
ruin," and he spoke of the cagey Modernists and their errors:
"they wrap them up in ambiguous terms and cloudy forms
which always allow them a way of escape in order to avoid
open condemnation, yet ensnare the imprudent." The reader
should go back now to page 11 and take a second look at
the quotation from *The Experience of Priesthood.* The moral
is that, while we can pity the man who has lost his faith,
and is afraid to show his true colours, and that, while we
can understand open disbelief in the Eucharist, since the
intellect is out of its depth, we must not be conned into

giving any respect to a pretence that a denial of transubstantiation is an allowable interpretation of it, that a reversal of Trent's teaching is consonant with it. Christians have to become like little children, and it was a child, in Hans Andersen's parable, who rejected the new interpretation of clothes and sang out that the emperor was naked. Heresy hates to have attention drawn to its nakedness, but it is the naked truth that some new interpretations fall under Trent's anathema (Dz. 884): "If anyone shall say that, in the most holy Sacrament of the Eucharist, the substance of the bread and wine remains conjointly with the body and blood of our Lord Jesus Christ, and shall deny that wonderful and unique conversion of the whole substance of the bread into the Body, and of the whole substance of the wine into the Blood—the species alone of the bread and wine remaining—which conversion indeed the Catholic Church calls transubstantiation: let him be anathema."

THE DOCTRINE OF THE COUNCILS

We set out the teaching of the Church before embarking on a discussion of what is being written today. Modern views must be assayed in the light of this teaching, and particular attention should be paid to the use of the terms *substance* and *transubstantiation*. The continuity of thought, language and meaning through the centuries will be unmistakable. To be a Catholic, we must (a) hold this doctrine, and (b) hold it in the sense in which the Councils taught it.

First, we have the retractation imposed on Berengarius by the Council of Rome in 1079: 'I, Berengarius, believe in my heart and profess with my mouth, that the bread and wine placed on the altar are, by the mystery of the sacred prayer and words of our Redeemer, *substantially changed* into the true, proper and life-giving flesh and blood of Jesus Christ our Lord; that after the consecration there is the true body of Christ, which was born of the Virgin and which, offered up for the world's salvation, hung upon the cross, and which sits at the right hand of the Father, and the true blood of Christ, which flowed from his side, and this not only through the sign and virtue of the sacrament but *in their natural reality and true substance. . . ."* (Denzinger 355.)

Next comes the Fourth Lateran Council of 1215: "There is indeed one universal Church of the faithful, outside which no one at all can be saved, in which the sacrifice is the priest himself, Jesus Christ, whose body and blood are truly contained in the sacrament of the altar under the appearances of bread and wine, the bread having been *transubstantiated* into his body and the wine into his blood by the power of God. . . ." (Denzinger 430.)

Remembering the anathema of Trent which we quoted above, we read now errors of Wyclif which were condemned by the Council of Constance in 1415:

"1. The material *substance* of the bread and in like manner the material *substance* of the wine remain in the sacrament of the altar.

"3. Christ is not in this sacrament identically and really by a genuine bodily presence (*propria praesentia corproali*)." (Denzinger 581, 583.)

The same doctrine appears again in the Decree for the Armenians drawn up by the Council of Florence in 1439:

"The form of this sacrament is the words of the Saviour . . . For by the power of those words the *substance* of bread is changed into the body of Christ, and the *substance* of wine into blood: in such a way, however, that the whole Christ is contained under the species of bread and the whole Christ under the species of wine." (Denzinger 698.)

We pass on to the teaching of the Council of Trent, our most eloquent witness to Catholic belief, even if the Council is looked upon with some disapproval by some today. "It is equally true," wrote Fr. Nicholas Lash in *His Presence in the World*, "that the definitions of Trent cannot, even implicitly, be regarded as a satisfactory starting-point for a eucharistic theology . . ." and Dom Philip Holdsworth echoed (in *The Tablet*, October 30, 1965): "I am not persuaded that Trent's canon is enough to make it (transubstantiation) *de fide*. Trent cannot be held to be an adequate representation of the Catholic Church." The infallible teaching of Trent is, however, what we must make do with, and, having already looked at its second Canon, we print, before giving Canon 1, what the Council taught directly about transubstantiation. . . . "Because Christ our redeemer said that what He offered under the appearance of bread was truly His body, the Church has always held and this holy Synod now teaches afresh: that through the consecration . . . there comes about the change of the whole substance of the bread into the substance of the body of Christ our Lord, and of the whole substance of the wine into the substance of His blood. This change is aptly and rightly called transubstantiation. . . ." (Denzinger 877.) Canon 1 runs: "If anyone should deny that the body and blood . . . the whole Christ, are truly, really and substantially contained . . . but affirm they are present in it only in sign or symbol, or in power, let him be anathema." (Denzinger 883.)

Again, and this is important although it is not a matter of a General Council, when the Jansenist Synod of Pistoia (1786) directed that it was enough to teach: (1) that Christ is, after the consecration, really and substantially under the appearances, and that (2) the whole substance of bread and wine has ceased to exist; but that there was no need to mention transubstantiation, implying that this was a mere scholastic issue, Pius VI condemned the error involved. He referred to transubstantiation "which the Council of Trent *defined as an article of faith.*" He castigated the Synod's omission as "pernicious, derogatory to the teaching of Catholic truth regarding the *dogma of transubstantiation,* and leaning towards heresy." (Dz. 1529.) Finally, in Denzinger, 1843 to 1846, we find the Holy Office dealing, in 1875, with a tortuous attempt to evade the clear meaning of the traditional term.

SUBSTANCE & TRANSUBSTANTIATION

But *is* the meaning of transubstantiation clear? It will help if we study the origins of the term. It first made its appearance in the twelfth century and appeared, in verb form, as we have seen, in the decree of the 4th Lateran Council, though 'substantially changed' cropped up in the recantation of Berengarius. The term *transubstantiation* was minted to fit one physical change and one only, just as *Homoousios* was coined to pin-point the truth about Christ's relationship to the Father. There is no other transubstantiation in the true sense of the term, even though many substances are changed into others—bread and meat, for instance, into our flesh and blood by digestion—since transubstantiation involves more than the word-structure indicates. To do justice to the full doctrine, one would have to compound a German-style construction, a verbal Dachshund, bringing in not only the change of substance but also the retention of appearances. It is used "aptly and rightly" to denote the conversion of bread and wine in the Eucharist, but it is not exhaustive of the full content of the doctrine; only a polysyllabic horror could be that, and our present term does what it can with six syllables. In practice, it serves perfectly to distinguish Catholic belief from heterodox and, as Calvin and Luther knew exactly what it meant, there is no excuse for ignorance today.

Though the term transubstantiation was not framed until the Middle Ages, it must not be thought that the term 'substance' was not adopted until then. Some have written as if it became current only when scholastics revived Aristotelian philosophy, but it was employed in the fifth-century homily *Magnitudo*, which had a strong influence on the shaping of doctrine. Nor must it be thought that the philosophy and terms of Aristotle were *terra incognita* before the age of Gothic. Boethius, who was canonised (and often passes incognito) as St. Severinus, translated and commented on the works of Aristotle in the early sixth century, and the fame of Boethius was so great in the Dark Ages that Alfred translated his *De Consolatione Philosophiae* into Anglo-Saxon.

What was, what is, meant by 'substance', and what by 'transubstantiation'? Here it is that some northern theologians have made such heavy weather, but there is no difficulty in establishing what the terms meant in the past for the good reason that a traditional Catholic uses them in the same sense today. The Church has not at any time since

Berengarius changed our doctrine, but has held determinedly to it, dealing firmly with innovators. What we were taught in church, in school and at home is what our parents were taught, and so back . . . the 'unchanging truth.' Pope Paul has rejected the right of anyone to give Eucharistic doctrine "an interpretation that whittles away the natural meaning of the words or the accepted sense of the concepts." There is, then, a natural meaning, an accepted sense, and Fr. Henry St. John was wrong when he wrote: "There may be more than one explanation of the meaning of substantial change in this context: none is *de fide* . . . To treat the *de fide* definition as the only explanation of transubstantiation . . . would be to put an end to all theological development."[1] To hold to the truth is to block not doctrinal development so much as doctrinal divergence, otherwise we could accuse our Lord of blocking doctrinal development when He imparted revelation. To possess truth is to be in a position to start on fruitful doctrinal development. We recall here the teaching of Vatican 1: "That sense of the sacred dogmas is to be retained forever which Holy Mother Church has once taught," and the terms of the anti-modernist oath.

The situation now is that some theologians would have it that we do not know the one sense when a well-instructed and intelligent school-child can tell them. It is to be found in a handbook like *The Teaching of the Catholic Church* (1948) as in any other handbook printed before Vatican II, though it will not be traced in the Dutch catechism. It was well known to those who rejected it, before Trent, and Calvin, for instance, proved that he knew perfectly well what the schoolmen taught. He argues against them: "When they say that the substance of bread is converted into Christ, do they not attach to him the white colour, which is all they leave of it? . . . the sum of all is, that that which was formerly bread, by consecration becomes Christ; so that Christ thereafter lies hid under the colour of bread." He will not have this change of physical reality and insists that "no other conversion takes place than in respect of men," which is, as

[1] *The Tablet,* October 30, 1970.

we shall see, the view which is being proposed now as a meaning of transubstantiation. The term, writes Dr. Schillebeeckx, "has lost its significance in our times—even Protestant theologians have discovered and accepted the suggested force of the word 'transubstantiation'. It has lost its function as a banner because it can now be used to fly over ships with different cargoes."[2] He is wrong. The term has not lost its one significance, nor has the attempt to fly the flag over different cargoes been successful, as we see from the words of Fr. Smits publicised in *Time*: "With transubstantiation we can't go forward." How have Protestant theologians accepted its 'suggestive force' if they do not subscribe to its meaning?

It was an eminent scientist who said that we must kneel down like children before reality. It is good science and makes also for good philosophy, and in places theology rests on sound philosophy, Pius X having warned us that he who threw over the metaphysics of St. Thomas could hardly avoid falling into grievous error. We kneel down before reality, then, and this is what we see: that there is a difference between what is permanent in a material thing and what is fleeting, between underlying physical reality and changing physical appearance. A child takes a handful of moist clay. He changes its shape by moulding it into a horse, and he now proudly calls it his horse, though he knows well that it is not a horse except in shape, but still clay. He puts it into the oven and bakes it. In the process, the clay suffers some colour change and emerges rougher and harder to the touch . . . but it remains stubbornly clay. The underlying physical reality, *whatever that may be*, stays unchanged. At the same time, the appearances have fluctuated. This underlying physical reality is what we mean by substance, and the term itself means only "that which stands under," which is a statement of what it does, rather than of what it is, a confession that it is mysterious. The appearances which vary are called accidents or species, the words being inter-

[2] *The Eucharist*, p. 41.

changeable; at Trent, an equal number of bishops voted for the use of each.

In addition to such change of appearances, there can, of course, be substantial change as when food is transmuted by process of digestion into flesh, or Moses' rod into a live, wriggling snake. Then the thing itself changes, not the surface appearances only; it is changed into something else. The lump of clay and the clay horse are both clay; but the hissing snake rearing and weaving is not a rod. Yet, in the realm of sensible experience, every substantial change is accompanied by a parallel change of accidents. That is why transubstantiation is unique, requiring the minting of a term, and why it is a flag which can never be made to fly over ships with different cargoes. Here the substance, the underlying reality, changes into Something else, while the appearances linger on, a veil for the physical reality of our Lord's body and blood. It requires faith to accept this and it is well termed *Mysterium fidei.*

We have echoed Pius X's warning against drifting away from Thomist metaphysics. Can it be said that our doctrine is tied to Aristotelian philosophy, whose terms it has borrowed, and whose fall, if it falls, it must share? "These formulas" of the Eucharist, the pope explained in *Mysterium Fidei*, "express concepts which are not restricted to any specific cultural system. They are not restricted to any fixed development of the sciences nor to one or other of the theological schools. They present the perception which the human mind acquires from its universal, essential experience of reality. . . . They are, therefore, within the reach of everyone at all times and in all places." This, as we have seen from our example of the clay horse, is common-sense, a view supported by Tangenot in the *Dictionnaire de Théologie Catholique*: "The Church has no intention of getting mixed up in purely philosophical questions. Whatever terms she employs are to be understood only in the light of the . . . very simple philosophy which one can no more dispense with in expounding dogmas than in any other rational discourse, a philosophy which can be understood without any study and . . . must underlie all systems, since without it the systems would fly in the face of common sense." This is why O. Schelfhout concluded "that the core of the Thomistic teaching does not belong to the area of free questioning, and that . . . its substance belongs to the authoritative teaching of the Church."[3]

We may add that Mr. Anthony Kenny drew the reddest of herrings across the student's path in his contribution to *Theology and the University*, maintaining that "It was not Trent, but Locke who defined substances as some thing . . . which supports the sensible qualities we find united in things"—true enough in so far as Trent did not *define* substance—and then pinning on the extraordinary suggestion that the scholastics' outlook on substance was that of Aristotle which he described as quite different from Locke's. The scholastics' 'substance' was Aristotle's 'first substance', he said, which is what is designated by a proper name (John Smith or Lassie). If one put one's mind to it, one could not get farther from the facts than this, and such extravagance, together with his travels in the twilight lands of modern philosophy, lead to his conclusion: "Thus the doctrine of transubstantiation appears in the end to fail to secure that for which alone it was originally introduced, namely the real presence. . . . I do not know of any satisfactory answer to this problem." One is left with the impression that everyone except a modern Catholic writer knows what Catholics held and hold. Almost a century and a half ago, Newman wrote in *The Via Media* that the Anglican Article which rejected transubstantiation opposed itself to 'a certain plain and unambiguous statement, not of this or that Council, but one generally received or taught both in the schools and in the multitude, that the material elements are changed into an earthly, fleshly and organized body. . . .'"

Mr. Kenny ended with "I do not know of any satisfactory answer to this problem." The most satisfactory answer is to listen with 'religious submission of will and of mind" to the teaching of *Mysterium Fidei*; the mystery of faith will remain, but the artificial confusion will disappear. Because the

[3] Cf. Joseph M. Powers, S.J., *Eucharistic Theology,* pp. 125-126.

Pope repeated our doctrine in its one meaning, and that meaning involves the idea of substance which Mr. Kenny thought that the scholastics did not envisage, he has been accused of betraying a Lockean philosophy. In fact, he reflected the experience of every man," and there is a salutary warning to be found in the fact that Charles Davis wrote early in 1964 (*Sophia*, April, 1964) that a strong point in favour of those theologians who demanded, in Eucharistic doctrine, a Thomist theology was "the failure of every other attempted theology so far," said openly that he could no longer hold the Thomist formulation, and left the Church in 1966, admitting that he did not accept her teaching on the Eucharist.[4]

It must be firmly stated that the Church defined not only the Real Presence but also the way in which it is brought about, that is, transubstantiation (Cf. Denzinger 884). We listen now to Pope Paul, raising his voice, as he said, "to give on behalf of all the People of God, a firm witness to the divine Truth entrusted to the Church to be announced to all nations," in his *Credo of the People of God*: "Christ *cannot* be thus present in this Sacrament except by the change into His Body of the reality itself of the bread . . . leaving unchanged only the properties . . . which our senses perceive. This change is very appropriately called by the Church transubstantiation." Thus he made his own, and the Church's, St. Thomas's conclusion that there cannot be the Real Presence without transubstantiation. (Cf. *Summa Theologica*, Parts Tertia, Q. LXXV, Art. III.)

THE DRIVE TO RE-EXPRESS

Herder Correspondence (July, 1968) reflected: "That there was need for re-thinking the theory of the Eucharist . . . not even a papal encyclical could deny, or would presumably want to deny." The present writer suspects that "theory" has been used when "doctrine" was in fact intended, and holds that the Pope would readily deny, as countless Catholics

[4] *A Question of Conscience*, p. 234.

would, that there was any need to re-think the doctrine. True, the Pope approved the desire "to investigate this great mystery, and to elucidate its riches, which are not yet exhausted, and to unfold its meaning to the men of our day," but he emphasised: 'It would be intolerable if the dogmatic formulae, which Ecumenical Councils have employed in dealing with the mysteries of the most holy Trinity, were to be accused of being badly attuned to the men of our day. . . . It is equally intolerable that anyone on his own initiative should want to modify the formulas with which the Council of Trent has proposed the eucharistic mystery for belief" (*Mysterium Fidei*). It looks as if a papal encyclical *had* wanted to deny the need for re-thinking and had gone ahead with the denial.

Bishop Butler has written: "In principle, then, the modern attempts to restate the truth which 'the Church aptly calls' transubstantiation, in concepts and language which will not distort the Church's meaning, are entirely justified. Certainly, the word 'transubstantiation' seems to create unnecessary difficulties for many modern minds. What ultimately matters is less the form of words than the meaning which the words were chosen to enshrine. . . ."[5] One must not overlook 'in principle', but, even with that caution, the words seem remote from the arena of reality. Experience with a long line of converts has taught me that the hallowed terms cause little difficulty, and the hard fact is that the attempts to recarve the cradle are killing the baby. Why should 'transubstantiation' cause unnecessary difficulties for modern minds? The doctrine was as hard to believe in the 16th century, and the term is as easily understood in the 20th. An article in *L'Osservatore Romano* (April 3, 1969) commented: "Some have feared that it might not be able to be understood by a modern mind. This does little honour to the modern mind. The idea of substance is one of the primordial notions possessed by every man and of which he constantly makes use. I cannot say that I feel cold without perceiving myself as a permanent subject, a substance, af-

[5] *The Tablet,* November 25, 1967.

fected by this unpleasant condition. . . . I may add that I have found Professor Marcuse using this very term transubstantiation in its true sense, and I think that this should be sufficient guarantee of its modernity (*The One-Dimensional Man*, 1968)." In reference to Christ's consubstantiality with the Father, *that* issue of *The Sower* says in glorious confusion: "We have long ago abandoned the ancient idea of substance as that which underlies the varying appearance of things. We are inclined to think of substance as 'stuff,'" and then there is talk of two loaves made from the same materials and so being composed of the same substance. One is left with the impression that, in an attempt to undermine the divinity of Christ, the writer has been betrayed into a statement that could be used to accuse him of believing in transubstantiation! God save the unwary Modernist from himself!

Anyone who can distinguish between a noun and its adjective knows the meaning of our terms. Converts may, on first hearing, have no, or a wrong, notion, but an explanation clears up the difficulties. We need not be alarmed if a scientist normally means something else by 'substance', for, though an American means something else by 'gas', we understand each other. Terms are soon shelled for their core. "What ultimately matters is less the form of words than the meaning . . . ." can be a false antithesis in practice. *This* baby is strapped tightly to *that* cradle; as Dr. Schillebeeckx observed, "the *mot juste* is important for faith." "This rule of speech has been introduced by the Church in the long work of the centuries," Pope Paul teaches, "with the protection of the Holy Spirit. She has confirmed it with the authority of the Councils. It has become more than once the token and standard of orthodox faith. It must be observed religiously. No one may presume to alter it at will, or on the pretext of new knowledge" (*Mysterium Fidei*). Some, however, felt that there was need of re-expression on one, or all, of three scores.

ECUMENISM THE SPUR

First, there was the drive of ecumenism which became, in spite of the Holy Father's warning of January 20, 1965, not merely an "apostolic programme" but a "temptation." Some years ago, Mr. Peter de Rosa wrote that, if the cause of ecumenism was to advance, there must be some blurring of the Church's outlines,[6] and it was soon apparent that unity with past Catholic belief was to be sacrificed at the altar of unity with present Christians. *Herder Correspondence* (November, 1967) grumbled that "Curial conservatism has of course no interest at all in ecumenical theology, which it suspects (rightly) of being tied up with . . . doctrinal reinterpretation." "Rightly" is an honest admission, and the same lid was lifted by the *Catholic Herald's* editorial on *Mysterium Fidei* which mentioned the general opinion that "the Pope had no alternative but to 'shoot down' some of the *avant garde* theorists . . . who were dismissing the Church's formulations in an effort to produce a formula more acceptable to other Christian Churches." This gives away more than the words suggest at a first hearing, since it is not directly the formulation but the *content* which is unacceptable to other Churches; to satisfy them, the truth wrapped in the formula would have to be disowned.

Some ecumenists had satisfied themselves that our doctrine was deficient. The *Catholic Herald* (August 30, 1968) reported a lecture in which "Fr. Donal Flanagan, Professor of Dogmatic Theology at St. Patrick's College, Maynooth, said that there was a primary ecumenical obligation on each Christian Church today to understand the deficiencies in its own theological understanding of the Eucharist." When Dr. Mascall reviewed Dr. Küng's *The Church*, he found that "the Catholicism which Dr. Küng desiderates . . . would differ very little from Lutheranism," and he deplored a "virtual obliteration" of the ordained priesthood in the book, remarking that the author was left in "much the same quandary as the sixteenth-century reformers."[7] The quandary is

---

[6] *Catholic Herald,* November 15, 1963.
[7] *The Tablet,* January 27, 1968.

the outcome of doctrine-corrosion by ecumenism, and we see how serious it is when we find the Swiss theologian teaching: "The sacrament of the Eucharist is given to the Church in precisely the same way as is the sacrament of baptism. Any Christian can baptise in case of emergency. What happens when a layman celebrates the Eucharist in a place where the faithful have not had a priest available. . . ? I am convinced that, in this case, there would be a valid Eucharistic celebration. . . . The very fact of considering that . . . any Christian can celebrate the Eucharist is very precious for us priests. . . . It means that other Christian denominations can carry out a valid Eucharistic celebration."[8] This, one assumes, is the kind of stuff which made Fr. Michael Hollings, former Catholic chaplain at Oxford, write with such obvious excitement (*Catholic Herald*, October 20, 1972): "The light"—apparently Christ, the Light of the World—" . . . sinks in despond at the voice of the establishment, it rises to high gusts at the words of Pope John, Bonhoeffer, Suenens, Bloom, Butler, Küng or Helda Camara." How very remarkable that the Light of the World should rise to a 'high gust' over Bonhoeffer's 'religionless Christianity' or Küng's Lutheranism and sink in despond at the voice of the establishment (Pope Paul?)!

The upshot of fevered ecumenism, together with other factors to be considered, has been confusion or loss of belief. Here is disbelief stated nakedly: " 'Orthodoxy is the tragedy of Christianity,' says the Rev. Joss Arts, the priest-editor of a Catholic weekly called *De Nieuwe Linie*. 'What we need is a rethinking of all the basics of Christianity. We must break away from the formal dogma of the Catholic Church.' "[9]

---

[8] Cf. *L'Homme Nouveau,* February 15, 1970. *A Catholic Herald* editorial (May, 1972) avers: "Validity, if linked only to external ritual acts, may indeed appear to represent a resurgence of the Pharisaic spirit. . . . The Joint Commission (on the Ministry) cannot ultimately avoid facing the question whether the Church . . . has the right to recognize or refuse recognition . . . to anyone wishing to stand up and say that he represents Christ." Apparently, if the Commission answers 'No,' then any non-Catholic may offer up Mass if he feels so inclined. And the Mass would be valid?

[9] Cf. *Time,* March 21, 1967.

And so we read 'atrocity stores' from Holland every few days . . . the bishop who rejects transubstantiation,[10] the Hosts, of toasted bread, which are thrown out when stale,[11] the Sjaloom group's interdenominational *agapes* which are intended to be full eucharistic celebrations,[12] the two vicars-general who investigated such a celebration but refused to condemn as "no one is fully justified in simply limiting one-self closely to Church law,"[13] and the priests who give Communion to pagans.[14] and nearer at home there is Fr. Gerald Hughes, S.J., chaplain at Glasgow University: "On one or two occasions I have served Communion to Anglicans. I had explained the Church's ruling on this, but they insisted on receiving and I felt I could not refuse." (*Catholic Herald,* June 2, 1972.)

As today's imbalance springs from an inferiority-complex, from a desire to take on the colour of surrounding society, it will not end with an advance towards conservative Protestant beliefs. Thanks to liberal Protestantism, the 'stout Protestants' have lost a lot of weight. The society around us is humanist, and, that being so, the wilder ecumenism is not a swing towards our Protestant brethren but a leap through the paper-hoop of liberalism towards humanism; Modernism is disbelief, not sectarian Christianity. The true kinship of the ultra-ecumenist is sometimes expressed frankly. . . . "Mr. Denis Rice, supervisor of adult education at Leicester University—and himself a Catholic—told the teach-in that he felt he had a closer relationship with Mr. Blackham (director of the British Humanist Association) than with Cardinal Heenan."[15] It recalls how Fr. Bouyer, in *The Decomposition of Catholicism,* wrote that Catholics having "long given up the idea of converting the world," "we

[10] *Volkskrant,* May 27, 1969.
[11] Douglas Brown, *Catholic Herald,* March 14, 1969.
[12] Desmond Fisher, *Frontier,* Spring, 1967; Fr. van der Weyer in *Those Dutch Catholics.*
[13] *Catholic Herald,* December 8, 1967.
[14] Brian G. Cooper, *The Dutch Quest for God,* in *Catholic Herald,* July 16, 1971.
[15] *Catholic Herald,* February 26, 1966.

should not be surprised that Catholics who go finally out to the world allow themselves to become caught by it like flies on fly-paper."

DISBELIEF SIRES DISBELIEF

Reckless ecumenism is the first ground for re-interpretation, and the second is disbelief in another doctrine on which the Real Presence depends. Just as the Docetist in the early Church could not hold that our Lord's Body was present in the Eucharist as he did not hold that He ever had a real body, so a man today may refuse to accept that bread is changed into Christ's Body since he believes that that Body decayed in the grave. St. Paul made it clear in 1 Corinthians, XV, that the resurrection is a key-doctrine of our religion—"if Christ be not risen again, then is our preaching vain: and your religion is also vain." As the Modernist could not tolerate that the Church's doctrine was true, this key-doctrine was an early casualty. Loisy picked at the dogma in *The Gospel and the Church*, Section 3: "The message of Easter (that is to say, the discovery of the empty tomb and the appearance of Jesus to His disciples, so far as these facts are taken for physical proofs of the resurrection) is not an irrefutable argument from which the historian can conclude with entire certainty that the Saviour rose in the body from the dead. The empty tomb is only an indirect argument and not decisive since the established fact, the disappearance of the body, can be explained in other ways. . . ." Tyrrell also hoped that, if he shuffled ideas around, the dogma would go away. From *Christianity at the Cross-Roads*, Chapter XII: "Now if we agree with Liberal Protestantism in taking symbolically what the early Church took literally, we differ in taking it all as symbolic of transcendental value . . . while not discarding the imagery, we recognise that it is an envelope and not the substance. Hence we claim to be true to the 'idea' of original Christianity. . . . He (St. Paul) was answering those who mistakenly supposed that the resurrection phenomena had to be fitted in with the physical series. .. . Yet, however subjective may be the imaginative

clothing of that reality, the reality itself is not necessarily
subjective. . . . The physical resurrection and ascension
could, at most, be signs and symbols of Christ's spiritual
transformation, of the fullness of His eternal and transcendent life; they could never be its substance. . . ." "At most"
is good. Doubting Thomas, with his hand stretched out to
test the reality of the wounded Flesh, had doubted like this,
and the Church crushed the errors in two condemned propositions (Denzinger 2036,2037): "The resurrection of the
Saviour is not strictly a fact of the historical order, but a
fact of the purely supernatural order, which is neither demonstrated nor demonstrable, which the Christian consciousness
gradually derived from other things"—"Faith in the resurrection of Christ was, from the beginning, not so much concerning the fact itself of resurrection as with Christ's immortal life with God."

But still they come, in spite of the *magisterium*. . . .
Here we find transubstantiation and the resurrection side by
side in the report (*Catholic Herald*, September 29, 1972) of
Fr. Hubert Richards's New Zealand lectures: ". . . modern
man does not admit miracles. . . . Therefore, there are no
miracles in the scriptures, including the virgin birth, the
raising of Christ's dead body to life, and the changing of
bread and wine into Christ's own body and blood." (Theologically, this is slovenly, since transubstantiation does not
qualify as a miracle, which is recorded by the senses.) *That*
number of *The Sower* (it is beginning to recall Pius X's
reference to Modernism as the 'compendium' of all the
heresies) teaches: "The resurrection stories are stories, and
not necessarily genuine descriptions of a factual event. They
are professions of faith in the risen Jesus. . . . One may
wonder whether the discovery of the empty tomb has any
historical foundation." In simpler language, one could put
all this as Loisy put it to Le Roy: "Your doctrine of the
resurrection is a beautiful poem; yet is it anything but a
poem?" "All that interests us to know," Tyrrell asserted,
"is to know that the resurrection is not fleshly. . . ." "Then,"
St. Paul would answer, "is our preaching vain," and Tyrrell
seems to have glimpsed the truth as he declared his bank-

ruptcy: "In the sense of survival and immortality the Resurrection is our critical and central dogma, 'If Christ be not risen' . . . etc. If I cannot maintain that, I will not stop at Campbell's halfway house."

Campbell's Halfway House, however, is the *poste restante* address for some now, though the voices of the Church's millions proclaim gladly and assuredly "And the third day He rose again." *Time* (March 31, 1967) reported: "Dominican Theologian Edward Schillebeeckx . . . proposes that the Resurrection of Jesus may not have been the physical recomposition of his body but a unique kind of spiritual manifestation. 'One generally likes to consider his Resurrection,' he says, 'as being the impact of his personality on his disciples and his presence in the hearts of all Christians.' "[16]

NO REDEMPTION, NO SACRIFICE

Wrong views on the redemption must also affect the idea of the Mass as a sacrifice and therefore the identity of the sacrificial Victim received in Communion. Loisy was condemned for, *inter alia*, throwing doubt on the redemption through the passion and cross, and it was not unnatural that he should have doubts in the matter since he had grown unsure about the very personality of God. In the nineteen sixties and seventies, sacrifice, not to a Person, but to the shapeless 'Ground of our Being' must also provoke difficulties. ("God cannot be thought of apart from this world. It is inconceivable that he existed before the world"—Fr. H. Richards is reported as saying.) *That Sower* states: "When reading the narratives of the passion and death it is misleading to have in mind analogies of justice, ransom, reparation, satisfaction, buying back. . . ." and thus Fr. Richard McBrien tells us in *What do we really believe?* (p. 50): "We need not believe that Jesus died on the cross to 'pay off a debt' to the Father. Our understanding of the sacrifice of the cross can therefore be altered and with it our understanding of the Mass as a sacrifice." *O crux ave, spes unica!*

---

[16] Catholics do not hold the 'physical recomposition' of the body of Jesus. It did not decompose.

We see, then, that 'no resurrection' spells 'no transubstantiation,' and 'no redemption' means no sacrifice and no sacrificial Victim under the appearances of bread and wine.

Reinterpretation has found justification, thirdly, in the new knowledge of matter. Linked to this has been a 'phenomenological' approach, the notion that the essence of things depends on their relation to man's mind. The Gospel tells us that a good father will not give a stone when begged for bread, but some modern fathers would counter that there is no such thing as bread. Charles Davis, in his *Sophia* article, denied that bread and wine were substances, alleging that "Bread as bread is knowable only to man, and that is because it exists as bread only in relation to man." There are two things involved there, one referring to the realm of physical science and the other to philosophy.

Bread, we are told, is a conglomeration of different substances, most of which could be separated from the others by a scientist with almost as much ease as we would separate the contents of a tool box. Bread is not so much a thing as a box of things and, as a result, it is asserted that we cannot rightly talk about changing the substance in a physical sense, since bread is not one substance. Therefore, the Church must speak in another sense and (it is argued) the only sense in which this conglomeration is 'bread' is in relation to man. Man *views* it as bread. Let him view it in another light and its reality will have been changed since its bread-reality is determined by its relation to man. Let him now look on it as Christ's body, and it will automatically cease to be bread. This is *transignification*. The line is not peculiar to Davis, of course, but is common currency among those who re-interpret, and it is no more transubstantiation than was Calvin's doctrine with which it has strong affinities.

THE 'BREAD-BOX' & UNREAL REALITY

If bread is only an assortment, is there no such thing as bread? The modernist answers: "It exists as bread only in relation to man." This is a fallacy. It is accepted that bread is made up of several substances, but bread is an objective reality, the name 'bread' being reserved for just such an amalgam. Iron is not bread; leather is not bread; none of the components is bread—only the sum-total is, and, if the whole human race perished suddenly, and a loaf was left upon a table, bread would exist without man. Here is the legerdemain which has been practised: the re-interpreter has said that a physical thing, bread, exists only in relation to man when he should have said that, in its *functional aspect*, as *food*, it made sense only in relation to man or animals. It is only in regard to man (or animals) that fruit can be regarded as food, and yet fruits have objective existence apart from man in their reality as physical things, even if Adam was required to bestow a generic and then an individual name.

The trick that has been pulled can be paralleled in this way: I pick up a shoe to hammer in a nail, and I remark that this is no longer a shoe to me but a hammer, since 'shoe' and 'hammer' denote man's usage. Therefore, if I suscribe to phenomenological philosophy, I claim that the object has undergone a substantial change of its reality, the shoe having been transubstantiated into a hammer. The answer is: certainly the shoe has been promoted to be an 'acting-hammer', but 'shoe' was not its physical reality. Leather was its physical substance and the substance has not been changed, since the leather has not been transmuted into steel. Change that leather shoe into a wooden shaft with a steel head and *then* you can talk realistically about substantial change!

The application . . . Bread is a physical reality whether I look upon a loaf as something to eat or to throw at a meeting. If I throw the loaf, I no longer look on this particular loaf in the light of food, but I certainly regard it as bread. Eat it, sit on it, throw it—it is bread used for food, coopted as a cushion, launched as a missile, just as truly as glass, air and water are physical realities even if "there is no one about in the quad."

If we turn to Calvin, we find how close his view came to the subjectivism exposed above. He tried to oppose the teaching of the early Fathers against that of the schoolmen, writing: "I admit, indeed, that some of the ancients occasionally used the term *conversion*, not that they meant to do away with the substance . . . but to teach that the bread devoted to the sacrament was *widely different from ordinary bread, and was now something else* . . . no other conversion takes place than *in respect of men*. . . . I willingly admit anything which helps to express the true and substantial communication of the body and blood of the Lord . . . understanding that they are received not by the imagination or intellect only, but are enjoyed in reality as the food of eternal life."[17]

A current Dutch Protestant joke runs: "Previously, nothing changed in the Catholic Church except the bread and wine. Now everything changes except the bread and wine." There is shrewdness in the gibe and, with Calvin's words, it gives us furiously to think. Though Calvin held that the Fathers did not mean to 'do away' with the substance, and that the conversion was only in respect of men—in our way of looking at the bread—he nevertheless advocated "a" real presence and that one received Christ's body and blood "in reality." From this we learn to look twice when someone writes that there is no longer ordinary bread after the consecration, and even when he speaks of the 'consecrated bread and wine'—though his intention may be innocent and orthodox—and to look a third time, perhaps in the direction of Luther and impanation or companation, when he tells us that Jesus gives Himself 'in the bread and wine.' We have to study also what is wrapped up in the term 'real' or the phrase 'in reality.' *It is so easy to state doctrine unequivocally that, today, we are right in asking questions when a Catholic pens ambiguities.* A true Catholic finds it second nature to speak in clear orthodox manner and is dismayed to find, for example, the Dutch catechism circling our doctrine but never touching it. Pope Paul, however, is all for manly openness: "Nor is it right to treat of the mystery of transubstantiation *without mentioning* the marvellous change of the whole of the bread's substance. . . ." (*Mysterium Fidei*).

---

[17] *The Institutes*, Book IV, Chap. XVII.

The case of Pope Honorius is raked up today, but it must be faced that the charge against him was that he left out when he should have spoken explicitly. The ambiguity with which we have to wrestle appears in these words written by Davis: the words of consecration "do not merely tell us of the change but they bring it about in the real order. But . . . what happens is not a change in the physical substance. . . ."[18] His 'real' is a relation to the mind, while ours is at the level of material reality. We shall see how carefully the Pope states that "the bread and wine have ceased to exist after the consecration," and this "in the reality itself, independently of our mind."[19]

MORE ABOUT MATTER

Does the fact that a scientist might describe bread as several substances affect the doctrine of the Church? In no way, since she has never committed herself as to the nature of material reality. She confines herself to stating that the underlying reality is changed at the consecration, without advancing any theory of matter. Put it this way, if I may do so without irreverence. Suppose that it was a question not of bread but of a chocolate biscuit. Theologians would speak as confidently about the change of the substance of the biscuit, though they knew that the object was originally chocolate as well. The academic question as to whether it was one, two or more substances would be irrelevant . . . it does not matter if the 'wall' of bread is built of five hundred 'bricks'; the whole underlying material reality is changed into another Substance.

Modern science, as everyone knows, has thrown new light on matter. "I have called my material surroundings a stage set," wrote C. S. Lewis in *Letters to Malcolm*, ". . . if you attack a stage house with a chisel . . . you'll get only a hole in a piece of canvas and, beyond that, windy darkness. Similarly, if you start investigating the nature of matter . . . . You will get mathematics." Others will say that matter is

---

[18] *Sophia,* April, 1964.
[19] *The Credo of the People of God.*

only a form of energy. Yet this does not affect Catholic doctrine, since it in no way conflicts with the reality which we all deduce when the child moulds his clay horse, with our awareness that there is basic reality and surface appearance.

We have all heard, too, of the atomic structure of matter, of molecules, protons, neutrons and electrons, but this does not touch our traditional belief, though there is need for care in case we compromise it. A Catholic has affirmed that, at the consecration, "there is no change in the molecular or atomic structure" of the bread and wine, classing atomic structure as an "accident' in scholastic terminology. It appears that he is mistaken and that differing molecular structure goes to *make* a substance, to make this thing bread or that thing flesh. I am buttressed in this view by Fr. C. Vollert, S.J., who writes in the *New Catholic Encyclopaedia* that the entire agglomeration of substance, i.e., protons, neutrons, electrons, atoms, is converted while properties like mass, electrical charges, energies, remain. Fr. Joseph Powers (*op. cit.*, p. 177) says rightly that an electronic microscope cannot reach the underlying reality, and then propounds as a conclusion that there is no change in molecular structure when the conversion takes place; this is a *non-sequitur*. The Real Presence escapes scientific tests since the scientists cannot dig beneath the 'accidents'—appearances, reactions etc. "He gives Himself," Fr. Powers adds, "in His own way, in sovereign freedom from all the conditions of our material existence" but it is one thing to be untrammelled by the ordinary *laws* of nature and quite another to act independently of the *nature* itself of matter.

MATERIAL, PHYSICAL PRESENCE

There emerges from the above the truth of Francis Clark's words that transubstantiation is "an intervention of divine power in the world of material creation. . . ." Some were annoyed when the non-Catholic Press reported that, in *Mysterium Fidei*, the Pope maintained "the material presence of Christ in the Eucharist," but the Pope *did* teach it, maintaining that Christ was "bodily present in His physical reality." This body, as Berengarius proclaimed, is the body that hung upon the cross, and Newman was right when he wrote in the *Apologia* that our doctrine "deals with what no one on earth knows anything about, the *material* substances themselves," though our knowledge of matter has since widened.

Why, then, did the present writer shy away earlier from saying that Christ was physically present in the sacrament? It was simply because the phrase is ambiguous and ambiguity can be deadly. If we say he is physically present, this may be taken as meaning that His physical reality is present, conveying *what* is present, and that is as orthodox as can be. On the other hand, and especially if the adverb is put last—"present physically"—it may be thought to describe the *way* in which He is present, and someone may translate it as "in a natural or normal way" instead of "sacramentally", and then we are in trouble, since our Lord is not present "physically" in the manner that physical objects are accustomed. The adverb should therefore be ruled out as favouring misunderstanding, and one can expound doctrine without its aid.

FRS SMITS, SCHOONENBERG & SCHILLEBEECKX

And now a hard look at the Fathers of transignification or transfinalization. . . . Most of us were unaware of trouble until we heard the first rumble in *Humani Generis*: "You will find men arguing that the doctrine of transubstantiation ought to be revised, depending as it does on a conception of substance which is now out of date. The real presence of Christ in the Holy Eucharist is thus reduced to a kind of symbolic communication, the consecrated species being no more than an effectual sign of Christ's spiritual presence. . . ." Pius XII reprimanded the "bolder spirits" who insist that "the mysteries of faith can never be expressed in terms which exhaust the truth—only in approximate terms, perpetually needing revision," and drew attention to "the contempt they show for the teaching commonly handed down, and for the terms which enshrine it." He voiced a warning that "the views which are put forward obscurely today, hedged about with safeguards and distinctions, will be proclaimed tomorrow, by other, bolder spirits, openly and extravagantly." He suggested that young priests in particular would fall victim to the wiles of the reinterpreters. The encyclical's reference to such doctrinal revision, Francis Clark reveals, was aimed at the work of Père Yves de Montcheil, S.J., and the rest of the genealogy of error is given by Fr. Powers (*op. cit.*). Until we come nearer home, we need mention only three names, Fr. Luchesius Smits, O.F.M., Cap., Dr. P. Schoonenberg, S.J., and Dr. E. Schillebeeckx, O.P.

Fr. Smits made world-headlines when *Time* (July 2, 1965) reported some Dutch theologians' advocacy of transignification, which it bluntly explained to mean "the change does not take place in the substance of the bread and wine but in its meaning." It revealed that the Capuchin compared Christ's giving Himself in the Sacrament to "the gesture of a Dutch housewife who offers her guests tea and cookies. Just as the housewife offers not food itself but her welcome 'incarnated' in the gift, Christ also offers himself, incarnated in the bread and wine." "With transubstantiation we can't go forward," *Time* reported him as saying, "but transignification? Now it is possible to be a Catholic in the modern world."

"Reckless journalism!" some have cried when they read the above, "Misrepresentation!" But the facts cannot be brushed aside as easily as that. The doctrine of Fr. Smits, given at length in *Actuele vragen rondom de Transsubstantiatie en de tegenwoordigheid des Heren in de H. Eucharistie* (1965) is in all important respects the same as that of Dr. Schoonenberg and, summarised in the book by Fr. Powers and Fr. Colman O'Neill's *New Approaches to the Eucharist*, fully lives down to its press reports. Even if the reader looks only at the précis supplied in *Herder Correspondence* (December, 1965), he should see why the Holy Father has been in such anguish. . . . "In the Eucharist our Lord embodies his love *in* bread and wine. . . . The doctrine of Transubstantiation was understood by Fr. Smits on the basis of the doctrine of the hypostatic union. Just as in Christ the human

nature . . . is taken up into a higher mode of being, so bread
and wine in the Eucharist are taken up into the mode of
existence of the risen Lord. Our Lord takes possession of
the bread and wine which become as it were part of his
heavenly corporal nature." We might add that Fr. Smits
would appear to have gone back to Guitmund of Aversa's
error, impanation, which alleged that Christ and bread are
united in a hypostatic union. "The consecrated bread is not
in itself the body of the Lord," he proclaims, "but it is only
the bread taken up by the Lord." No wonder that he could
not go forward with transubstantiation, as he was in flight
to Calvin and 16th century Geneva! Yet his elaboration of
the Real Presence has been echoed in *Bible Catechism* by
Fr. John C. Kersten, S.V.D.,—"Jesus is present in the bread
and wine as the giver in the gift. . . . Neither is there a
physical or chemical change of bread and wine. What happens
at the Consecration is a 'trans-signification,' a sign-change."
Dr. Schillebeeckx has rallied to Fr. Smits' aid, explaining
that "His central idea was the uniqueness of Christ's giving
of himself in the gift of bread and wine" (*The Eucharist*, p.
121) but this is merely to confirm that Fr. Smits is in confusion, since Christ cannot give Himself in bread and wine
which have ceased to exist.

For Dr. Schoonenberg's views, one may read the works
by Fathers Powers and O'Neill, *Herder Correspondence* for
December, 1965, for March, 1967, and for May, 1967, and
his own article in *Cross Currents*, No. 1, 1967 (summarised
in *Herder* that May). All these are in tune with the words
attributed to him in the *Time* article: "I kneel not for a
Christ who is supposed to be condensed in the host, but for
the Lord who through the host offers me his reality, his
body." The teaching which emerges is: bread and wine are
given to eat and drink in the Sacrament. We cannot speak
of a physical transformation of the bread and wine. Transubstantiation *is* transignification. . . "The bread signified our
Lord's real self-giving. Precisely because this giving takes
place under the species of bread, which must be eaten, the
physical reality of bread must remain after the consecration. . . ." (This reverses Catholic doctrine which holds that

Christ's body will not be present unless the bread 'goes';
Schoonenberg holds that He will not be present sacramentally
unless the bread *stays*.) Dealing with the complaints of the
Dutch traditionalists against the new catechism, he thought
to minimise them by replying, "Their complaint is concerned
with transubstantiation, not with the presence of Christ,"
and by teaching that bread's new relation to man is "con-
structive of the essence" and thus, as Davis urged, the change
of relationship or viewpoint marks a real change.

We have listened to the Capuchin and the Jesuit. Now
we come to Dr. Schillebeeckx the Dominican, on whose behalf
the Dutch bishops sent a telegram to Rome attesting that he
had always shown the greatest possible care for the maintenance of the orthodoxy of modern theology. He is of the
opinion that Pius XII was shadow-boxing in *Humani Generis*:
"I have never been able to discover a purely symbolical interpretation of the Eucharist in Catholic theology prior to
1950. Rome's criticism is probably based on a misunderstanding" (*The Eucharist*, p. 110), and he laments that "some
theologians of the Roman school must judge the theology of
the whole world. . . . Rome has got itself into such a panic
that it can no longer distinguish between true attempts at
renewal and other kinds" (*Herder Correspondence*, December, 1968). It will be interesting to see, then, if a symbolical
interpretation has reared its head in his own writings and if
he has given Rome grounds for concern, if not 'panic'.

Dr. Schillebeeckx tries to write of the Eucharist "in a
manner that is open to the experience of modern man and
above all as an authentic dogma which every Catholic can
accept and with which he can feel at home in the . . . thought
of the twentieth century." It is the kind of thing which drew
from Chesterton: "An imbecile habit has arisen in modern
controversy of saying that such and such a creed can be held
in one age but cannot be held in another. Some dogma, we
are told, was credible in the twelfth century, but is not
credible in the twentieth. You might as well say that a certain philosophy can be believed on Mondays, but cannot be

believed on Tuesdays."[20] If Dr. Schillebeeckx feels a need
to adjust doctrine to the taste of today, it is not because the
doctrine has become less credible, but, because he has abandoned the Dominican Aquinas for the German semi-rationalist
Kant. The scholastic distinction between substance and accident, he holds, "has been philosophically untenable since
Kant," thus placing himself on the path which led Charles
Davis into the theological wasteland. Kant, it may be remembered, held that things in themselves were unknowable—
"that objects must conform to our knowledge, not our knowledge to objects."

"If we abandon any attempt to re-interpret the Eucharist," he lays down, "we shall then either have to live with a
double truth, which will result in an increasing gulf between
our lives in the Church and our lives in the world, or else we
shall be letting the reality of what we celebrate in faith in the
Eucharist sift out imperceptibly." (*Op. cit.*, p. 156). It is not
clear what he means by a 'double truth'—probably one truth
and one falsehood—but he has revealed the quandary in which
he ("we") has placed himself. Having rejected the common-
sense view of nature, embodied in the scholastic theology,
which alone makes sense of transubstantiation—"an Aristotelian distinction between substance and accidents cannot
help us in interpreting the dogma of transubstantiation" (p.
145)—he has either to give dogma a new meaning, that is,
deny the old truth, or live a lie. He does not see that to
reinterpret in this way *is* to live a lie. Davis saw it and left.

The reality of the bread, he believes, is changed because
it becomes a sign of Christ's presence, which makes one
wonder if he would hold that the reality of a flag (bunting)
changes when it flies over a palace and becomes a sign of
the Queen's presence, and, indeed, one reinterpreter has compared transubstantiation to the change in a piece of cloth
when it is adopted as a national flag. This for him is substantial change. Does the bread remain throughout the Mass?
He would prefer to say that "the bread remains, but not the
'bread-reality'." It should not be called *simply* bread, and

[20] *Orthodoxy.*

transubstantiation, as a concept in natural philosophy, can be set aside if it is no longer in agreement with present-day philosophy . . . whereas *Humani Generis* was acid about "impermanent fashions of speech, borrowed from our up-to-date philosophies, which today live, and will feed the oven tomorrow."

"The Tridentine statement," the Dominican is confident, "is, therefore, apart from its specifically Catholic significance, first and foremost a denial that the bread can still be called bread after the consecration. . . . A further analysis of what the bread is, for example, physically or metaphysically outside this context, is irrelevant." (*Op. cit.*, p. 133) It is not clear what the qualification "apart . . . significance" is intended to convey, but we have here nonsense to which no one should be asked to extend serious consideration. The Tridentine statement is not primarily the denial stated, but an affirmation that the whole substance of the bread has been changed into Christ's body, with a barb of anathema fitted for anyone who holds that the bread remains. It deals with what things are objectively. The bread is unchanged in its material reality in Dr. Schillebeeckx's view, as in the view of Smits and Schoonenberg, however they make play with terms like 'real', 'reality', 'simply' or 'primarily.' Unhappily their approach is shared by the body of their country's bishops. They teach in their catechism that ". . . one should therefore say that the reality, the nature of material things is what they are . . . for man," and so, in place of *Mysterium Fidei's* teaching that "nothing is left of the bread and wine but the appearances alone," we get after much nervous circumambulation: "It is better to say that the bread is essentially withdrawn from its normal human meaning. . . ." In consequence, the Commission of Cardinals laid down: ". . . it must be explained that the bread and wine in their deepest (not phenomenological) reality . . . are changed." The Dutch should heed Abraham Lincoln. He was determined to be so clear, he said, "that no honest man can misunderstand me, and no dishonest man can successfully misrepresent me." "I am never easy when I am handling a thought, till I have bounded it north, bounded it south, bounded it east, and

bounded it west." If a catechism cannot get round to lucid
Eucharistic doctrine in sixteen pages, charity does not bar
us from scenting disbelief. And now we are in a position to
evaluate Fr. Corbishley's words—"As to the doctrine of the
Real Presence and the idea of the Mass as a sacrifice, it is
emphatically not true that any reputable theologian has done
any more than try to safeguard the essential truth by pre-
senting it in a more acceptable way" (*Catholic Herald*,
October 22, 1971). "Reputable"? And "more acceptable" to
whom? Loisy and Renan?

I suggest that disbelief in transubstantiation lurks in
these words of the Dutch catechism: "Little particles which
may have been left behind on the altarcloth are not in any
sense the presence of Christ." This thought is not 'bounded'—
note the slackness of "particles are not the presence"—and
the view is phenomenological. "The point," according to the
catechism, "is this. What would be called bread by ordinary,
sensible people?" We are back to the Kantian idea that the
essence of things hang upon man's outlook. "So too a piece
of bread which has been reduced to dust is no longer called
bread." Again—"called"—and a trick concealed in ambiguity. If bread powders into dust through corruption, then it
is no longer bread, but, if there is a metamorphical 'dust' of
bread in a bin, fragments, "ordinary, sensible people" talk
of tiny breadcrumbs. They do more than talk—these are
bread and a starving man will brush them into a pile with
infinite care. In a parallel way, particles of the Host are
that to us, not dust, not breadcrumbs . . . 'This is my Body.'
Even on phenomenological grounds, the Modernist case is
faulty, for a man, who had no further use for crumbs and
threw them out, would still say that he threw out breadcrumbs. Our grounds are deeper . . . . *Fracto demum sacramento, ne vacilles, sed memento, tantum esse sub fragmento,
quantum toto tegitur.* Faith is our ground.

Before ending this section, might I address a word of
respectful criticism to the German bishops? In their letter
of September 22, 1967, which defended traditional teaching,
they sought to see genuine values in transignification, putting
forward the idea that "the doctrine of transubstantiation can

be elaborated in terms of transignification and transfinalization, but not replaced by these." "The terms are indeed new,"
they said, "but their content is old; the one emphasizes the
fact that the natural bread becomes spiritual bread, the
other that the new food is food for eternal life." I can only
say that that is what the terms might have emphasized, but
is not in fact what the terms were created to mean; that I
have never heard anyone elaborate genuine transubstantiation in terms of transignification and every attempt has been
at substitution. Is the German bishops' fatherly smile not
rather like beaming at the man who comes with matches and
petrol to burn down your house, greeting him with a cry that
these will be splendid for a bonfire of weeds in the garden?
The gentleman is not *interested* in a garden bonfire. There
is a vital difference between transignification and Pope Poul's
teaching that not the bread and wine, but their appearances,
acquire a new significance. I suggest then, that the attempt
to meet the opposition half-way can only generate confusion,
and that the gambit tends to appear weak-kneed. "Dead is
all the innocence of anger and surprise," Chesterton wrote
of the Reformation era, and, though we must keep anger as
far as possible out of sight, we have to remember a saying
of C. S. Lewis—"Such anger is the fluid that love bleeds
when you cut it."

On pages 334 and 341 of their catechism, the Dutch
bishops teach: "It (the Church) is convinced that the Spirit
of God will not permit it to err in this matter."—"And we
also believe that the Spirit of Jesus does not allow the Church
to err in its interpretation of this gift." The traditional
teaching of the Church, then, on the Eucharist, is infallibly
true and must not be changed.

MYSTERIUM FIDEI: 'THE MATTER IS SETTLED'

In 1965 the magisterium spoke. Pope Paul swept aside
the attempts to replace transubstantiation and stood firm by
old doctrine and ancient formulation. His encyclical, *Mysterium Fidei*, was published a few days before the opening of

the last session of Vatican II, which gave it an air of fore-stalling discussion, and was greeted in some quarters with contempt. "I should not have accepted the document as a piece of work from a student," was the reaction of Charles Davis.[21] *Commonweal* (September 4, 1965) was hardly more happy. *Herder Correspondence* found the Pope guilty of having a "Lockean concept of substance" (July, 1968). The remarkable Fr. Gregory Baum, in *The Canadian Register*, September 25, 1965, accused the Pope of stressing Trent as against Vatican II, of wishing to slow down the movement of renewal. Thomas Sartory alleged in *A New Interpretation of the Faith* that the Pope had "missed the actual question which interests every theologian who knows the actual data of the New Testament."

And there were those who saw beyond the letter to a hidden spirit. . . . Dr. Schillebeeckx spoke of living with a double truth if we abandoned attempts to reinterpret, and appended: "it seems to me that the deepest meaning of the encyclical . . . is that it points to this as a very real danger." (*Op. cit.*, p. 157.) "What the Pope is doing',, maintained the *Catholic Herald* bravely, ". . . is to encourage the desire to find new and fuller expressions of the faith." Though the Pope insisted on the vital importance of our fixed rule of speech, Fr. Nicholas Lash wrote in *Dogmas and Doctrinal Progress*, in the symposium *Doctrinal Development and Christian Unity*: "Notice that it is the concepts which he says are not tied (to any specific cultural system), not the formulae" and then, from Olympus: "May I add that it is not my intention either to approve or to question some . . . presuppositions of the theologian employed by the Pope to write the encyclical. . . ."

We go on now to break down the encyclical into its main affirmations, but first we remind the reader who has, we hope, learned the lesson of the previous chapter: this is a very solemn act of the papal magisterium, and the teaching of "the teacher of the whole Church" closes debate. Transignification is now ruled out as an explanation of, or substi-

[21] *The Observer,* January 1, 1967.

tute for, transubstantiation. Some, we know, have rejected
the teaching of *Humanae Vitae* and some of these same people
will disdain *Mysterium Fidei*. There will be others, however, who, while resisting *Humanae Vitae*, will be horrified
by the tattered faith of those who dismiss the teaching of
the Pope on the Eucharist, and these must look in the mirror
and see their true face. It is the same authority which
teaches, with equal right and weight, in the two encyclicals.
We leave aside the devotional aspects of the pronouncement
and list the main principles and implications, with one or
two cross-references to the *Credo of the People of God*.

(1) Theologians are causing "considerable mental confusion in matters of faith" by their writings regarding transubstantiation.

(2) No interpretation is acceptable which "whittles
away the natural meaning of the words or the accepted sense
of the concepts."

(3) It is wrong to treat of the topic without mentioning the marvellous change of the whole substances of the
bread and wine; these changes cannot be reduced to transignification or transfinalization.

(4) This is the mystery of faith, and we must shun
poisonous rationalism; human arguments ought to be hushed
and we should "follow the magisterium of the Church like
a star."

(5) Careless language breeds false opinions. The
Church has elaborated a rule of speech which has been a
"token and standard of orthodox faith. It must be observed
religiously. No-one may presume to alter it at will or on
the pretext of new knowledge." It is *intolerable* that a Catholic, independently of the magisterium, should want to modify
Trent's formulations.

(6) These formulae express concepts which are timeless, not being the offshoot of passing cultures, scientific
views or particular theologies. The terms are "appropriate
and certain" and the concepts present concrete experience
of reality; "They are, therefore within the reach of everyone
(a) at all times and (b) in all places."

(7) As Vatican I taught, the original meaning of a doctrine must be retained.

(8) Christ is truly present in the Church in many ways, but the supreme form of real presence is the "substantial presence by which Christ is made present, whole and entire, God and man" in the Eucharist. It is a "true, real and substantial presence." (*Credo*) This is not an omni-presence, a pneumatic presence, of Christ's Body in glory.

(9) Our Lord becomes present precisely by the change of the bread's whole substance into His Body and the wine's whole substance into His Blood, the singular change aptly termed transubstantiation. The Real Presence can come about *only* through transubstantiation (*Credo*).

(10) "Nothing is left of the bread and wine but the appearances." It is not a matter of the bread and wine no longer being *ordinary* bread and wine, or of the so-called bread-reality, as distinct from the bread, having changed. The appearances contain another Being "for beneath these . . . there is no longer what was there before but something quite different."

(11) This is not a re-valuation arising from the Church's belief. "This is so in very fact." It is not a matter of the use of bread and wine as determined by man. "To be in accord with Catholic faith," we must "maintain that in the reality itself, independently of our mind, the bread and wine have ceased to exist. . . . (*Credo*). Kant is thus relegated to the world of unreal shades.

(12) Bread and wine do not take on a new signification, since they no longer exist after the consecration but their appearances acquire a "new expressiveness and a new purpose." Christ does not give Himself in the bread and wine— even God cannot give Himself in the no-longer-existent.

(13) Christ is bodily present, in His physical reality, whole and entire. This is the fundamental difference between the Real Presence and other 'real presences' of our Lord; it is first and foremost physical, material.

(14) But He is not present in the manner in which

bodies occupy and are circumscribed by space, and so we say "sacramentally", this case being unique.

There, then, is the teaching of the Church. And as the encyclical was greeted with disdain by some Catholics, so also was the *Credo*, to the authority of which Canon Drinkwater rightly drew attention. The Dutch paper *De Volskrant* said it merely repeated old teaching, in old words, "as if the world and man have not changed in the meantime," while *De Nieuwe Linie* was confident that many Catholics who *thought* about these thinkings "are for the most part thinking differently from the Pope."[22] How often are the phrases "thinking Catholics" or "educated Catholics" introduced by way of argument! Professor Butterfield contended: "More often than people generally recognise, it is true that a moral element—pride or wilfulness or a tendency to wishful thinking, for example—enters into the constitution of even our intellectual mistakes" (*op. cit.*, p. 30).

THE STRAW CROZIERS

Near the end of *Humani Generis*, Pius XII emphasised that his warning about false teaching was addressed to all bishops and heads of religious houses. One false trend concerned transubstantiation. The Pope ordered the bishops and superiors to "take every possible precaution against the utterance of such opinions in schools, in gatherings for discussions, in writings of whatever sort, and against their being passed on in any fashion either to clerics or to the faithful at large." The next words were addressed to professors in seminaries, pointing out "that they cannot with a clear conscience, exercise the office so entrusted to them unless they dutifully accept the principles we have here set forth, and observe them narrowly in educating their pupils. Mind and heart of their pupils must be impregnated with the same spirit of loyal reverence towards the teaching authority of the Church. . . ."

It is undeniable that some bishops have failed in their duty and have allowed those under them to obscure the Faith.

[22] Cf. *Catholic Herald*, July 19, 1968.

The present section of this chapter will indicate that we have not been beyond reproach in these isles, nor have those elsewhere in the English-speaking world. It was for this reason that I confessed to being only partly convinced by Cardinal Heenan's "Since nobody knows which theologians are being condemned (by the Pope), it is impossible for bishops to take any action." We may not be certain as to the identity of all the theologians censured, but we are certain about the *views*, and Pius XII's command stands with regard to schools, publications etc.

On page 69 of *Dialogue*, the Cardinal mentioned the Austrian bishops' reaction to attacks on the Eucharist and commented, "We have heard echoes here of this iconoclastic thinking, but in England the exponents of false thinking on the Eucharist have been so few that the bishops have not found it necessary to make any official pronouncement on the subject." Are they so few? And is there not a fallacy in the idea that a statement solves problems? If the pope's utterances are disregarded, so will the bishops', and problems are solved by *action*. (Everyone talks now about 'failure to communicate.' What about 'failure to excommunicate' or suspend?) We refer again to St. John Fisher who had seen it all happen: "We go nothing nigh to the matter. . . ."

One recalls that, when Frs. Charles Davis, P. de Rosa and H. J. Richards were moved from their seminary posts to important posts at Heythrop College and Corpus Christi College, *Herder Correspondence* intimated that Cardinal Heenan had rid St. Edmund's College, Ware, of an *avant-garde* group, only to be told by the Cardinal that this interpretation was false and unflattering. Yet it was widely known that they were of uncertain orthodoxy, the magazine of their old college gave them a woundingly cool farewell, and Davis has left the Church, Fr. Richards is pounding the Loisy trail, while de Rosa, who issued from Corpus Christi two round robins, one (addressed to the bishops) demanding that a priest who rejected his vows should be allowed to marry after a month, the other a letter to *The Times* denouncing *Humanae Vitae*, has given up his priesthood to fight against papal error, saying that the Cardinal had resisted any plea to sack him and that the sole restriction imposed on him had been that he was not to make *public* pronouncements against the pope's teaching, which left him free to indoctrinate students in unofficial conversation.[23] Yet Cardinal Heenan is a man of passionate general attachment to the Church; perhaps his enormous kindness of heart, a marvellous priestly quality, has here betrayed him. The root of disappointment in the bishops is not that, in the main, they lack faith. The nerve of the matter *is* nerve, the bowstring (as the Latin suggests) which launches the arrow. If Cardinal Heenan regrets that the pope does not pin-point individuals or books, may we not voice the same complaints against our bishops? Thus it is that the views condemned in *Mysterium Fidei* circulate.

IT COULDN'T HAPPEN HERE?

Newman wrote in the *Apologia*, "It is not at all easy . . . to wind up an Englishman to a dogmatic level." Thus we do not expect to find much theological writing here, or much in it that is original, but there has been some work which verged on Cranmer's teaching in Tennyson's *Queen Mary*:

> "It is but a communion, not a mass;
> A holy supper, not a sacrifice;
> No man can make his Maker. . . ."

and parroting of Smits-Schoonenberg-Schillebeeckx has gone on to an extent which seems to have escaped the eye of authority.

Davis' article in *Sophia* appeared before *Mysterium Fidei*, as did also an article from the pen of Fr. Herbert McCabe, O.P., in *The Clergy Review*, December, 1964. We repeat here some passages from the latter and the reader may compare them with the points laid down in the encyclical. . . . "It is sometimes thought"—Fr. McCabe put forward—"that the real presence is due to transubstantiation . . . transub-

---

[23] *The Daily Telegraph*, September 1, 1971, and *Catholic Herald*, January 14, 1972.

stantiation is simply the form that the real presence takes in the Eucharist. . . . To say that Christ is present in the sacraments through our faith will sound Protestant to some Catholics; they will want to say: 'Yes, but . . . there is also his sacramental presence in the Eucharist.' The man who makes this objection reveals that he has himself a Protestant conception of faith." (Actually, the man who made the objection turned out to be the Pope, who wrote: "He [Christ] is present too when she is administering the sacraments . . . Yet there is another form of presence, the supreme form, in which Christ is present in his Church in the sacrament of the Eucharist. . . .") Again—"There is no more question of a physical change in the bread and wine when they are consecrated than there is in the man when he is baptised. . . . Christ is present in the same way (ecclesially) in the Eucharist and in baptismal character. The fact that in the Eucharist transubstantiation occurs does not mean that Christ is present in a different way . . . the Council of Trent, so far from teaching the physical presence of Christ, need not even perhaps commit us to the physical absence of the stuff that was bread and wine."

In fairness, it must be remembered that this article appeared before *Mysterium Fidei*. Have the English-speaking voices which jeopardised Catholic belief been *de facto* silenced so that our bishops need recognise no duty either of making statements or of dealing with the obdurate? The answer involves two considerations. First, books written in other countries are finding their way here. Fr. Joseph Powers, for example, is American. He claims in the introduction to *Eucharistic Theology* that his book is written in the spirit of *Mysterium Fidei*, gives this only the briefest mention in his text, and proceeds to disregard it, writing: "It is in the genuine reality of this transignification, *in the change of the meaning* (italics mine) of this bread and wine . . . that the substantial realities involved are changed . . . one cannot speak of bread and wine unless one situates them in a concrete action."

Secondly, not only do tendentious imports continue to arrive, but the effects are seen in the writings of British

priests. Let me give a few examples, leaving the reader once
more to check with the encyclical if necessary.

First we look at *For All Men* by Fr. John Baptist Walker,
O.F.M., which contains lectures given to parents, teachers
and catechists at a Brentwood diocesan catechetical centre,
and which was reviewed by Fr. Michael Richards, editor of
The Clergy Review, as "a most admirable achievement,"
giving "A deep and inspiring insight into Catholic belief as
the best theologians are expounding it today."[24] Fr. Walker
tells us that we have interpreted transubstantiation in too
materialist a fashion, and explains its meaning as the change
by which what was *ordinary* bread and wine becomes
Christ. . . . "And though it does so by referring to 'substance' and 'accidents', what it *really* says is. . . ." He goes on
to show that he does not know what 'substance' is, writing,
"Most of us do not nowadays believe that all the things
around us are made of a spiritual substance coated with a
covering of material accidents. . . ." (Because substance is
invisible, he has taken it to be spiritual.) "Nor does the
Church require that we should. She simply states that, *for
its time* (italics mine), the explanation . . . was the best way
of putting the truth. . . ." (This is a contradiction of the
Pope's "at all times and in all places".) Then he leads us
into the fairyland of transignification, showing first that he
does not know what transubstantiation means, as he says
that, when a carpenter takes wood and makes a table, he
has 'transubstantiated' the wood. "We know that it *is* something different from what it was because it has been given
a new *meaning*. . . ." and, finally, "the bread . . . now stands
for and signifies the risen Lord . . . this bread is something
different from what it was before. . . ." It is most depressing,
this disregard of *Mysterium Fidei*, for it means that Catholics
are parroting views which are far further from orthodoxy
than was the doctrine of Luther. Luther wanted to deny
the Real Presence, since he was all for giving the Papists
"a really hard slap in the face," but he found himself "im-

---

[24] Fr. Walker has since left the priesthood.

prisoned by the text of the Gospel" and held at least for consubstantiation and impanation. When he met Zwingli in conference, he chalked on the table 'This is my body' and refused to be won over to a symbolical interpretation. Luther did hold, in a heterodox way, the material presence of Christ which is what the 'transignificationists' certainly do not.

Just as disturbing as Fr. Walker's catechesis was that contained in a teaching aid circulated to secondary schools by the Liverpool Catechetical Centre in 1969. The director of the Centre is Fr. Anthony Bullen who brushed aside criticism of the Dutch catechism by writing, "there are people who are really intent on sniffing out heresies in each new book: and, of course, you can make almost any sentence read like heresy if you try hard enough,"[25] which was the same line as adopted by Fr. Corbishley, S.J., who, declaring the catechism "profoundly orthodox and immensely enlightening," thought some rewriting might be needed "for the benefit of those who are determined to find the catechism unsound."[26] We are content to print some of the handout's sentences, leaving the reader to assess them. . . . "If we think about it, we will see that it is not a question of several different real presences but only the one Real Presence which we encounter in many ways and that has its centre and climax in the Eucharist . . . after the consecration what lies upon the altar is no longer *ordinary* bread and wine (italics mine); it is truly Christ's body and blood . . . no physical or chemical change has taken place at the consecration. . . . Unfortunately, many people . . . do tend to think in terms of some sort of physical change. Young people especially are unable to think about Christ's words except in a completely literal sense. This leads to them thinking of Christ being somehow physically present in the host; a physical presence, 'screened' by the bread and wine. . . . The term transubstantiation for them signifies the removal of some inner part of the host and Christ taking its place. But within the bread nothing is removed, nothing physical happens to the bread

[25] *Catholic Pictorial,* December, 1967.
[26] *The Universe,* December 8, 1967.

or wine. . . . If Christ were physically present then we really would eat his body as cannibals eat people[27] . . . He is not present in order to bring us physically closer to himself. That would be quite impossible and of no significance anyway." Yet Fr. Bullen carries a certificate of orthodoxy. When the staff of Corpus Christi College resigned, Archbishop Beck hastened to send his clergy a letter announcing, "I think I am right to reiterate the expression of the confidence I have in Father Anthony Bullen. . . ."

We have glimpsed the catechesis given in two English dioceses and, without any expenditure of energy in heresy-hunting, one comes across frequent examples of Dutch theology in articles or reports of lectures. The *Catholic Herald* editorial of April 23, 1971, dismissed as "amateur theology" the statement that "Christ is present whole and entire, bodily present in His physical reality", a statement taken from *Mysterium Fidei.* The homely magazine *The New Franciscan* printed in July, 1968, an article by Fr. Godric Young, O.F.M., which championed transignification, and concluded not surprisingly: "When we see more clearly how Christ is present in his people, in us, we shall not feel that something is missing even in a church in which the Real Presence is not there." The editor, coming to the writer's defence in subsequent issues, turned out to belong to the same camp, and warmly recommended Fr. Walker's *For All Men.*

Another case is that of Fr. John Coventry, S.J., who, reviewing the Dutch catechism, lodged only one complaint in regard to the evasive pages on the Eucharist and that concerned merely the terminology of the statement that we "receive the whole Jesus."[28] The *Catholic Herald* for August 30, 1968, reported a paper given by him at Maynooth Union Summer School, and we print from the report, with a minimum of comment. . . . ". . . no one formulation could purport

---

[27] St. Thomas, *Summa,* Pars Tertia, Q.LXXV, Art. V: "Christ wished to put forward His body and blood in the Eucharist for our consumption, under the appearances of bread and wine, so that faith might gain in merit, unbelievers would not be able to mock, and there would be no trace of that disgust which men associate with the eating of human flesh."

[28] *The Tablet,* September 23, 1967.

to explain the Real Presence. . . . It was not a special . . . not a physical presence; if the word was to attain any assignable meaning, not a corporal or bodily presence, as Christ's humanity was not present in corporal form. It was . . . the unique presence of a heavenly reality to faith." (We interject that the Council of Constance defined a "propria praesentia corporali".) "One had to say something like a change of substance. . . . Fr. Coventry said that centuries of Eucharistic devotion had brought about a serious imbalance, at least in the popular mind. . . ."

Mention of the popular mind, and the ambiguity of Eucharistic interpretation, brings back to mind the story of Berengarius which may fittingly end this section. C. E. Sheedy in the *New Catholic Encyclopaedia* tells us that he approached the Eucharist as a rationalist, looking down on the common belief which he dubbed 'the opinion of the mob.' He was contemptuous of Rome's authority, and "the distinction between substance and accidents was lost on him. . . ." At the Council of Rome in 1079, his eel-like quality showed. Traditionalists took pains to see that the word 'substantially' was inserted into the oath proposed for him, and he was enraged, feeling himself trapped. He seized the document, read through it, looking for an escape, inserted the clause 'saving the substance of the bread' and said that he was ready to take the oath. The bishops would have none of this evasion, and the upshot was that Pope Gregory came down on him 'like a bolt', ordering him to prostrate himself and admit his error in omitting the key word 'substantially.'[29]

The Catholic world has not seen a 'bolt' for a long time. "Dangerous writing on ecumenism and the Eucharist incurs no episcopal censure," admitted Cardinal Heenan. And truth suffers.

THE WINDSOR STATEMENT

At the end of December, 1971, the Press announced that the eighteen members of the joint Anglican-Roman

---

[29] Cf. *Berengar and the Reform of Sacramental Doctrine,* by Rev. A. J. Macdonald, D.D. (non-Catholic), 1930.

Catholic International Commission had reached substantial agreement on the doctrine of the Eucharist. The Catholic theologians included Bishop Christopher Butler, Bishop Alan Clark, Professor J. J. Scarisbrick, Fr. Herbert Ryan, S.J., from Woodstock College, New York, and Fr. E. J. Yarnold, S.J., Master of Campion Hall, Oxford. Among the Anglicans were Very Revd. Henry Chadwick, Dean of Christ Church, Oxford, and Rev. J. W. Charley, Vice-Principal, St. John's College, Nottingham. The statement of 'substantial' agreement which they published occasioned an outcry in the Catholic press. Why? Was it only Catholic Colonel Blimps reacting according to form? That this was not the case may be deduced from the post-agreement reflections of two of the Anglican theologians. Dean Chadwick explained: "We tried to escape from the assumptions of the past and the immovable positions formerly adopted"—which rings an alarm bell for any Catholic who holds to traditional teaching—"We wanted to preserve the activity of God in the Eucharist without anything 'thingly' remaining around to be manipulated. The word activity occurs frequently, not the traditional language of substantiation. It is not that we were trying to avoid its use but we thought emphasis on action made things clearer."[30] But it is obvious that they *were* trying to avoid its use . . . and—"anything 'thingly' remaining around to be manipulated"? Surely, 'thingly' here means 'substantial', and the idea is that there is no transubstantiation, and no Blessed Sacrament after Communion to be placed in tabernacle or monstrance. How could sane men speak of substantial agreement when the one thing they had taken care to dissemble was the key matter of change of substance?

The Rev. Julian W. Charley published an historical introduction and theological commentary with the text of the Agreement (Grove Books, Bramcote, Notts). The Catholic signatories, in order to achieve substantial agreement, had incredibly allowed the doctrine of transubstantiation (without which there is no 'the' Real Presence) to be relegated

[30] *Catholic Herald,* December 31, 1971.

to a footnote which ran: "The word transubstantiation is commonly used in the Roman Catholic Church to indicate that God acting in the Eucharist effects a change in the inner reality of the elements. The term should be seen as affirming the fact of Christ's presence and of the mysterious and radical change which takes place. In contemporary Roman Catholic theology it is not understood as explaining how the change takes place." The Catholic theologians, therefore, uninfluenced by *Mysterium Fidei*, had allowed 'contemporary Roman Catholic Theology' (Smits, Schoonenberg and Schillebeeckx?) to guide the Agreement. Not unnaturally, the Rev. J. W. Charley commented: "The footnote to paragraph 6 concerning transubstantiation shows the suspicion of contemporary Roman Catholic theology for the philosophical ideas of substance and accidents. . . . If the term (transubstantiation) has had to undergo modification in its usage by Catholic theologians, it would seem appropriate to discard it. However much it were to be re-interpreted, its retention could only prove a major obstruction to Anglicans." Mr. Charley did seem to find hope in the fact that Anglican theologians from Jewel onwards regarded the consecration "as an action whereby God set apart bread and wine for their holy use, which might be called trans-signification." In his conclusion, he suggests that "This consensus should cause Roman Catholics to re-evaluate the relation between their current eucharistic theology and that contained in the dogmatic decrees of the Council of Trent." This was the impression made by our Catholic representatives at Windsor, though one of them, Bishop Butler, had recalled to us (*The Tablet*, March 7, 1970) what Vatican II laid down in the Decree on Ecumenism: "Of great value . . . are meetings between the two sides, especially for discussion of theological problems, where each can deal with the other on an equal footing. . . . *It is, of course, essential that doctrine be clearly presented in its entirety. . . .*" The italics are mine, and I add the words implied by the last dots: "Nothing is so foreign to the spirit of ecumenism as a false conciliatory approach which harms the purity of Catholic doctrine and obscures its assured genuine meaning."

Bishop Alan Clark, for his part, suggested that "We had to find a new language to express it (the Real Presence)." With all respect, new language was required only if the old doctrine was to be bypassed, since non-Catholic theologians *do* understand our terms; if not, the terms are easily explained. He, too, published a commentary on the Agreement, and the commentary did nothing to allay concern. ". . . it would be wrong," he said, "to expect to find in the Agreed Statement . . . the familiar terminology of Trent or of the Anglican Articles. The whole purpose . . . is to express the understanding of the Eucharist that underlies these formulae, to express the present faith of both Churches, and do so in language which people can understand today." He has suggested that *one* understanding underlies both Trent and Anglican Articles though Article XXVIII declared transubstantiation repugnant, and he has left himself open to a charge of holding that the 'present faith' of the Church is not that of Trent. Further the bishop treats papal teaching in cavalier fashion. He tells us that "the Council had no wish to lock itself to a particular philosophy of substance and accident," and adds that the development of the notion of transubstantiation "rests on a particular philosophical framework." Not so Pope Paul in *Mysterium Fidei!* And, in reference to the relegation of transubstantiation to a footnote, we read: "It was therefore no attempt to avoid doctrinal controversies or divergencies that made us relegate an explanation of the term to a footnote, but a conviction that this Catholic doctrine can be misinterpreted even by ourselves." May one say to this that no Catholic, reading *Mysterium Fidei*, can misinterpret transubstantiation . . . but Mr. Charley, re-reading the Agreement, interprets Bishop Clark as no longer believing in the traditional doctrine.

"THE STILL LOWER DEPTHS"

The vital weakness of the Agreement is that it merely papers over differences of belief with vague terminology; there is no Catholic doctrine of the Mass as sacrifice; there is no clear doctrine of the Real Presence. I have, indeed, seen a more Catholic-sounding 'Agreement' drawn from Calvin's *Institutes* and Calvin did *not* share our beliefs. It is apposite here to quote the splendid editorial which *The Tablet* published on July 4, 1896, when Leo XIII spoke out manfully in *Satis cognitum* on papal authority and the real problems of reunion: "He might have led Reunionists on, dangling as a bait before their eyes the hope of possible compromise, or of one or other of those small ecclesiastical mercies which some men have agreed to magnify into 'informal communion.' Or, without committing himself to any doctrinal statements, he might have studiously used the language of platonic generalities, dwelling unctously on points of concord, and adopting the cheap policy of burking the points of disagreement . . . he might have stooped to the still lower depths of the deliberate use of a nebulous speech— of phrases designedly chosen as sufficiently loose and vague to cover both a Catholic and an Anglican meaning, adaptable at will by each class of readers—in a word, to those childish devices by which men are led to play at believing they are one, because the antagonisms of sense are hidden in the sameness of sound. . . . From the chair of *Peter* he has given to mankind the example of the charity and dignity of Apostolic honesty." This is what has angered Catholics—that our theologians at Windsor chose 'the still lower depths'.

One of the best critiques of the Agreement will be found in Chapter XII, *The Royal Supremacy and Theology*, of Professor Scarisbrick's fine book *Henry VIII*. There he studies the doctrinal utterances of the latter part of Henry's reign to determine whether the king was moving from Catholic orthodoxy as he had moved from papal allegiance. He passes the judgments "by Catholic standards, a very inadequate statement," "not an impressive performance," etc., on doctrinal statements which are more truly Catholic than anything set down at Windsor.

Windsor, therefore, has been one more move against the key doctrine of transubstantiation. Defending the Agreement, Fr. Peter Hebblethwaite, S.J., wrote in the *Catholic Herald* (January 21, 1971)—"when Trent declared that 'transubstantiation' was the 'most appropriate' way of speaking of the 'remarkable change in the bread and wine,' it did not say, and should not be made to say, that it was the *only* appropriate way of stating the nature of the change." This is a sophism. What Trent did, as we have seen, was to state the one and only nature of the change, and then to say that this precise change was most aptly termed 'transubstantiation.' The Modernist pretends that his debate is over a term; but it is in fact over a statement of fact. And the result of all this theological fog can be seen in Fr. David Woodard's account of church-sharing with the local Anglicans: "We are all united in asking for the reservation of whatever Eucharist is celebrated." (*Catholic Herald*, January 21, 1972.)

6

Churchquake.....Humanae Vitae

The test of loyalty and orthodoxy is, and will always be, sincere assent to the decisions of the magisterium.

BISHOP BUTLER,
The Tablet, September 28, 1963.

Generations of Catholics have been brought up to the view: 'You are safe if you follow the Pope.' Now I think . . . that this is an oversimplified statement . . . when he is not speaking with full infallible authority, it is possible that what he says may need to be modified from other sources.

BISHOP BUTLER, five years later, The Dictates of Rome, in the Sunday Times Weekly Review, October 6, 1968.

'Then, with a defiant flourish, 'if the Pope does not decide in my favour, I (Henry VIII) shall declare the Pope a heretic. . . .'

GARRETT MATTINGLY, Catherine of Aragon.

If the Pope does not allow the pill very soon, I will refuse to recognize his authority.

Quoted in Herder Correspondence, July-August, 1967.

In the days of the apostles, St. John Fisher wrote, there "were no chalices of gold, but many golden priests. Now be many chalices of gold, but almost no golden priests." Any Catholic who has dined in the ancient Recorder's House in Thaxted, and let his eye wander from the portrait of Thomas More to the lugubrious features of Archbishop Warham, the least likely representative, as Mgr. Hughes said, of the spirit of Thomas Becket, may have meditated that the lack of golden priests made for a famine of golden bishops, though there were passably good and learned bishops. "The anger of a king is death to men," Warham muttered over and over, relegating to second place for so long the anger of God. *Episcopi anglici semper pavidi* ('the English bishops are always timid') ran an old saying and it was verified in 1531, which seems a fitting year to recall on the threshold of this chapter.

In 1531 Henry VIII demanded from the clergy an acknowledgement that he was "Protector and Supreme Head of the English Church and Clergy." He did not reject papal supremacy but claimed only to be local Head which did not debar him from recognising the Pope as Head of the universal Church. The poison lay in the ambiguity of the words, since they could mean as little or as much as the King chose. Ambiguity is a far more deadly weapon than falsehood since it disarms the weak and patches lesions of conscience; and it was ambiguity which shattered the Church in England since all the other disasters followed from it.

"There was, on the part of most of the bishops," Mgr. Hughes wrote,[1] "a careful avoidance of the fundamental question which the title raised. . . ." The exception was John Fisher who, according to Hall's account, "never spared to open and declare his mind freely in the defence of the Church." He begged his fellow bishops "to consider and take good heed what mischiefs and inconveniences would ensue to the whole Church of Christ by this unreasonable and unseemly grant," and argued for outright rejection. It was only when he saw them on the point of abject submission to

[1] *The Reformation in England,* Part II, Chapter III.

Henry's pressure that he "stood up again, all angry," and tried to salvage something from the surrender by suggesting a qualifying clause. "Finally," Mgr. Hughes wrote, "the aged Archbishop of Canterbury, William Warham, put it to the assembly in Fisher's words . . . 'as far as the law of Christ allows, even Supreme Head, we acknowledge his Majesty to be'. And when he did so a long silence followed. *'Qui tacet consentire videtur.'* said the veteran lawyer . . . 'Then are we silent all,' said a prelate . . . And so, *ambiguously* (italics mine), the thing went through." Afterwards Tunstall wrote a letter of complaint to the king and received a reply which was "yet another vast ambiguity," a "masterpiece of evasion." Incredibly, he accepted it, and yet the implications of the matter were so clear to anyone who would face them that Fisher was physically ill, More thought of resigning office, and Anne Boleyn was "as much delighted as if she had gained paradise," while her father was already looking forward and offering to prove from Scripture that "when God left this world He left no successor nor vicar." The Act of Supremacy and the loss of England to the Church were still to follow but they followed with something approaching inevitability, since the strength of the Church in England had already shattered on ambiguity.

What is the relevance of the weakness and ambiguities of the English hierarchy in far-off 1531 to 1968, the year of *Humanae Vitae?* Consider . . . . on July 25, 1968, Pope Paul gave to the world the long-awaited answer of the Vicar of Christ to the reconsidered question of contraception; the answer was a forthright rejection of birth control by any other method than abstinence or use of the infecund period, and he asked priests throughout the world to expound his teaching *without ambiguity.* After some delay, the hierarchy of England and Wales issued their expected statement (September, 1968) on this vital question of the Church's teaching. The relevance of 1531 will appear from some of the Press reactions. First, the leader of the *Daily Telegraph* (September 25): "A long-expected statement from the . . . bishops . . . on the Pope's recent Encyclical has left confusion worse confounded. . . . Either the Pope . . . is right or he is wrong.

If he is . . . right, then why do the bishops not affirm this categorically? If he is wrong, then why do they not state, equally categorically, that his guidance in this affair is to be ignored?" *The Times* leader of the same date: "The mild and inconclusive statement . . . sets out two apparently conflicting positions without giving priority to either or indicating how they are to be reconciled. . . . On the face of it, and without interpretation, this does not appear to leave room for conscientious disagreement. Yet elsewhere the statement says, 'it must be stressed that the primacy of conscience is not in dispute' . . . it may be inferred that there are circumstances in which a Catholic may allowably dissent from particular articles of the teaching of the Church. . . . But in another passage . . . the bishops leave the last word with the Pope. . . . The statement therefore does not offer a clear resolution of the conflicts of mind generated by the encyclical."

The Tablet, a determined opponent of the Encyclical's doctrine, reflected: "A composite document, such as this, must meet with a mixed reception. Compromises, which are inevitable in joint authorship, tend to leave the single mind unsatisfied . . . a composite document has corresponding defects, notably a lack of consistency and a certain ambiguity of language and purpose . . . the statement makes room for a variety of interpretations. . . . It will be tragic if this generous intention of the hierarchy as a whole is taken advantage of and exercised in a spirit of rigorism by individual bishops."[2] The *Catholic Herald* confessed, "Admittedly the statement is not without ambiguity," but felt that "Perhaps even the vagueness is a point in its favour," and then added unexpectedly, "The bishops give full support to the encyclical. . . ." followed by, "But . . . the statement does not condemn out of hand those who are practising contraception." (September 27, 1968.)

It is my contention that a wound of consequence was given to the Church in England in 1968, that the oracular answer of the hierarchy was in the tradition of 1531, and the

[2] September 28, 1968.

unity of the Church was lacerated. Consider: the See of Peter gave its verdict, a confirmation of what the ordinary and universal magisterium of the Church had taught from time immemorial and therefore taught infallibly. The verdict, therefore, was *binding.* ("To repudiate the teaching on contraception . . . throws open the possibility of repudiating all of these other positions [divorce, sterilisation, abortion, euthanasia] as well. *The skein simply unwinds.*"—B. A. Santamaria, *Contraception.*) The Scottish bishops said of the suggestion that the papal decision did not demand assent, "Such an assertion is destructive of all that Catholics understand by the teaching authority of the Church. . . . The obligation of a Catholic to accept the teaching of the Church on any grave moral problem can never justifiably be regarded as an offence against the freedom of his conscience." ("God bless the hand that wrote that pastoral!" a rueful English bishop wrote to a Scottish confrère.) In Armagh cathedral, Cardinal Conway insisted, "This teaching is authentic and binding," while Cardinal O'Boyle of Washington classed it as "authentic teaching of the Church—which is binding in conscience." The Australian bishops taught that to refuse to accept Pope Paul's decision "would be a grave act of disobedience" and they, like their Scottish brothers, gave the lie to *The Tablet's* suggestion that compromises are inevitable when there is joint authorship. They are inevitable only when belief is fragmented.

When the bishops in 1531 fashioned their ambiguous clause, it was, in Fr. Bridgett's splendid phrase, "a bolt without a ward," and the phrase describes perfectly the Bishop's statement in 1968. The bolt was shot into place by talk of the assent due, and then the ward was ripped out by reference to the primacy of conscience. In addition, two sentences came close to falsehood: "The Encyclical makes no sweeping condemnations," and "There is no threat of damnation." Not only did it claim to repeat unchanged teaching, with references to *Casti Connubii* which condemned forthrightly, but it did contain sweeping condemnations— "To be absolutely excluded"—of abortion, sterilisation and contraception, and while the *term* 'Damnation' was not used, the Pope taught that contraception was contrary to the natural law, fulfilment of which was *necessary for salvation,* and reminded couples that "the gate is narrow . . . that leads to life," which involved a reminder about the broad way to death.

CONFUSION WORSE CONFOUNDED

Cardinal Heenan had issued a pastoral letter on August 4th, directing that "Those who have become accustomed to using methods (of birth control) which are unlawful may not be able all at once to resist temptation . . . they must not abstain from the sacraments." There was compassion in the words, but no mention was made of a firm purpose of amendment, an essential of true repentance. It could have been implied, but this was an hour when things needed to be spelled out. Charles Davis pounced (*The Observer,* August 4): "What this means is that Catholics, while accepting the papal teaching . . . should solve the problem . . . by constantly confessing their sin. . . . This is to preserve intact the papal teaching at the cost of fostering permanent guilt-feelings. . . ." Obviously, both those who rejected the encyclical and those who accepted it were not going to be satisfied with anything suggesting moral compromise, but the question raised most loudly was: what about Catholics who reject the decision?

An unhappy part-answer was given by the Cardinal in a Press Conference on September 25th. "The priest," he explained, "is never bound to go against his conscience but he is bound to make clear that the encyclical is the teaching of the Pope. He can then say that as a matter of conscience he does not agree with it." This left a priest free to reject the teaching of the Holy See—a far cry from Vatican II— and revealed how unsettling membership of the papal commission on birth control had been. The following month, the Cardinal defended the bishops' statement, in an address to members of the legal profession. . . . "Although . . . the magisterium itself was not in doubt, many who spoke with some authority . . . had led many to believe that a change was imminent . . . some organs of the secular press gave misleading accounts of what the bishops said . . . newspapers do not usually have moral theologians on their staff." But . . . had the press misled? And, as the statement was addressed to the Catholic public, did the newspapers require theologians to decode it? He came nearer the point by adding, "It is serious, however, when priests and laymen reading our words fail to grasp their meaning," but he failed to indicate where the fault lay or to grasp the authority-conscience nettle and inculcate absolute duty.

Consultation followed among the bishops and, as a result, the Cardinal addressed a letter to the clergy of his archdiocese. "Many," he said once more, "were led to expect a different answer" from the pope. He himself, however, had given precisely that lead. Though he had been firm in his Lenten pastoral of 1964,—"What is wrong and immoral can never become right. Nor can any doctrine of the Catholic Church ever be changed."—and in a later statement of that same year, issued in the name of the whole hierarchy—"It has even been suggested that the Council could approve the practice of contraception. But the Church . . . has no power of any kind to alter the laws of God"—he had led people to expect the green light for contraception when, in his pastoral letter for Trinity Sunday, 1966, published on the day that he left for a meeting of the Commission on Birth Control, of which he was co-president, he had written: "Some of our notions of right and wrong have also undergone change. . . . Moral principles, of course, remain the same . . . loyal Catholics will all accept his verdict when the Vicar of Christ makes his long-promised announcement." His article in *The Tablet* for May of 1968 had reinforced the impression given: "Until the Pope gives the promised guidance most bishops will continue to act with restraint. . . . If indeed the old principles are to be adapted to the changed conditions of our times, Catholics resent this prolonged period of suspense. . . ." In addition, as Douglas Brown and Barry Cox revealed to the public in *The Sunday Times* (August 25), Archbishop Beck of Liverpool had also wavered in his allegiance to our principles, having "informed the Holy See that pending the Pope's pronouncement he would not feel able to instruct his priests to withhold absolution from penitents who had genuine reasons for transgressing the birth-control ban."

Now, in his letter of 1968 on behalf of the whole hierarchy, Cardinal Heenan taught "that no priest in the exercise of his ministry may repudiate the solemn teaching of the supreme authority of the Church. . . ." and he announced the hierarchy's agreement that: "Priests are required in preaching, teaching, in the press, on radio, television or public platforms, to refrain from opposing the teaching of the Pope in all matters of faith and morals. If a priest is unwilling to give this undertaking the bishop will decide whether he can be allowed without scandal to act in the name of the Church. Although he need not be required to cease celebrating Mass, a priest may not normally hold faculties to hear confessions without undertaking to declare faithfully the objective teaching of *Humanae Vitae* in the confessional and when giving spiritual guidance." It was a deadly compromise; the bishops had not even been able to agree that a priest who publicly attacked the encyclical *must* not be allowed to act in the name of the Church whose teaching he repudiated. A public mask could be worn over the private face, the priest being allowed to attack the magisterium's teaching 'in private' and, as no sin was involved, to offer up Mass. If he did not promise to uphold *Humanae Vitae*, he might not 'normally' hold faculties. It was not consonant with unity of faith. A month later, the Holy Father, in a message to the West German Catholics' rally at Essen, cut across ambivalent responses which had come from German and Belgian bishops, suggesting that people had the right in this to follow their own conscience—"His reply to this was that individual conscience has no validity in such matters." This has been misrepresented as a trampling on liberty, but it is never an infringement of honest rights to require consistency and integrity. The man who is expelled from the Conservative Club for voting Labour has no call on our sympathy, and neither has a Catholic who plays the Protestant.

Conscience was to the fore again in David Frost's interview with the Cardinal on television, on December 6th, and, though there was talk of the duty to inform the conscience, there was none of the duty of submission of will and mind or of sincerely adhering to papal judgments. "The teaching of the Church is very clear," the Cardinal said, "A man is bound to follow his conscience and this is true even if his conscience is in error. . . . Now it's the duty of a Catholic to inform his conscience. But it could happen . . . that a couple might say conscientiously: I'm quite sure that this is the right thing for me to do . . . then, of course, they must follow their conscience. There is no dispute about this."

David Frost pressed the point: "And if they go to their priest and say that they're doing precisely that, what should the priest say?" The Cardinal answered: " 'God bless you!' If they're really following their conscience in the sight of God, which is all that matters—the priest, the bishop, the Pope doesn't matter compared with God."

Another question followed: "But if a person is really following their conscience and using some form of contraceptive and goes to the priest and says so, then the priest should say, 'God bless you!', and not refuse them the sacraments?" The reply was: "Of course not, of course not! Perhaps you don't know, but in the pastoral letter I wrote immediately after the Encyclical was published, I insisted on this. I said, don't let this prevent you from receiving the sacraments. Remember?" Frost answered with truth: "Yes, I do. I read that, but you've never said it as clearly or forthrightly."

Those who had felt that Charles Davis had been unfair when he pounced on the Cardinal's pastoral were aghast, for Davis had indeed underrated the aberration, and the Cardinal was teaching that a Catholic could reject papal teaching, practise contraception, declare that he intended to continue doing so, and be absolved and given Communion. The connotation was that, if a Catholic squared abortion with conscience, the Sacraments were his for the asking. The skein simply unwinds.' That month a Scottish bishop sent his priests a circular which ended: "These are difficult days and I sympathise with you in your problems and especially when you are fulfilling your weighty responsibility in the confessional. A recent broadcast has complicated your work even more. Follow the Pope and—*sursum corda!*"

It is only fair to mention that Bishop Ellis of Nottingham, in his August pastoral, warned the sin-deniers: "Let them ponder the awful words of St. Paul: 'Whosoever shall eat this bread . . . unworthily shall be guilty of the body and blood of the Lord. . . . The Church is . . . full of love and mercy . . . But . . . her children must acknowledge guilt and, in seeking pardon, have a sincere determination to avoid sin in the future". In the same way, Archbishop (now Cardinal) Gray of the Scottish archdiocese of St. Andrews & Edinburgh laid down: "There will be absolution for those who fail to maintain the standard, but who show their intention to abide by it," adding that absolution would not be granted to those who rejected the papal ruling.[3] This was not in any way to show lack of understanding of the difficulties involved in breaking a habit of sin, but was a 'No' to schismatic rebellion however agonised. It was evidence of the disunity in the Church that, four months later, Fr. John Symon's *Catholic Herald* Question & Answer column, written from the seminary in that same diocese, taught the reverse, that "the priest may quite conscientiously decide that he should be absolved." This, of course, would leave a Catholic free to disobey the highest authority in the Church and be doctrinally selective, though the 7th ecumenical Council decreed: "If anyone does not accept in its entirety the Church's tradition, whether written or unwritten, let him be anathema." (Dz. 308.) It should be remembered that Pius XI had stern things to say, in *Casti Connubii*, about confessors who connived in wrong opinions or even gave them the benefit of tolerant silence— 'They are blind and leaders of the blind . . . both fall into the pit.'

[3] Cf. *Catholic Herald,* August 9, 1968.

CONSCIENCE & PRINCIPLES

In August, while Bishop Ellis spoke well of the "specious appeal to conscience," the Holy Father complained of those who "have recourse to ambiguous doctrinal expressions" and of others who were conferring on their own opinion the authority which they challenged in the Pope. He hinted that they were falling into Protestantism and said that they were confused about freedom of conscience.[4] To help clear the confusion, we draw attention to two vital principles. The first is that *a Catholic does not fashion his own moral principles*, but inherits them, receiving them from the Church, and it is never the role of his conscience to challenge these principles; his conscience comes into play in their *application*. To reject one of these moral principles is to exercise not freedom of conscience but Luther's private judgment.

The second is this: conscience has in the past come into collision with authority—usually civil authority when Caesar ordered Christians to do what was contrary to the Church's doctrine, and theologians have elaborated, in this regard, the rights of conscience. But it is a sin against truth to attempt to justify, in terms of this theology, defiance of the Church when it does not command something sinful but condemns an action as sinful. A Catholic's conscience is bound to work within the Church's moral code and principles and not declare itself free from them.

THE CAMPAIGN TO DIMINISH

Archbishop Beck, we saw, had 'cracked' before *Humanae Vitae* appeared, and Douglas Brown and Barry Cox, in their *Sunday Telegraph* article, classed him with Bishop Worlock of Portsmouth, Bishop of Arundel, and Dom Christopher Butler . . . "whose ambiguous public statements or private advice have tended to subordinate the encyclical to private conscience and to give the impression that the discussion about contraception is far from closed," and they contrasted the attitude of Archbishop Murphy of Cardiff who had uttered

---

[4] Address to Latin American bishops' conference.

a resounding "Now that the Holy Father has spoken, let no one be so foolish as to disobey." Archbishop Beck produced a pastoral in August as others did, and laid some dangerous trails. . . . "How different is the tone"—of *Humanae Vitae*, he said—"from that of Pope Pius XI's Encyclical. . . . Pope Pius XI spoke severely . . . of those who frustrate the natural power to generate life as doing something shameful and vicious. Pope Paul, in striking contrast, makes no such condemnations. Only once does he mention sin, and then in a gentle and pastoral way." This had every appearance of an attempt to de-fuse the encyclical, since it was adamant that it repeated the "moral teaching . . . proposed with constant firmness by the teaching authority," carried more than one reference to *Casti Connubii* which condemned contraception as "intrinsically vicious," and, though the actual word 'sin' may have been used but once, it was presupposed time after time as follows: "The faithful fulfilment (of the natural law) is equally necessary for salvation"; husband and wife "*must* conform . . . to the creative intention of God"; ". . . is in contradiction with the design constitutive of marriage, and with the will of the Author of life"; ". . . is to contradict nature . . . it is to contradict also the plan of God and His will"; ". . . are to be absolutely excluded as licit means"; "intinsically disorder"; "condemning, as always being illicit"; "intimate and unchangeable opposition to the true good of man"; "practices contrary to the natural and divine law"; and the reminder—"the gate is narrow. . . ." Could one say after reading these terms that "Pope Paul, in striking contrast, makes no such condemnations"? The fact is that Pope Paul has a very different type of mind from Pius XI, and favours a more complex and less direct approach, circling his topic more nervously; but he says the same.

That same week, there appeared in the *Catholic Herald* answers given by the Archbishop to questions put to him. "In a moral crisis of this kind," he stated, "I think the only thing one can tell people is that they must do what they think is right." He went on to say that Pope Paul had advanced a "very noble concept . . . an ideal many people would call it, that perhaps is very difficult to live up to," and then came out with the unexpected claim that the Pope's meaning was "not yet clear to us." (From *The Times*, July 30: "Cardinal Heenan . . . made only the briefest comment: 'The encyclical is clear enough.'") Archbishop Beck continued: "I would advise my priests to maintain the ideal in principle" and, holding that the encyclical's teaching "isn't intended to be, I'm quite sure, a practical programme of action," he thought that "most people would accept it as the ideal," and felt "bound to say that I must set before them the ideal that the Pope has put to all of us."

THE 'IDEAL'

Archbishop Dwyer of Birmingham also made considerable use, in his pastoral, of 'ideal.' The fourth time, it was wed to an adjective which lifted it to a high peak: "The Church would be false to its calling if it did not give even an heroic ideal." The notion caught on. Fr. Michael Richards wrote (*The Times*, August 8) that the Pope "has set out to teach the way of Christian perfection," and he gave comfort by asserting: "New Testament morality is not a set of implacable laws, damning equally all those who turn aside. . . ." He identified "the language of persuasion and exhortation, not of command," and judged: "If the highest authority in the Church does not at present see any more certain principle . . . that does not mean that we cannot go on trying to find one. . . ." "At present" turned up again in Fr. Symon's *Question & Answer* column in the *Catholic Herald* (March 26, 1971): ". . . the encyclical is certainly the best guidance which the Church can offer us at present. . . ." This was a curious way of rendering Pope Paul's "We now intend, by virtue of the mandate entrusted to us by Christ, to give our reply. . . ." *The Times* editorial, two days after Fr. Richards' letter, said, "Contraception remains a sin, but its gravity appears to have been diminished especially as a bar to the sacraments," but this was not enough for Canon Drinkwater whose letter, the next day again, decided: "it begins to look like a problem of ascetics and counsels."

The quotations which we have given from *Humanae Vitae*, when reflecting on Archbishop Beck's remarks, show how wrong was the attempt to 'reduce' the document in this way. Those who openly opposed the pope showed courage, but it is not easy to muster respect for attempts to get round clear teaching. What value was there, for example in Fr. Richards' axiom that "New Testament morality is not a set of implacable laws. . . ."? If it was meant to mean that every New Testament law admits of an exception, it is simply not true. Some modern theologians who deny intrinsic right and wrong would, for instance, excuse St. Peter for denying his Master, or early Christians for denying their faith, in the face of pressing danger, but St. Peter would not have accepted the vindication. He was right to weep to the end of his days, for what is intrinsically wrong can never be right, however circumstances may lighten personal responsibility.

This was the hour of the hollow axiom, the rigged choice and false antithesis, and even so distinguished a son of the Church as Mr. Christopher Hollis was guilty. Writing in the *Catholic Herald* (July 11, 1969), he said: "the commandments are not absolute but are to be interpreted according to circumstances," and he concluded that, in the matter of contraception, "the rules should be, as most people now agree, more flexible." What most people may agree may reflect the ethos of the permissive society, but it must not be advanced as theological argument, and Mr. Hollis's first principle is baseless. Some commandments *are* absolute with the result that we are bound to keep them every minute of the day and night . . . e.g., thou shalt not commit adultery, thou shalt not covet . . . and such are those which deal with acts intrinsically evil. His principle reflected the type of ethics to which Fr. John Coventry subjected us in his letter to *The Times* on August 13, 1968—the Pope has "reaffirmed a moral imperative" but "an imperative is not a rigid rule governing all possible cases . . . our moral decisions cannot simply be deduced from such universal rules," which, amazingly, the *Catholic Herald* classed as "not inconsistent with the encyclical." Fr. Coventry wrote this in the spirit of the paper on *Christian Conscience* which he contributed to *The*

Heythrop Journal in April, 1966, casting doubt on the possibility of universal moral principles and suggesting the impossibility of any action's being intrinsically wrong. *Pace* the *Catholic Herald*, this teaching—moral anarchy resprayed and marketed on the situation-ethics counter—is not only inconsistent with *Humanae Vitae* but is destructive of all Christian morality.

Fr. Coventry's *Times* letter unhappily proposed a second fallacy which had already been sponsored in Vatican II by Patriarch Maximos IV Sayegh of Antioch when he declared: "The faithful find themselves driven to live in breach of the law of the Church, far from the sacraments . . . for want of being able to find the viable solution between two contradictory imperatives: conscience and normal conjugal life." Fr. Coventry's version was "But there are many imperatives in marriage . . . they will sometimes be seen to conflict." The first comment to be made is that it is a sad day when a Patriarch classes contraception as "normal conjugal life," and the second must be a denial that there can ever be a conflict between two *moral* imperatives since God's laws never involve a contradiction. Obeying God's law by refusing to do what is intrinsically wrong may involve physical, social and emotional difficulties, but these would never justify one in breaking the law; even the best of ends does not justify a sinful means. It is in fact a *suggestio falsi* to speak as if moral duties ever came into conflict, making sin permissible; a bit of honest thinking always reveals that there is only one real imperative and that the conflict is imagined. Loyalty to God and His commandments, of course, inevitably involves the cross but, for adults, the only way to heaven is the way of the cross.

The "presents-an-ideal" line of escape proved, however, more popular than the 'pick-the-imperative' hatch, not only in this country but throughout the world, but it was scouted by Charles Davis with this comment: "Openly to grant such freedom of conscience . . . would nullify the purpose of the encyclical."[5] Another, minor, attempt at minimising

---

[5] *The Observer,* August 11, 1968.

appeared in Fr. M. Richards' letter: "The avoidance of artificial birth control cannot be the touchstone of Catholic
morality," and Bishop Worlock's pastoral—"it is scarcely
the acid test of being for Christ or against him." Both laid
a false scent with their definite article, one before 'touch-
stone' and the other before 'acid test'. No one had suggested
that contraception was *the* test but now it was insinuated that
it could not be 'a', because it was not 'the', test. Every
grave obligation is in fact a touchstone, and the encyclical
gave in advance the answer to all such attempts to water
down: "To diminish in no way the saving teaching of Christ
constitutes an eminent form of charity towards souls."

VENIAL SIN OR DISORDER & THE LESSER OF TWO EVILS

The bishops of England and Wales had shown themselves to be a house divided against itself. It was not true
that, as Canon Drinkwater asserted, Pope Paul "left it to
the various national episcopates to fit the principle to the
concrete situations,"[6] but some hierarchies proceeded to
do so, if burying the principle qualifies. The Austrian bishops denied in September that those who used contraceptive
pills needed to confess it, as "the Holy Father did not define
the usage of the pill as a mortal sin." Yet Paul VI had
neither directly nor indirectly 'demoted' contraception to
venial sin. In addition to facing up to the passages quoted
from the encyclical, we must recognise that the Pope stated
that the Church has always provided a "coherent teaching,"
appended a footnote reference to *Casti Connubii*, which was
explicit about the seriousness of the sin, and to Pius XII's
address with its famous words: "no alleged 'indication' or
need can convert an intrinsically immoral act into a moral
and lawful one. This precept is as valid today as it was
yesterday, and it will be the same tomorrow and always. . . ."
(The English hierarchy quoted these words in the statement
of May, 1964.) Later, he objected that the Commission's
Majority Report—which Mr. Paul Johnson hailed with the

---

[6] *The Tablet*, August 11, 1968.

cry "The Roman Catholic has finally turned Protestant!"[7]—
had departed "from the moral teaching proposed with constant firmness by the teaching authority." Yet once more,
he told married couples that they must obey the "constant
teaching" and gave a reference to Vatican II's *Gaudium et
Spes* with its categorical "must" and "may not." In the
next section we heard again of "constant doctrine" and were
referred as before to Pius XI and Pius XII. Later again, the
Pope recalled that the Church had frequently declared direct
sterilisation sinful and told us that any contraceptive act
was similarly ruled out, pinning the inevitable reference to
Casti Connubii and Pius XII. The burden of *Humanae Vitae*
is, therefore, the "constant teaching" given in *Casti Connubii*,
and, if any further evidence of the 'mind' of Paul VI is required, one has only to read Fr. R. M. Wiltgen's *The Rhine
Flows into the Tiber*, pp. 268-272, and learn how the Pope
personally saw to it that, in spite of the disobedience and
evasion which he met in the process, references to *Casti
Connubii* and Pius XII's address were incorporated in
Gaudium et Spes.

What the defusers are in practice arguing is "Don't be
fooled by smooth talk about 'constant teaching' or by references to Pius XI and Pius XII. The Pope is downgrading
contraception to venial sin, but is an indecisive Hamlet-
figure who lacks the courage to speak out loud and clear.
Read between the lines and you'll see what is meant by the
omission *in* the lines—he has dropped the idea of this being
mortal sin." Put thus in its nakedness, the suggestion is an
insult to his integrity and bears the hall-marks of a desperate
attempt to wrest victory from defeat. The honest reaction
was expressed in the headline with which the *Catholic Herald*
announced the encyclical on August 2nd: AN ABSOLUTE
'NO CHANGE' DECISION.

We have seen the "two imperatives" line of attack on
traditional teaching raised in Vatican II and in *The Times*.
In November, the French bishops met at Lourdes and came
out with a variation of it in a document which had seen ten

[7] *New Statesman,* April 28, 1967.

drafts and 700 amendments. They were of opinion that "contraception can never be a good thing. It is always a disorder but this disorder is not always sinful." It was the lesser of two evils, the bishops held, for the individual who finds himself in a "real conflict of duties," his duty to obey the Church's teaching, and his duty to maintain a harmonious married life. They recalled "the constant moral teaching: when one faces a choice of duties, where one cannot avoid an evil whatever the decision may be, traditional wisdom requires that one seek before God to find which is the greater duty." Not only had they bypassed Pope Paul's words about "always illicit" but they had circumnavigated his warning that "one cannot invoke as valid reasons the lesser evil." Their whole statement brings to mind our warning about the tendency of northern Europeans to distil moonshine theology, since the good men had proposed a simple error as constant teaching. They spoke of occasions "where one cannot avoid an evil," which is to class moral, social, physical and economic evils on much the same plane. *There is no occasion where one cannot avoid moral evil,* and no other evil must be set in the balance against it; to do so is to turn one's back on the Redemption. "Traditional wisdom," they said, "requires that one seek . . . to find which is the greater duty," and that is true in the sense that the greater duty is of obedience to God, to avoid sin, and one *can* avoid sin, come hell or high water. "Constant moral teaching" cannot depart from Romans 3:8.

We note here that Mr. Hugh Kay had raised, as far back as 1961, the lesser-of-two-evils solution in a tentative way, asking if one could not do moral evil to avoid social or physical (though not in those blunt terms),[8] and that, in June, 1968, Fr. F. X. Murphy, C.S.S.R., had tried to hallow a right to choose moral evil "as in keeping with an age-old practice of the Church,"[9] to be told by Mgr. L. L. McReavy, a noted moral theologian: "I know of no responsible moral theologian who holds that one may ever do an act which

[8] *Catholic Herald,* May 1, 1961.
[9] *The Tablet,* June 29, 1968.

one's conscience declares to be sinful. . . . A moral evil may never be deliberately done, that good, or the lessening of evil, may come of it." Traditional teaching allows *toleration* of evil, in certain pressing circumstances, but never its *commission*.

Bishop Boillon, acting as spokesman for the French hierarchy, explained the bishops' line. He drew upon his experience, which he magnified into a 'dilemma', as a member of the French resistance. "I killed four Germans," he said, ". . . but I did not consider it a sin to kill because I faced a conflict of duty . . . Killing those Germans was an evil but not a sin." By this he justified the idea that contraception may be sinless and no bar to the sacraments, but the catch is obvious. The Church does not teach that killing in a just war is sinful, but she has always taught that contraception is inherently sinful. There was no dilemma of choosing between two moral evils, picking the unavoidable smaller sin. Killing did in fact happen to be the good man's duty. If the French bishops deny the Church's teaching, that is honest enough, and *The Observer's* headline reduced their statement to such blank rejection—"Birth control evil, but not a sin"—but they must not bury the issue under sophistry.

MORTON'S FORK & PAPAL PRONOUNCEMENTS, 1964-1968

When *Humanae Vitae* appeared, *The Daily Telegraph* columnist 'Peter Simple' asked, "Can the Vatican in some sense have fallen into a trap set for it by liberals, progressivists. . . . ? After raising an intolerable uproar about contraception in the knowledge that the Pope could not possibly pronounce otherwise than he did, these people are now gleefully extracting the utmost possible advantage. . . ." One doubts if the writer meant the idea of a calculated trap to be taken seriously, but we can see that the reconsideration of the morality of contraception *acted* as a trap. The very fact that the Holy See agreed to consider was bound to make some think that change was possible, whatever warnings authority issued in the interval.

The Pope had, indeed, been confronted with a modern version of Morton's Fork. If he had refused to let the modern world have its say, he would have been accused of closing his mind to modern thought and scientific discovery. When he agreed to reconsider, it was at once put out that traditional teaching was now of doubtful binding force.

Was Peter Simple correct in saying that the Pope could not possibly pronounce otherwise? As we shall see, he himself asserted so, and support can be found in unexpected quarters. Dr. Schillebeeckx wrote in 1963: "It is unthinkable that in such an important question of daily life the Church could err in its solemn teaching",[10] while John T. Noonan had written of the great authority of *Casti Connubii*, in *Contraception: A History of Its Treatment by Catholic Theologians and Canonists*, considering that, by standard theological criteria, the condemnation of contraception was infallibly proclaimed. Considerations of this kind, too, drove Dr. Küng to demolish and rebuild 'infallibility.'

Let us now look at the facts which should have kept Catholic ranks solid from 1964 to 1968. Vatican II decided on November 20, 1964, by 1,592 votes to 427, to reserve the decisions on marriage morality to the Pope. Pope John had himself withdrawn the matter from the Council agenda before this and Pope Paul was his unlucky legatee.

During the following years, the Pope spoke out at intervals. He announced in June, 1964: "so far we have no sufficient motive to regard as superseded or not compulsory the rules outlined by Pope Pius XII. . . ." Clear enough; he had found the case for change unconvincing. Yet this was passed over by many in favour of the next sentence, which, from the point of view of public relations, was disastrously worded, and, human beings being what they are, was bound to be interpreted by many in a sense opposed to the Pope's conviction. . . . "Therefore, they must be considered valid at least until such time as we may conscientiously feel

---

[10] Cf. *Herder Correspondence*, September-October, 1966.

obliged to change them." The next sentence was gently phrased but it should have brought Independents to heel: nobody was for the time being to "make pronouncements in terms that differ from the existing rule," and yet, even there, it was only natural if people saw traces of 'wobble' in "for the time being." The inevitable result was that many acclaimed the possible loopholes to the detriment of the pronouncement's structure which consisted of (1) The arguments against traditional belief are in my eyes without weight; (2) the Church's rule must still be considered valid; and (3) nobody must make a pronouncement in a contrary sense. Those who turned the declaration against the Pope's "manifest mind and will" did not see that they had been told not to pre-judge the issue, and that to deduce that the teaching could be changed was precisely to pre-judge. If there was doubt in their minds about the Pope's meaning, they had only to listen to his following utterances.

Early in 1965, the Pope rebuked "those who throw doubts on, or deny, the validity of the Church's traditional teachings so as to invent an untenable theology," and, though the marriage issue was not mentioned, the principle obviously applied.

Later that year, in his address to the General Assembly of the United Nations, he counselled with an imbedded condemnation: "You must . . . not favour an artificial control of births, which would be irrational. . . ."

He addressed the Italian Society of Obstetricians on October 29, 1966, and his words rang through the Church. The Church, he said, was in a "state of reflection, not of doubt." How clear that was for those who faced it squarely! "The mind and rule of the Church have not altered," he added, insisting that the rule bound Catholics. In view of this, can we not say, without breach of charity, that any priest or bishop who taught otherwise was rebelling against Petrine authority?

The encyclical *Populorum Progressio* appeared in March, 1967, and stress was laid upon God's law authentically interpreted, with a footnote referring the reader to *Gaudium et Spes*, Pius XI and Pius XII. The Pope drove in a final nail in September when addressing the General Chapter of the Redemptorists, ruling out any possibility of chameleon morality: "Never let it happen that the Christian faithful be led to another opinion, as if . . . certain things were now permissible which the Church declared intrinsically evil."

NO SMALL SIN?

Pope Clement wrote to the Corinthians, "If some do not obey what God has said by us, let them know that they will be involved in no small sin and danger." One wonders how often he was forced to repeat it. In any case, Pope Paul, we have seen, raised his voice in warning six times between 1964 and 1968, but a section of the Catholic community had developed immunity. He warned in 1964 against any contradiction of the standing doctrine and rebuked in 1965 those who threw doubts on, far less denied, it. Yet, early in 1965, appeared the symposium *Contraception and Holiness*, the work of ten Catholics who must at least have heard the warning of June, 1964. By April, 1965, Rosemary Haughton was confident that the searching study in progress "will inevitably modify previous thinking on birth control,"[11] while, in November, she told a meeting: "We cannot say with certainty that what *seemed* (italics mine) to be the teaching of the Church some time ago will be the teaching of the Church forever . . . the matter is far from clear."[12] On December 5, *The Sunday Times* divulged that Archbishop Roberts, S.J., was convinced that he was on the winning side and that he felt free to give guidance according to his own conscience. The following week that same paper carried an article by Dr. Küng which spoke of "an urgently necessary Papal decision in favour of birth control." These last three utterances were all made close on the heels of the Pope's address to the United Nations, and drove home that progressive Catholics seemed to have grown incapable of listening; their certainties were utterly unrelated to the realities of the situation. It was the hour of Dr. Strabismus,

[11] *Duckett's Register,* April, 1965.
[12] *Scottish Catholic Herald,* November 19, 1965.

and the world in truth was turning madder than Beach-comberland . . . in America a seven-year-old-boy, born deaf and dumb, sued two doctors for allowing him to be born. His lawyer claimed that "every person has the right not to be born."[13]

Populorum Progressio was published in March, 1967 . . . and *The Tablet* of May 20, 1967 bore a report that the 'pill' was now in common use in Ireland, as "the papal pronounce-ment has been anticipated." August saw the Canadian Hierarchy's centenary congress in Toronto, at which Fr. Bernard Häring alleged that science made nonsense of the Church's teaching, and Dr. Schillebeeckx contradicted the Pope, affirming that the Church was in doubt, and "When the Church is in doubt, the laity may have important messages for us."[14]

A few weeks later, Pope Paul spoke his lapidary words to the Redemptorist Chapter: "Never let it happen. . . ." Alas, it happened in less than a month, for Dr. Enda Mc-Donagh, professor of moral theology at Maynooth, said on television that the Church could not clarify its mind, and that priests could tell a couple that "they could use another effective means of contraception for the moment."[15]

THE SUPREMACY OF INTELLECT

Some had patently forgotten the *raison d'être* of the papacy and were backing intellect against the papal charism. Fr. N. Lash expressed the idea as follows: "Most intellectual Catholics have already solved the problem. It remains a problem for people who haven't got the equipment—or the arrogance, if you like—to solve it for themselves,"[16] while Fr. F. X. Murphy wrote of those who "feel that most of the Church's intelligent and conscientious thinkers have already settled the issue,"[17] and Dom Sebastian Moore affirmed that

[13] *Daily Record,* October 25, 1966.
[14] *Catholic Herald,* September 1, 1967.
[15] *Herder Correspondence,* December, 1967.
[16] *The Observer,* August 4, 1968.
[17] *The Tablet,* May 11, 1968.

the fallacy involved in the encyclical had "been exposed and rejected by every Catholic thinker of any standing."[18] Seventy-six "leading" laymen added the weight of their talents to the scales in October.

Those who had settled the issue in advance, in a contrary sense to tradition, had however overlooked two factors of vital importance. First, as *The Sunday Times* stated on August 4: "They forgot about Paul." To forget about Paul is to forget about Peter, and that is to dismiss Christ and His divine assistance. Secondly, they had overlooked the fallacy in the idea that cleverness gives a truer spiritual insight as to what is right and wrong, while assuming that all clever people must be vociferous and on their side. It was our Lord Who said that God revealed to little ones what He hid from the clever and self-assured. Education, especially education in a secular University atmosphere, can indeed be a source of pride and spiritual error and can dim the eye of the spirit.

Nevertheless, a qualification has to be made. It might be imagined from the foregoing that only those clergy who were arrogant—to follow Fr. Lash's thought—had begun to waver in their adherence to doctrine before July, 1968, but there was also a strong temptation for the priests who had the lovely virtue of compassion. The veto on contraception, equally with our Lord's 'No' to divorce, can cause great hardship, and, the warmer a man's heart is, the more it is moved by the plight of others. Many priests succumbed to the urge to abandon principles, especially as the principles were being challenged. We must not underestimate the pressure brought to bear when Catholic publishing houses and periodicals trumpeted anti-tradition. It resulted in an extraordinary, twilight 'certainty'. "The Holy Father is studying . . ." wrote Canon Drinkwater in April, 1968, "and the ultimate result can be expected with confidence,"[19] and then in June: "it is beyond imagination that any authority

---

[18] *The Times,* August 6, 1968.
[19] *The Universe,* April 5, 1968.

would just reiterate the former teaching."[20] It took great
fidelity for a kind-hearted priest to adhere to Rome, and, if
compassion shook a man's steadfastness and he sold the pass,
how hard for him to retract! If one has even a minimal
vestige of pride, it is difficult to admit to one's flock that
one has been a blind leader, albeit blinded by tears.

THE HEART OF THE MATTER

Herder Correspondence, commenting on Pope Paul's
insistence that every marriage act must remain open to the
transmission of life, expostulated: "What is remarkable about
this passage is its reliance upon mere assertion rather than
reasoned argument when dealing with a question which does
not seem to be in any way dependent upon revelation but is
merely a matter of the natural law—as the encyclical states
in §11 quoted above and as it recognises when earlier it
stresses the competence of the Church's teaching authority
'to interpret even the natural moral law.' "[21] I cite this remark regarding independence of revelation—'merely a matter
of the natural law—as the encyclical states' as startling evidence of the way in which anger blinds. Far from advancing
natural law without benefit of revelation, the pope stressed
early in the encyclical that the Church's teaching was "founded on the natural law, illuminated and enriched by divine
Revelation." He went on to say that the problem of birth
had to be considered in the light not only of man's "natural
and earthly, but also his supernatural and eternal vocation,"
and later proclaimed that the Church taught "with humble
firmness the *entire* moral law, both natural *and* evangelical,"
drawing attention to the limitations of her freedom in the
matter: "Of such laws the Church was not the author, nor
consequently can she be their arbiter; she is only their de-
pository and their interpreter. . . ." Later again, he under-
lined that Christ's law was "that law proper to a human life
restored to its original truth and conducted by the Spirit of

---

[20] *The Tablet,* June 1, 1968.
[21] *Herder Correspondence,* September, 1968.

God." If there is one thing certain, it is that Pope Paul did not base his teaching on naked natural law.

Let us go back for a moment to Chapter 19, verses 2 to 10, of St. Matthew's Gospel. Christ has dismayed His apostles by ruling out divorce, and they come up with a splendid argument against what must have seemed unfeeling teaching devoid of compassion, since a bar on divorce can result in so much unhappiness. "Why then did Moses allow divorce?" they ask. The interesting thing is that our Lord turns the tables—it is not His heart that is hard but theirs that are. "By reason of the hardness of your heart," He retorts. He is not lacking in compassion as He closes the door on divorce; it was failure in true humanity which opened it. And He does not give them a convincing explanation why God will not have divorce; instead, He makes a laconic, definitive statement: "From the beginning it was not so." That, He says, is not how men were designed to behave, that is a failure in true humanity. He gives them the correct way of viewing man's nature, the angle of God. Now anyone who has lived into middle age could point out a dozen cases where compassion seems to cry out that divorce be allowed. Equally, one who followed, some years back, the *Saturday Evening Post's* investigation into what divorce has done to hundreds of thousands of American children would not be stuck for an argument against *all* divorce. Who is to decide the truth as arguments are tossed from one side to the other? God. Our Lord gave us no argument since arguments do not convince all; He cut across argument, telling us how we must look at man's nature and duty. And that is how the Church has looked at them ever since. On this matter of divorce, we have "the natural law, illuminated and enriched by divine revelation."

That scene in St. Matthew's Gospel was recalled when I quoted above Pope Paul's words that Christ's teaching on marriage was "that law proper to a human life restored to its original truth and conducted by the Spirit of God." This is true of the Church's teaching on contraception as it is of her marriage teaching in general. Just as the apostles could have argued that our Lord's ban on divorce was deaf to the cry of human need, so one can bring forward this line of 'argument' against the teaching on contraception. *And in neither case, if we rely only on reason, without benefit of revelation, can a completely convincing answer be given.* (Which, no doubt, is why the attack on the Church's teaching on birth control is being accompanied by a sally against her teaching on divorce.) The Minority report of the papal commission said with common-sense: "If we could bring forward arguments which are clear and cogent based on reason alone, it would not be necessary for our commission to exist, nor would the present state of affairs exist in the Church. . . ." It could have added that, if overwhelming arguments from reason were forthcoming *against* tradition, the crisis would not have come about.

Man's reasoning powers are limited, his judgments often unconsciously biased, and Pius XI warned us, in *Casti Connubii*, of the special danger of error in marriage matters "where the inordinate desire for pleasure can attack frail human nature and easily deceive it. . . ." But it has to be replied to those who describe themselves as unconvinced by the encyclical's arguments, that it does not really advance an argument, except from tradition, which is not a proof from the inner nature of things. *Humanae Vitae* gives an *answer,* and here we should focus on two key-points of an article by Fr. F. X. Murphy, champion of contraception, which appeared before the Pope broadcast his verdict.[22] He wrote: (1) "What seems obvious . . . is that the issue cannot be solved by logical argument alone;" (2) "What the Catholic people and the world want is a clear statement." The Pope's crystal-clear statement cut through the endless argument, but, alas, it was greeted by Fr. Häring with a shout of "Rescue the Pope!",[23] by Rosemary Haughton with a cry of "Nightmare!",[24] while Mr. St. John-Stevas was left wondering why he and the "poor old heretical and schismatical

---

[22] *The Tablet,* May 11, 1968.
[23] *The Tablet,* August 31, 1968.
[24] Cf. *Catholic Herald,* August 2, 1968.

Church of England" were right while "the Spirit-guided Universal Church" was wrong.[25]

Humanae Vitae gives the answer by laying down the true viewpoint on marriage, together with observations about the fact that God has given man only limited right over his body. This is Christ's revelation passed down under the guidance of the Holy Spirit of which Mr. Stevas spoke. Here we interject a reminder that *man* cannot make Solomon-judgments on sex. Mr. Donald Nichol of University College, Keele, put this tellingly: "As I listened to advanced Catholics . . . I couldn't help thinking that, in spite of all their claims, they don't know the first thing about sex. For the first thing to know about sex . . . is that it is a mystery."[26] A mystery requires revelation, and Christ has enlightened His Church.

THE UNNATURAL NATURAL

Again, we have to be wary about any argument from what is "natural." What seems natural may be highly unnatural—"From the beginning it was not so"—since our nature is wounded. When we say of a tendency, "It's only natural," it may be that we are in fact white-washing our bias to evil. In a true sense, it is natural to be selfish, to lose one's temper, to lie, and to be lecherous, and that is why our parents spent so much time correcting our natural bents. It is no exaggeration to say, then, that what is truly natural will seem to many unnatural as it will run counter to the grain of fallen nature.

The Holy Father provided us with no remorseless syllogism but, as Christ did, gave the true viewpoint. He spoke early on "of an integral vision of man and his vocation," and the mentions of natural law occur because this law is "inscribed in the very being of man and women," and is "that law proper to a human life restored to its original truth"; this is both "the human and the Christian vision of marriage." This teaching, springing from revelation, pinpoints "the objective

---

[25] *Ibidem,* August 16, 1968.
[26] Quoted by Archbishop J. Murphy, *Ibidem,* August 2, 1968.

moral order," "the design constitutive of marriage," "the will of the Author of life," "the plan of God." This is not argument as we know it. "And they were astonished at his doctrine. For he was teaching them as one having power, and not as the scribes." (Mark 1,22.) In addition, we said, the Pope drew attention to the fact that man has been given only limited rights over his body. Here again we fall back on revelation held in the amber of tradition, in face of modern Christians who advocate abortion and euthanasia. ("Keep the last bullet for your wife!" is the accepted morality of the Westerns as the Apaches hit the wagon-train.) In the first chapter of the encyclical, the Pope speaks of man's domination of nature, adding, "he tends to extend this domination to his own total being." Later we read, "Just as man does not have unlimited dominion over his body in general, so also, with particular reason, he has no such dominion over his generative faculties." God has to guide us if we are to know where the limit of our self-dominion falls, and He does so through the magisterium.

And so to the kernel of the matter. . . . Pope John taught in *Mater et Magistra* that the solution of the population problem was not to be found in expedients *which attack human life at its very source.* Pope John, be it noted, did not advance an argument but looked at the matter in a startling way which may be new to the reader. *Contraception is outlawed because it attacks human life at its source.* Here, in fact, is the Natural Law basis for the ban, and it is a thing that you either do or do not see, being in the nature of a first principle; it is the key to the sinfulness also of abortion and infanticide. Contraception attacks human life at its source; abortion attacks it before birth, and infanticide launches an assault after birth.

It may be that this way of looking at the matter is fresh to the reader and, as it is new, he may have trouble in adopting it, but would he be certain that this was not the right way? Only a rash man would enter his private opinion in the lists against the Church's teaching strongly reaffirmed in this century by four popes and a Council. This is the belief of the Church of "Jesus Christ, yesterday, and today, and the same for ever."

WHO SHALL ASCEND . . . ?

Some claim that the teaching of *Humanae Vitae* is impossible of fulfilment and, in some circumstances, they are right. The doctrine is difficult to follow, in some settings, even for those who lead a fully Christian life and here it is that the 'impossible of fulfilment' camp have seized on a half-truth: it *is* impossible for those who lack the true conviction *and* do not lead a deeply Christian life, especially as modern society has loaded the dice against purity and some insist on playing with the dice even when they are free to avoid them. A section of the encyclical is entitled *Creating an atmosphere favourable to chastity* and it warns about the harm done by the mass media, and cries out to married people to turn to the Sacraments and persevering prayer.

"And he spoke also a parable to them, that we ought always to pray and not to faint" . . . and there we come to the nub of the matter. *That* is essential to a real Catholic life, not a glance shot at God twice a day, but substantial prayer and it is impossible to keep God's law, in a world drenched with sex, without such prayer and the penance on which the Church insists *ad humanae naturae nauseam*. There are vital questions, therefore, which we put to the Catholic who claims that the Church's teaching is too hard. . . . First, how long do you spend in prayer each day? What time do you devote to spiritual reading to counteract the pagan blast to which you are exposed? In detail—what penance do you practise? What occupies your imagination for the last hour before you retire?

This last question has special urgency because, as we said, Christians *will* play with the world's loaded dice. Some Catholics spend their evening reading novels which are pagan through and through. I heard one young Catholic girl boast in mixed company, "I flatter myself that I can read anything." Many spend their last hours before retiring watching scenes of near-nudity on television or in a cinema. They are so conditioned to this pattern that they never suspect that they have become, in St. Paul's phrase, "lovers of pleasure more than of God" (2 Tim., 3:4). They have in fact abandoned the Christian day even if they maintain the legalities of the Christian Sunday. The Church's teaching is impossible for them because they have made it so, and, when we find a priest who has been so—not brain-washed but—brain-soiled, we know that he will teach according to his own light.

Cardinal Heenan said something at the Maynooth Union Summer School in 1969 which should have shocked authority into action since he is not given to foolish exaggeration. "It is astonishing," he said, "how many young priests do not recite the Divine Office, much less say the Rosary, visit the Blessed Sacrament, or make any attempt at meditation or mental prayer. It cannot be by chance that *this neglect is worldwide.*"[27] Now that lets the cat out of the bag and explains in part why fallen nature has risen against *Humanae Vitae* and cried out against celibacy, obedience, and so much else. Let us listen now to an outsider telling us what has been the outcome. According to Mr. Malcolm Muggeridge, "The Pope's real offence was that he had impugned the only thing that was truly and inviolably sacred in our Western consumer societies—pleasure."[28]

Continually we come across evidence that God and the supernatural are being pushed into the background. Hear, for example, the teaching of Fr. Richard P. McBrien: "To be a Christian does not mean to be religious in a particular way. We are proceeding towards a time of no religion at all, men as they are now simply cannot be religious any more. . . . I suggest that Charles Davis' criticism of the Church is not nearly radical enough . . . I am not even sure that he has departed from the Church."[29]

And so it goes on. Priests and Religious throw away the armour of prayer, finally abandoning priesthood, Order

[27] *The Universe,* August 29, 1969.
[28] *The Observer* Colour Supplement, December 12, 1969.
[29] *Do we need the Church?*

or even the Church, giving a new meaning to Kipling's lines about the legionary:

> "But his shield was picked up in the heather
> And he never saw Rome any more!"

I reproduce now, in evidence, sentences from two reviews of recent books by priests, a sentence from an article written by a priest (2), and one from a published letter criticising a priest's article on the priesthood:

1. "There is scant trace of that hunger for souls that marks the real priest."
2. "In the Church there is a search for a new style of Christian life: the development of non-sectarian humanitarianism."
3. "Personal relation to God, though central, is by-passed."
4. "An article about the priesthood . . . is surely somehow defective if it does not mention God, Christ or the Mass."

Cardinal Heenan said that the neglect of prayer by young priests was world-wide, and the questions inevitably rise: what has gone wrong with our seminaries? why have the instructions laid down in *Humani Generis* regarding ecclesiastical institutions, etc., been ignored in so many places? This would seem an appropriate moment to voice concern regarding a kindred matter, and that is the suitability of those appointed to be university chaplains, since they are placed in an environment where they can do endless good or harm. Three of the British Catholic chaplains either publicly attacked *Humanae Vitae* or expressed reservations, one protesting point-blank that married couples need not confess contraception, and being obdurate that he would continue to teach so. In addition, another 'contestant' has since

been appointed assistant-chaplain and has subsequently de-
rided the magisterium in print. These priests have never
publicly retracted their views and, as far as the public knows,
they have not retracted in private either. To complain of
this will no doubt raise a cry of 'Persecution!' but even sage
non-Catholics have brushed the cry aside as inconsistent.
This is how *The Observer* editorial (August 18, 1968)
summed up: "The remarkable aspect of the controversy . . .
is not that the Catholic hierarchy has suspended priests who
have publicly disagreed with the Pope's encyclical. . . . To
criticise the Catholic Church for this . . . is to criticise the
whole historical basis of its existence. . . . Far more remarkable is the extent to which some of the Church's dignitaries
in this country are conceding the right of private dissent."

Paul VI put forward in *Humanae Vitae* the "saving
teaching of Christ," and opposition to the encyclical reduces
in bitter practice to an attack on Christ's redemptive doctrine; it is a move to return to the darkness which Jesus
dispelled. Unhappily, the saving teaching was not received
universally with the traditional "The matter is settled!" but,
by some at least, with the words of Fr. Kevin Nicholls, head
of the Education Department of Christ's College, Liverpool:
"Rome has spoken; business is wide open!"[30] If this was
only ancient history, we could gladly bury it, but the trouble
is that the 1968 attitudes hardened and persisted, so that the
Catholic Herald of January 15, 1971, reported: "today some
priests pass over admissions by penitents that they have used
contraceptives and, in fact, encourage the faithful not to
mention it." We print for the second time Bishop Butler's
words: "the Roman Church teaches that schism is a grave
sin, and that a schismatic is one who refuses to be subject
to the Roman See." This is the undeniable criterion of schism
and, by that standard, many of our priests and lay-people,
with perhaps an occasional bishop, are in schism, and yet,
if it had been suggested to them, say, twenty years ago, that

---

[30] Address to British Conference of Youth. *Edinburgh Evening News,*
July 31, 1968.

they would one day publicly contest the teaching of the Vicar of Christ and lacerate the unity of the Church's doctrine, they would have been indignant and incredulous. "Yes," said Luther, "I cannot deny it, these things often terrify me; above all when my conscience reminds me that I have destroyed the present state of the Church, so calm and peaceable under the Papacy."

7

Newman and Conscience

The claim of conscience in the end took the place of the claim of Rome.

SIR MAURICE POWICKE,
The Reformation in England, p. 107.

Freedom of conscience, in terms of freedom of thought and doctrine, was the lever used to lift the Christian idea off its hinges.

E. W. ZEEDEN, The Legacy of Luther, p. 208.

The spirit of John Henry Newman, it has been said, hovered over the second Vatican Council, as the Spirit moved over the waters at the creation. Whether that be true or not, it is remarkable how often, since the churchquake of 1968, he has been summoned from the dead and made to stand, in uncharacteristic pose, with raised glass, toasting conscience before he drinks to the Pope. It must embarrass that sensitive shade since, when he penned the now-famous words, he hesitated over their propriety. . . . "If I am obliged to bring religion into after-dinner toasts (which, indeed, does not seem quite the thing), I shall drink—to the Pope, if you please—still, to Conscience first, and to the Pope afterwards."

The wine that this abstemious saint has been asked to down since July, 1968, would run into hundreds of gallons, and, of course, it has all been to one end, to drown the Pope's authority, like Clarence, in wine. I am not sure who had the honour of playing this card first; either, I think, Bishop Butler in *The Tablet* for September 21, 1968, in his article *Con-*

science and Authority which was patently prompted by "the current dispute among us, a dispute brought to a sharp point by the encyclical *Humanae Vitae*," or Mr. John Wilkins in *The Moment of Truth* in Frontier, Autumn, 1968. It has appeared again and again since then in anti-papal argumentation, and it is about as legitimate as a fifth ace.

Bishop Butler pointed, in his article, to Newman's "defence of conscience" in the *Open Letter to the Duke of Norfolk*. "In that great work"—he said—"Newman is engaged on a double task: he is defending the Church against Gladstone's attack . . . and he is defending middle-of-the-road Catholicism against the exaggerations of neo-ultramontanism." "His treatment of conscience," the bishop advocated (and this is the urgent content of his article surfacing), "is to be commended to all who feel drawn to take sides in the current dispute. . . ."

Now what the Bishop has written about Newman's double task is true, but he misleads since he suggests that Newman's remarks about conscience are here situated in the arena of pure doctrinal or moral teaching. Nothing could be further from the truth as their setting is political and social and Newman's teaching, as given in the *Letter*, would be, "You are bound to accept the teaching of Pope Paul." One has only to hear the name of Gladstone's pamphlet, which Newman was refuting, to realise this. It was *The Vatican Decrees in their Bearing on Civil Allegiance*, brought out with a nice sense of timing on Guy Fawkes' Day, and its theme was that a Catholic's civil allegiance was now at the mercy of the Pope's whim, that 'Depose Queen Victoria or go to hell' could prove to be a Catholic dilemma. This was the context of Newman's reply; it was not papal teaching on faith or morals *versus* conscience, but hypothetical political direction from Rome in clash with private conscience and allegiance. Thus Newman wrote in his Introductory remarks: "The main question which Mr. Gladstone has started I consider to be this: Can Catholics be trustworthy subjects of the State? has not a foreign Power a hold over their consciences such that it may at any time be used to serious perplexity and injury of the civil government. . . ?" His reply was second only to his *Apologia* in its effect and Gladstone said that it was "of an intellect sharp enough to cut the diamond, and bright as the diamond which it cuts."

The passage which Bishop Butler brought to uphold conscience against the Pope was the following and, even by itself, it gives the game away: " 'The Divine Law,' says Cardinal Gousset, 'is the supreme rule of actions . . . and this law is the rule of our conduct by means of our conscience. Hence it is never lawful to go against our conscience.'. . . . Conscience is the aboriginal Vicar of Christ, a prophet in its information, a monarch in its peremptoriness, a priest in its blessings and anathemas, and, even though the eternal priesthood through the Church could cease to be, in it the sacerdotal principle would remain. . . . Did the Pope speak against conscience in the true sense of the word, he would commit a suicidal act. He would be cutting the ground from under his feet. . . . On the law of conscience and its sacredness are founded both his authority in theory and his power in fact. . . . Conscience cannot come into collision with the Church's or the Pope's infallibility. . . . *A collision between it and the Pope's authority is possible only when the Pope legislates, or gives particular orders, or the like* (italics mine). But a Pope is not infallible in his laws nor in his commands, nor in his acts of state, nor in his administration nor in his public policy. . . . Since then infallibility alone could block the exercise of conscience, and *the Pope is not infallible in that subject-matter in which conscience is of supreme authority*, no dead-lock . . . can take place between conscience and the Pope. . . . If in a particular case it (conscience) is to be taken as a sacred and sovereign monitor, its dictate, in order to prevail against the voice of the Pope, must follow upon serious thought, prayer and all available means of arriving at a right judgment on the matter in question. And further, obedience to the Pope is what is called 'in possession'; that is, the *onus probandi* of establishing a case against him lies, as in all cases of exception, on the side of conscience . . . in the fact that, after all, in extraordinary cases, the conscience of each individual is free, we have a safeguard and security, were security necessary (which is a most gratuitous supposition) that no Pope ever will be able . . . to create a false conscience for his own ends. . . . Certainly, if I am obliged to bring religion into after-dinner toasts (which, indeed, does not seem quite the thing), I shall drink—still, to Conscience first, and to the Pope afterwards."

"The very moment the Church ceases to speak, at the very point which she, that is, God who speaks by her, circumscribes the range of her teaching, then private judgment of necessity starts up; there is nothing to hinder it. . . . *A Catholic sacrifices his opinion to the Word of God, declared through his Church;* but from the nature of the case, there is nothing to hinder him having his opinion and expressing it, *whenever, and so far as, the Church, the oracle of Revelation, does not speak.* . . . I acknowledge one Pope, *iure divino*, (but) I acknowledge no other, and . . . I think it a usurpation, too wicked to be comfortably dwelt upon, when individuals use their own private judgment, in the discussion of religious questions . . . for the purpose of anathematising the private judgment of others."

In the last sentence, Newman has made it absolute that he holds by one Pope and will not listen to mini-popes, and his whole viewpoint raises a problem disconcerting to the progressive who wishes to match him against Pope Paul. The problem is that the Cardinal attributes infallibility to encyclicals, though Bishop Butler was confident—rightly, I think—that he defended middle-of-the-road Catholicism against neo-ultramontanists. "Conscience," he said, "cannot come into collision with the Church's or the Pope's infallibility." What he meant was that conscience never has a right to challenge the Church's or Pope's teaching in the field of doctrine or morals, and this is seen in the switch from 'infallibility' to 'authority' in the next sentence—"A collision . . . is possible only when the Pope legislates, or gives particular orders, or the like."

He centres therefore on the area, in line with Gladstone's attack, where collision is possible. . . . "I shall, with him, put aside for the present the Pope's prerogative of infallibility in general enunciations, whether of faith or morals, and confine myself to the consideration of his authority . . .

in matters of daily conduct, and of our duty of obedience to him." So he moves to the charges regarding civil allegiance: "I say, *till* the Pope told us to exert ourselves for his cause in a quarrel with this country, as in the time of the Armada, we need not attend to an abstract and hypothetical difficulty. . . . Again, were I actually a soldier or sailor . . . and sent to take part in a war which I could not in my conscience see to be unjust, and should the Pope suddenly bid all Catholic soldiers and sailors to retire from the service, here again, taking the advice of others, as best I could, I should not obey him."

The reader should now have a different view of the occasions on which Newman was prepared to drink that toast. Collision was possible "only when the Pope legislates, or gives particular orders. . . . Since then infallibility alone could block the exercise of conscience, and the Pope is not infallible *in that subject-matter* in which conscience is of supreme authority, no deadlock . . . can take place. . . ." If we leave aside the infallibility question for the moment, we see Newman distinguishing between two fields, that of religious teaching and that of particular dictates; only in the latter can conscience, aboriginal Vicar of Christ, clash with Peter, present Vicar of Christ. (He clarified in his *Development of Doctrine*: "The supremacy of conscience is the essence of natural religion; the supremacy of Apostle, or Pope, or Church, or Bishop is the essence of revealed. . . .")

And even in that narrow field conscience has the right to defy only under stringent conditions; the *onus probandi* falls upon it. . . . *"Prima facie* it is his bounden duty . . . to believe the Pope right. . . ." Newman had,therefore, enormous respect for papal authority when he would allow conscience to challenge the Pope, only under rigid conditions, and only in the subject-matter of practical Roman dictates, not of doctrinal or moral teaching.

Why could there not be a clash with the Pope when he acted as teacher of the Church? It was because the whole point of the papacy is to guide conscience in faith and morality, and Newman sounds like an echo of *Humanae Vitae* when he writes of "those truths which the Lawgiver has sown in our very nature." He says of the Pope: "It is his claim to come from the Divine Lawgiver, in order to elicit, protect, and enforce those truths which the Lawgiver has sown in our very nature. . . . The championship of the Moral Law and of conscience is his *raison d'être*. The fact of his mission is the answer to the complaints of those who feel the insufficiency of the natural light; and the insufficiency of that light is the justification of his mission."

". . . the sense of right and wrong, which is the first element in religion, is so delicate, so fitful, so easily puzzled, obscured, perverted, so subtle in its argumentative methods, so impressible by education, so biased by pride and passion, so unsteady in its course, that . . . this sense is at once the highest of all teachers, yet the least luminous; and the Church, the Pope, the Hierarchy are, in the Divine purpose, the supply of an urgent demand." Poor aboriginal Vicar of Christ, it was weak and needy indeed!

On an earlier page, we drew attention to the vital fact that it is not the function of a Catholic's conscience to draw up moral principles, but to work at their application, and Newman teaches exactly this: " 'Conscience,' says St. Thomas, 'is the practical judgment . . . by which we judge what *hic et nunc* is to be done. . . .' Hence conscience cannot come into direct collision with the Church's or the Pope's infallibility; which is engaged on general propositions, and in the condemnation of particular and given errors."

Elsewhere in Bishop Butler's quotation, we see Newman's distinction between the two fields. . . . "The very moment the Church ceases to speak, at the very point which she, that is, God who speaks by her, circumscribes the range of her teaching, then private judgment of necessity starts up . . . there is nothing to hinder his having his opinion . . . whenever . . . the Church, the oracle of revelation, does not speak." Within "the range of her teaching," conscience, then, must accept.

Newman, we said, appeared to attribute infallibility to encyclicals and we interpreted his view that conscience cannot come into collision with infallibility as meaning that it cannot challenge the Pope's teaching in faith or morals, giving only one support for the view. We must now give further justification. First, he separated two fields, the religious area of the Church's teaching office, and the mundane area of civil allegiance etc. He did not sub-divide the first into sectors of fallible and infallible teaching, and he was emphatic that conscience may never here challenge. He laid down in the *Apologia* his general principle: "I submit myself to those other decisions of the Holy See, theological or not . . . which waiving the question of their infallibility, on the lowest ground come to me with a claim to be accepted and obeyed." This was his general rule, but, when it was a matter of faith or morals, his *Letter* was adamant about instant acceptance: "cases may occur now and then, when our private judgment differs from what is set down in theological works, but even then it does not follow at once that our private judgment must give way, for these books are not utterances of Papal authority."

Speaking in the *Letter* of Pius IX's *Syllabus of Errors*, he assured us: "The *Syllabus*, then, is to be received with profound submission. . . .", unsigned as it was, adding, "If, indeed the Pope should ever make that anonymous compilation directly his own, then of course I should bow to it and accept it as strictly his. He might have done so; he might do so still; again, he might issue a fresh list of Propositions in addition, and pronounce them to be errors, and *I should take that condemnation to be of dogmatic authority, because I believe him appointed by his Divine Master to determine in the detail of faith and morals what is true and what is false.*" (Newman then would have been horrified by Rosemary Haughton's un-Catholic: "what is the will of God about sex? . . . the way to answer this is not to look up the opinions of dead theologians and Popes but to observe living people. . . ." *The Clergy Review*, November, 1965.) The *Syllabus* was without technical signs of infallibility; nor does Newman require, if a new list be issued to the Church by the Pope in person, that it carry such hall-marks. It is enough that the Pope is fulfilling his function as supreme teacher.

Dealing with the objection to infallibility which springs from the case of Honorius, he drew the distinction between

Honorius's two letters "written almost as private instructions" and the encyclical *Quanta cura* which is addressed to "All the Venerable Brothers, etc" and contains the condemnatory terms "reprobamus, proscribimus, atque damnamus." He says that Honorius did not "actually intend to exercise *that infallible teaching voice which is heard so distinctly in the Quanta cura*." This was, then, for Newman an infallible utterance, although many a modern theologian would be chary of calling it so. Perhaps Newman was right, perhaps wrong. But it is definite from the above that he would have considered the teaching of *Casti Connubii* and *Humanae Vitae* impregnable to private conscience, both addressed to the whole Church, the first a raising of the Church's voice "in token of her divine ambassadorship," the second issued "by virtue of the mandate entrusted to us by Christ."

Newman himself lays down in the *Letter* how we are to know when the Pope speaks infallibly: "He speaks *ex cathedra*, or infallibly, when he speaks, first, as the Universal Teacher; secondly, in the name and with the authority of the Apostles; thirdly, on a point of faith or morals; fourthly, with the purpose of binding every member of the Church to accept and believe his decision." By these criteria he held *Quanta cura* to be infallible; by the same criteria, he would consider *Humanae Vitae* infallibly true in its teaching.

Then he adds: "Another limitation is given . . . in the *Pastor Aeternus* . . . the proposition defined will be without any claim to be considered binding on the belief of Catholics, unless it is referable to the Apostolic *depositum*, through the channel either of Scripture or Tradition. . . ." But, as we saw, he maintains that "the Pope is the judge whether it is so referable or not."

Church history books reveal that, with the publication of the decree of the first Vatican Council, controversy over the scope of infallibility did not end. Dr. Ullathorne, in his pastoral of October, 1870, gave a very calm and restrained account of it, while Cardinal Manning produced another pastoral, running to two hundred pages, in which he extended the scope of papal infallibility "so as to include dogmatic facts, censures less than heresy, canonizations of saints, approbations of religious orders: all this is roundly asserted. . . ."[1] An 'Old Catholic', Dr. Schulte, brought out some pamphlets, out-manning Manning, with the purpose of making the Vatican decrees ridiculous, and it fell to Bishop Fessler, who had been the General Secretary of the Council, to echo Ullathorne and common-sense in a pamphlet, *The True and False Infallibility of the Pope*, which appeared in 1871 and laid many ridiculous ghosts. Before publishing it, he put it in the hands of Pius IX who passed it to his theologians for examination, but also had it translated into Italian that he himself might study it. The outcome was that the Pope wrote to the bishop, thanking him for "having brought out the true meaning of the dogma of Papal Infallibility," which gave the pamphlet a claim to be the most authoritative interpretation available of the Vatican decrees.

"Fessler showed that the dogma was strictly limited to questions of faith and morals, and, 'the Pope must express his intention, by virtue of his supreme teaching power, to declare this particular doctrine on faith and morals to be an integral part of the truth necessary to salvation revealed by God, and as such to be held by the whole Catholic Church; he must publish it, and so give a formal definition in the matter.' . . . Newman welcomed Fessler's pamphlet as he hoped it would see the end of 'tyrannous *ipse-dixits*'; it 'clearly proves to us that a moderation of doctrine . . . is not inconsistent with soundness of faith.' "[2]

"The burden of his (Fessler's) tract," Dom Cuthbert Butler stated, 'is the necessity of *definition*." But that does not compel the Pope to use the actual word define' as if it were an essential seal. Fessler put the terms of the Vatican decree *doctrinam de fide vel moribus definit* in his own words:—'issues his final decision that a certain doctrine is to be regarded as an essential part of the Catholic faith or of Catholic morality, and to be maintained as such by the universal Church."

---

[1] *The Vatican Council,* 1969-1970, by Dom Cuthbert Butler, p. 461.
[2] E. E. Reynolds, *Three Cardinals,* p. 220.

"Fessler's interpretation," according to Dom Cuthbert—and this may surprise some readers—"has been found by some theologians unduly *strict*; yet the Pope's commendatory letter certainly implies that he had set forth 'the true meaning' of the definition."[3]

Newman drew upon Fessler in his *Letter*, and, weighing Fessler's words and seeing the reasonable interpretation which he gave to "defines", we are in no doubt that Newman would have had stronger grounds for being convinced of the infallibility of the encyclical of 1968 than he had for that of 1864. A modern Catholic might argue that Fessler, far from being 'unduly strict' was not strict enough, and that Newman was wrong in taking encyclicals as infallible. This may be so, or perhaps the spirit which hovered over Vatican II was an inspired one. Whatever the truth, the old man—as he then was, being 74 when he wrote the *Letter*—must not be dragged to his feet to drink a spurious toast. He had sadness enough that year. His close friend, Fr. Ambrose St. John, translated Fessler's book and died on May 24, exhausted by his many labours. When an Old Boy of the Oratory School came to visit Newman shortly afterwards, he said to the visitor, "You must have something to remember him by." He went to the bookcase to pick out one of his dead friend's books and, suddenly, holding on to the bookcase, began to sob. His little group of friends was so precious because so many others misrepresented him. He is misrepresented still.

CHRIST IS LORD

Preaching in Guildford Cathedral on August 18, 1968, Bishop Butler referred to *Humanae Vitae* and then, six sentences later, told the largely non-Catholic congregation, "The rights of conscience (a conscience which has tried to instruct itself adequately) are absolute." To amplify this, we repeat Newman's words: "the supremacy of Apostle, or Pope . . . is the essence of revealed (religion)," and we can make the

[3] *Op. cit.,* p. 465.

truth clearer still if we remember what the Irish Hierarchy taught in their Lenten Pastoral of 1969. They wrote: "The Corinthians were fond of appealing to conscience against St. Paul. They took their ideas of conscience from the sophisticated pagan culture around them. St. Paul keeps saying to them that it is not conscience as such which is supreme, *but Christ the Lord.* . . . The Vatican Council repeats the same doctrine of the Lordship of Christ over conscience, and the obligation of all to form their conscience by the teaching Christ gives through the Church."

We conclude this section by adducing two more statements of profound truth. The first is from a pastoral letter written by Bishop Philbin of Down and Connor in 1968: "As Christians we have already exercised our conscience, that is our moral judgment on the larger and more fundamental question of whether we accept Christ and His Church as holding authority from God to teach. Once we have made this acceptance, we are obliged, and obliged by our conscience, to follow the authoritative guidance that comes from these sources." The second is from the American Hierarchy's *The Church in our day,* also dated 1968: "That Word speaks to us and still enlightens us in the Church of Jesus Christ which carries the double burden of human conscience and divine authority. The only sufficient norm for conscience is authority established in a person . . . the Church sees (herself) not as institution but as person since she is the Body of Jesus vivified by the Holy Spirit and present in the world."

AUTONOMOUS MAN

"Soft cheveril conscience" is the phrase used by an old woman in Shakespeare's (Fletcher's?) *Henry VIII* in regard to the conscience of Anne Bullen, cheveril being pliable kid-skin. It reminds us to retain a grain of scepticism when conscience sanctifies the sinful, and it takes us back to another age when conscience was exalted against authority, with what dire results we know. We read of the Renaissance-Reformation period that it was the age of "autonomous" man. This self-dependence was written even in the names of

the English ships—*Lion, Tiger, Revenge,* and *Dreadnought*—
while the Spanish fleet recalled the litany of the saints. It
was written again across the map of America, in Pittsburg,
Harper's Ferry, Fort William Henry, while the Spanish held
to Sacramento, Los Angeles, Santa Fe, or San Francisco.
It was this self-reliance which shattered Christendom; it is
a pointed coincidence that the 'Holbein school' portrait of
Henry VIII, standing with legs straddled, hands on hips, is
a replica of Pride in the Seven Deadly Sins as carved in
Roslin Chapel. "Conscience's rights are absolute" and what
conscience more absolute than that of a Tudor? "I alone
have acted with the purest faith," King Henry assured himself and others, in those exact words. It may be that there
is some link between this throwing-off of religious authority's
reins and the widening of man's earthly horizons with the
discovery of the New World. If so, it could explain the pattern of rebellion in our day when man is moving his frontiers
out into space. The world is wider. Man asks: are laws to
remain as narrow?

It should be added that, half-way between the Reformation and our time, there was another period of violent up-
heaval when established authority travelled by tumbril. The
intellectuals judged then that the papacy was done for. "That
had been supposed before, and would be supposed again. . . .
But in 1799, when . . . the intellectuals were still talking about
the new age of philosophy and reason, it did seem as though
there might be something in it."[4] Man's autonomy reached
its peak in 1793 when the Christian God was made to give
place to Reason. It was the hour of the degradation of Notre
Dame Cathedral. An actress of unsavoury reputation was
enthroned on the altar to personify Reason. Man was dei-
fying Man's own faculty.

In our times, we have come full circle even if we are
less histrionic, and reason in its role of conscience has been
set up on the altar that is truly Christ's. In the April, 1969,
number of *The Sower*, a contributor asked, "What, then, am
I to do if on a particular point of doctrine . . . I conclude

[4] E. E. Hales, *Revolution and Papacy*, p. 129.

that the body of bishops including the Pope, are mistaken?" and came up with no answer. *Herder Correspondence* suffered no such inhibitions—"However strong our attachment to the Church, we must always bear in mind the possibility— a purely theoretical possibility, it is to be hoped—of finding ourselves forced to leave it for much the same reasons as forced Charles Davis to his painful and lonely decision."[5]

[5] April, 1968.

8

The Antinomians

*Pope Paul asked at his weekly general audience:
"How do you explain today's pronounced tendency
to interpret the Council as a 'liberation' from moral
obligations which Christian custom had always regarded—if not, unfortunately, always observed—
as serious and binding?"*

Catholic Herald, July 23, 1971.

*Fr. Kevin Kelly, of Upholland, said he didn't like
the word (lapsing). He preferred to say 'non-
churchgoing.' 'Surely there is real Christian holiness in the lives of many non-churchgoing Catholics,' he said.*

Catholic Herald, September 22, 1972.

*This open-minded attitude (i.e., to Dr. Küng) was
followed through in the speaker's (Bishop Butler's)
belief that 'the notion was gathering strength in
the Catholic Church that ethics cannot be fixed
down to a code.' . . . . Many Catholics will wish
that this notion gathers enough strength to reach
the givers of missions and other hard-liners.*

JOAN MCGARRY, reporting in
Scottish Catholic Observer, April 9, 1971.

"Loving God," St. John wrote (1 John 5:3), "means
keeping his commandments" but the letter either reached
Corinth too late or was coldly received, since, Ronald Knox
wrote in *Enthusiasm*, "It seems clear that there were those

231

at Corinth who adopted the antinomian attitude; who
claimed that sexual purity was a Mosaic scruple which had
disappeared with the other Mosaic scruples. Christian life
was a life of the spirit, not of the body; the Christian, therefore, should be above these materialistic taboos." Those
who have read Knox's remarkable book will have registered
how often 'the antinomian attitude' in one form or another
has reappeared in the history of Christianity; it is one more
example of the "hoary old mistakes."

It was a mistake which Wesley brought opprobrium on
himself by renouncing and, when his disciple Fletcher of
Madeley published his seven volumes of *Checks to Antinomianism* to vindicate Wesley's change of outlook, he threw
a fascinating light on the ways in which the error could
cloak a multitude of sins . . . there was the highwayman who
had salved his conscience by it . . . there were the deeds
which the preachers rated as "damning sins in Turks and
Pagans, but only spots in God's children" . . . the Member
of Parliament whose book pronounced that "murder and
adultery do not hurt the pleasant children (the elect), but
even work for their good. . . . Hence, in the midst of adulteries,
murders and incests, he (God) can address me with, Thou
art all fair, my love, my undefiled; there is not a spot in
thee . . . adultery, incest and murder, shall, upon the whole,
make me holier on earth and merrier in heaven!"[1]

That member of Parliament was well advanced down the
lunatic line but antinomianism is a recurring infection. It
is pushing up just now in the Church like poppies all over
a field. It may show itself mildly in a cast of mind. I note,
for example, that Mr. T. S. Gregory, reviewing Bishop Butler's *The Theology of Vatican* II, remarked, "He is always
on the side of life and sacrament as against law and institution. . . ."[2] Or it may appear in a forgetfulness of the key
importance of obedience—when Vatican II's schema on the
Church's missionary activity was submitted to Pope Paul,
he pointed out that every requirement in a missionary had

[1] Cf. Bishop Milner, *The End of Controversy,* pp. 117-118.
[2] *The Tablet,* February 10, 1968.

been listed, except obedience.[3] Or it may burst out in hatred of any fixed system of moral precepts. "Do you imagine," Tyrrell asked Cardinal Mercier, "that the coming world will listen to a Church that has identified itself . . . with the moral standards and conceptions which the line of casuists represented by Gury have developed to their profoundly immoral consequences? Will men long be content to estimate human acts from the outside as separate atoms or entities torn from their living context in the personality that gives them their unique unclassifiable character?" Here was a first Blast of the 'Catholic' Trumpet in favour of situation ethics, and how ill-judged it was! Fr. Jean Pierre Gury, who followed the gentle St. Alphonsus, helped to root out the narrow spirit of Jansenism in moral theology, and was no ivory-tower moralist. While a professor, he kept in close touch with reality by preaching and hearing confessions, teaching catechism in villages and acting as spiritual director to priests. He knew far more about the 'living context' than Tyrrell did, but still adhered to Christ's "Sin no more!" rather than turn it into "It's no more sin."

"At the heart of the meaning of Christian obedience is the one great Commandment"—Fr. Haring is reported to have told a meeting of the Scottish 'Renewal' Movement in Glasgow—"Love each other. . . ."[4] He went on to remind his hearers that "there is nothing new in opposing legalism. . . . Maturity in the Bible means people open to the spirit. . . . We were going into a period of protests . . . And we need them to overcome the last remnants of paternalism." But "Love each other" is *not* the one great Commandment, as there is a prior command to love God, which love we prove by keeping His laws *and* loving one another. We have to be careful about the legalism and the paternalism which we oppose. Are these God's laws, the Church's authoritative laws, and the authority of the Holy Father?

Readers of the *Catholic Herald* for August 13, 1965, were met with the headline "Catholics told 'Don't be slaves

[3] *The Rhine Flows into the Tiber,* p. 257.
[4] *Scottish Catholic Observer,* July 11, 1969.

to rules' ", and it was followed by "Catholics urgently need to throw off the selfish and false security of slavishly following rules. This was the dominant note of an eight-day conference. . . . 'Standards that are compulsively imposed will not endure,' Mr. Denis Rice . . . told the conference. 'God makes man free for a purpose. . . . There is a sin-bound mentality in Catholicism.' " There is, of course, a sin-bound mentality from cover to cover of the Bible. We do not know if the Corinthians extended St. Paul the courtesy of a reply, but, if they did, Mr. Rice could have been plagiarising.

Whereas our Lord cried out that, if our eye scandalised us, we were to pluck it out, we are asked to take another view and look on evil as an indispensable nursery for spiritual growth. Rosemary Haughton, writing in *Married Love in Christian Life* (p. 59), puts it thus: "It would be a good idea if Christians were less smug about irregular sexual relationships. We should be more anxious to discover and encourage in them the seedling of good which may well be growing up among the weeds than to root up the weeds and probably pull up with them the growth of real goodness and love. It may well be that the only chance of spiritual growth for a particular person lies in a situation which is, in an objective sense, wrong." But are we smug about adultery, etc.? Pope Paul taught in *Ecclesiam Suam*: "The Gospel of Christ recognizes the existence of human infirmities. It recognizes and denounces them. . . . Yet it also understands and cures them." And what grounds are there for Mrs. Haughton's 'probably'?

We are continually being subjected today to a rigged choice between Spirit/maturity/honesty *versus* Law/obedience. "Maturity . . . means people open to the spirit," said Fr. Häring. It is at a premium today, but the drawback is that people assume that physical or intellectual maturity is interchangeable with spiritual. They would do well to ponder this extract from a sermon preached in 1927 by Fr. Charles Miel, S.J. . . . "At what moment in the destiny of the individual does the child become a man? Do you think that your manhood dates from the day when by some act of violence or rebellion, some success or other, you asserted yourself before your fellows or yourself? Nonsense! How often are such things but childish pranks. In reality, the precise moment at which we become adult is rather that in which after some personal failure, struck by the feeling of our own helplessness, we at last exclaim: 'Lord, deliver me from myself, I am only a poor, wretched man.' It is only at that moment of honest humility that childhood comes to an end. Then man has grown up."[5] Maturity is not, therefore, a question of independence, but a realisation of insufficiency and dependence, with a gratitude for the protective hedges of God's laws. Yet . . . . "Even God's laws"—wrote the late Fr. V. Rochford—". . . are not the laws of the New Covenant and may help to obscure it."[6] No comment.

Fr. F. Somerville, S.J., contributed an article on *Conscience and Law* to *The Sower* (April, 1969) of which he was editor. He assured us: "The legalism rampant in the Church is destructive of true Christian morality and conscience." He went on: "We may succeed . . . in making some students understand the necessity and usefulness of external laws. But we are under no illusions that we will convince many of them." (Was he really talking of *Catholics*?) Again: "The moralists have changed the gospel into a code and given precedence to rules over persons. The vast majority of the faithful think of the Christian life as believing certain truths, keeping the commandments and being faithful to certain religious practices, in particular 'going' to the sacraments. In contrast to this legalistic man-centred mentality our catechising is to be God-centred." How extraordinary that accepting revelation, keeping God's commandments and receiving the body of our Lord should be classed as man-centred! We get in conclusion that, if there is doubt about morality, people must seek guidance from the Church "but in the final analysis they themselves judge."

To return to Mrs. Haughton: *Herder Correspondence* (October 23, 1967) reviewed together her *On Trying to be Human* and *The Transformation of Man* and gave us this di-

---

[5] Quoted in Fr. de Lubac's *Catholicism*, p. 281.
[6] *Duckett's Register*, July, 1967.

gest: "Mrs. Haughton feels that it is a waste of time to try to 'adapt traditional theological structures to the existentialist attitudes of modern man'. The thing about modern man is that he refuses to be classified: 'He isn't modern man but just himself' . . . Herein lies the very apparent tension within the Church between 'moral principles and dogmatic formulations as worked out by former generations and the pressure of the spirit of the age—to which indeed the Vatican Council bade us pay attention. But this spirit is the Spirit of God, and it is an explosive force.' "

This, again, borders on the incredible. The permissive spirit of the age, which presses against the moral and dogmatic teaching of the Church (the Church is infallibly guided in these fields by the Holy Spirit), *is* the Spirit of God . . . or so we are asked to believe. If we are to listen to the Spirit, then, we must throw overboard our moral principles (and our hoary dogmas) and adopt an existentialist attitude.

And this attitude is at the root of much of our present trouble. The Minority Report of the Papal Commission on Birth Control picked out the way in which existentialist ethics underlied some of the arguments advanced against the traditional teaching of the Church. Referring to the commission's session of March 25th-28th, 1965, it quoted a member's axiom: "It suffices in a particular moment if the judgment on a moral matter is true 'for the moment' "—an axiom which obliterated any idea of absolute right and wrong. Later the report amplified the existentialist approach: "However, many theologians, who maintain that contraception is not intrinsically evil, seem to come to this conclusion from a more general principle: that, namely, which denies *all absolute intrinsic morality* to external human acts, in such a way that there is no human act which is so intrinsically evil that it cannot be justified because of a higher good of man. In stating this, they apply the principle that 'the end specifies the means' and that 'between two evils the lesser is to be chosen'. . . . If this principle is admitted, it would seem that more serious evils can yet be expected. . . . Thus, for example, that masturbation is for the good of personal equilibrium, or homosexuality good for those who are affected with abnormal inclinations. . . . The same could be done for the use of abortives or of abortion directly induced to save the life of the mother."

We have already seen Fr. Coventry throw doubt on absolute morality. He has returned to the attack in *How Conscience Works*,[7] and this is his line: "Surely, you may be thinking, adultery is always wrong. Well, of course it is, if 'adultery' is already a morally loaded word. If we met a defensible instance, we would not call it adultery. We need a neutral description . . . e.g., sexual intercourse between two people, one of whom is married to someone else. The moral question is then whether *that* is in every possible set of circumstances wrong. If so, how do we know?"

Mr. St. John-Stevas, to take another example, wrote under the heading *Rules are needed: but love is greater than law* that "Catholicism has been bedevilled . . . by legalism for centuries." He might have illustrated this thesis by laying a finger on some pettifogging legislation, since all systems of law score misses, but instead he picked on the irregular 'marriage', dignified as the lesser of two evils—"If less than a sacramental marriage it can clearly be more than sinful self-indulgence." "Rules," he would have it, "are necessary but . . . Love is greater than law," and he suggested that a sacrilegious Communion should be permitted in the name of love.[8] St. John-Stevas, one is forced to comment, but not St. John the Baptist or St. John Fisher! How can love be greater than God's law, when God is love?

The Minority Report feared that the existentialist principle would lead to condonation of masturbation and abortion. In *The Catholic Herald*, January 17, 1969, Dom David Bird, O.S.B., informed us that masturbation is no longer a mortal sin, and revealed later that he had been encouraged in his view by a visit to the Higher Catechetical Institute at Nijmegen in Holland. Abortion? Many were grateful to Fr. W. P. Crampton for his no-nonsense letter to *The Tablet* (November 23, 1968): "your television critic

[7] *The Month,* January, 1971.
[8] *Catholic Herald,* January 5, 1968.

Mary Crozier wrote: 'I should not have thought that today even in the most severe Catholic circles such expert medical advice would be opposed by priest or relatives.' The advice was that a pregnancy should be terminated. Here is one priest at least who would always oppose it. . . . I should have thought that Vatican II had made sufficiently clear to all Catholics its abhorrence of abortion." ("Abortion and infanticide are unspeakable crimes" taught *Gaudium et Spes* and the iron principle should silence existentialists.)

It is the Dutch, however, who have been wildest in their legal iconoclasm and their rush for maturity and grace-without-strings. The preparatory commission of the Dutch Pastoral Council recommended: "There should be no moral constraint. Thus men holding office in the Church should bear witness and not enforce rules."[9] A year later, we read the report of the Marriage and Family Committee of the Pastoral Council and their fresh approach to divorce: "Perhaps it must be said that if there is no human tie any longer, there is no sacrament . . . the bond does not exist any more if it is humanly impossible to live together in peace . . . the marriage has dissolved itself."[10]

Antinomianism had found its way into the teaching of the Dutch catechism, and the Commission of Cardinals ordered: "The text of the catechism is not to make obscure the existence of moral laws which . . . bind our conscience always and in all circumstances. Solutions of cases of conscience should be avoided which do not sufficiently attend to the indissolubility of marriage."

Time (December 9, 1966) gave a précis of an article contributed by Dutch-born Bishop Simons to *Cross Currents*. Here are excerpts: "Simons rejects Bible-based morality on the grounds that Jesus himself imposed no detailed code of behaviour, but rather gave a general injunction that man should live according to the highest standards and seek perfection through love. . . . Now, Simons believes, a consensus is developing outside the church that permits abortions when

[9] *The Tablet,* November 25, 1967.
[10] *Ibidem,* November 16, 1968.

a mother's life is in danger, birth control and even steriliza-
tion. . . . Masturbation is another act that Simons thinks
should be . . . condoned under particular circumstances. . . .
The Catholic Church's inflexibility in condemning remarriage
after divorce is also not in accord with the modern view of
human welfare."

Bishop Simons' views are shocking, and yet we must
not forget that, at the third session of the Dutch National
Pastoral Council, *all* members of the Dutch hierarchy voted
in favour of a resolution which ran: "All absolute norms for
the guidance of moral conduct must be rejected, one alone
excepted, namely 'Christ's self-giving and sacrificing love' "
while, by a majority of seven to two, the bishops approved
a resolution in these terms: "Ecclesiastical authorities should
abstain from giving definitive directions on premarital sex,
abortion, euthanasia, and other new problems, and wherever
possible should leave room for experiment."[11] Dr. Schillebeeckx described the report as a "pearl", and the assembly
adopted a motion declaring its regard for the New Catechism
without the Roman corrections. Since then, Cardinal Alfrink
has ventured to say that "the bishops feel uneasy about
legalisation of abortion," while Bishop Bluyssen maintained
that "just exceptional cases of utter emergency can make
abortion unavoidable." In contrast, that good Pope's man,
Bishop Gijsen, "called abortion in all cases downright murder."[12]

There is, then, an epidemic of antinomianism in the
Church. But is there any sign of the extreme form which
Fletcher of Madeley attributed to a Member of Parliament,
the form which sees sin as not merely neutral but even preferable? A reviewer of Rosemary Haughton's *The Transformation of Man* found in it " 'sin mysticism' . . . the implication seems to be that sin brings a man closer to God"[13] and
she writes in *On Trying to be Human*: ". . . the insistence
in the gospels on . . . the advantage of being poor and neg-

[11] See *Triumph,* February, 1969.
[12] *Catholic Herald,* June 30, 1972.
[13] *Catholic Truth,* Autumn, 1967.

lected and even sinful. . . . The poor in spirit are likely to be . . . poor, either financially or morally or both. . . . The 'publicans and harlots' will go into the Kingdom of Heaven before the well-behaved. . . . The sinners he (Jesus) associated with were not people to whom he had come to do 'good' but people whose obvious moral incompetence gave them a head start in the search for freedom on which . . . he was himself engaged. . . ." (pp. 147-148).

"Not really antinomianism," the reader may be of opinion, "but only confusion!" It may be so, but such writing can have an ill-effect among the easily-confused, especially as Geoffrey Chapman advertised Mrs. Haughton in *The Clergy Review* as "England's most discussed Catholic theologian" and in *Duckett's Register* as "England's most discussed Catholic thinker."

At the end of this section, we must ask: is antinomianism to be allowed to spread? In the guide-lines laid down for the teaching of religion in the fortunate Baltimore province and archdiocese of Washington, one reads: "The teacher must impress upon his students that there are objective unchanging moral principles. . . ." Yet, if we turn to Dom Peter Flood's review[14] of *Morals, Law and Authority* (edited by J. P. Mackey), a symposium whose authors are mainly teaching in seminaries, we hear of one contributor: "He is terrified at the possibility of finding any positive law in the teaching of Jesus or even in the Decalogue . . . he lectures the Church as a teacher of morals . . . 'the Church must never consider herself as a last bulwark against a permissive society . . . she must as a teacher propose rather than impose.' " We are told of another contributor: "Later he says, 'appeal to authority is never sufficient justification for a moral judgment,' " and Dom Peter demands, "Is he so sure that this is so in the case of all authority? What about the Decalogue? The article shows no cognizance of the authority of the Supreme Pontiff reaffirmed by Vatican II."

What about the Decalogue? Dom Peter's question rings through the Church.

---

[14] *Catholic Herald,* October 10, 1969.

9

In Other Words

*I must not be supposed to be forgetful of the sacred
and imperative duty of preserving with religious
exactness all those theological terms which are
ecclesiastically recognised as portions of dogmatic
statements, such as* Trinity, Person, Consubstan-
tial, Nature, Transubstantiation, Sacrament. . . .
*In this curious sceptical world, such sensitiveness
is the only human means by which the treasure of
faith can be kept inviolate.*

> JOHN HENRY NEWMAN,
> On Consulting the Faithful.

*Professor T. F. Torrance, of the Church of Scot-
land, is reported as saying, concerning the recent
Brussels Theological Conference: "I was fascinated,
astounded and horrified to find Roman theologians
lapsing back so easily and rapidly into bad Protestantism."*

> Cf. Catholic Herald, July 14, 1972.

Pope John announced the conservative purpose of Vatican II on its first day: "The greatest concern . . . is . . . that
the sacred deposit of Christian doctrine should be taught
and taught more efficaciously". He spoke of our "renewed,
serene and tranquil adherence to all the teaching of the
Church . . . as it still shines forth in the acts of the Council
of Trent and the first Vatican Council," and looked to further
"doctrinal penetration . . . in . . . perfect conformity to the

241

authentic doctrine," which, however, "should be studied and expounded through the methods of research and through the literary forms of modern thought." "The substance of the ancient doctrine," he explained, "is one thing. The way in which it is presented is another."

It was the last section which unleashed the dogs of war. "Perfect conformity" was forgotten, and "modern thought" mounted the rostrum forbidden it by *Humani Generis*. The result has been that his alarmed successor deplores "the appearance . . . of the works of some teachers and writers who aim at expressing Catholic doctrine in new ways . . . but who, in fact, would often adapt the dogmas of faith to secular thought and language rather than follow the norms of the Church's magisterium."[1] Some might comment that Pope John was simply asking for trouble when he spoke in that way; perhaps, but it was Pope Paul who inherited the trouble. What precisely did Pope John have in mind when he encouraged the 'literary forms of modern thought'? I think it unlikely that he had anything precise in mind, just as, I am sure, the dear old Scottish archbishop who used to tell his priests. "The hour is now come when we must sweep forward to victory!" had drawn up no plan of campaign. In the same way, Pope John had no idea of what his General Council would involve or how long it would last. All that he had in mind in regard to 'literary forms' is, probably, that we must 'get it across' to our contemporaries. We might arrive at the modest truth if we mark that Pope Paul, in *Ecclesiam Suam*, wrote of the encyclicals of Pius XI and Pius XII: "Providentially they strove to bridge . . . the gap between divine and human wisdom, using not the language of the textbook, but the ordinary language of contemporary speech." Pope John wrote in much the same way as had the two Popes mentioned, and so *Ecclesiam Suam* continues: "As for our immediate predecessor, John XXIII, he laboured with masterly assurance to bring divine truths as far as may be within the reach of the . . . understanding of modern man." Later we read: "All of us who feel the spur of the

[1] Cf. *Herder Correspondence,* November, 1967.

apostolate should examine closely the kind of speech we use. Is it easy to understand? Can it be grasped by ordinary people? Is it the currrent idiom?" I think that, if we ruminate on this, we will come up with the conclusion that all that Pope John was saying came to: "Be faithful to our doctrine, and put it clearly as we Popes do!"

Perhaps there is a touch there of Johannine saintly simplicity. Certainly, many would smile at the idea that encyclicals were trendy and modern in style. They might hint darkly at elements of the Baroque, Byzantine or at least Pontifical . . . and yet, pick up *Casti Connubii, Humani Generis* or *Populorum Progressio* and see how clear they are!

Now the paradoxical thing is that it is those who have tried to stretch the papal recommendation into something quite different who are the worst offenders against simplicity and clarity. "Is it easy to understand? Can it be grasped by ordinary people?"—asked the Pope, and the answer is a mystified negative. Fr. N. Lash, if I remember rightly, when reviewing a book by Dom Sebastian Moore, admitted that the author was at times unintelligible, while Dom Christopher Delaney, reviewing Fr. Lash's *His Presence in the World*,[2] warned: "it is not easy reading in places. Take for instance the following passage: 'In other words, to deny the necessity, and indeed the centrality, of that sacramental actualisation of the Church which is the Eucharistic assembly is seriously to over-eschatologise our present situation.' Oh, dear!"

Dr. Schillebeeckx's *Christ the Sacrament* was a bestseller, but people did not buy the book on its merits; it is almost unreadable. Fr. Karl Rahner is a far saner theologian than Dr. Schillebeeckx but, nevertheless, Fr. Schoof remarks in *Breakthrough* (p. 130)—"Not all Rahner's fellow theologians have been equally impressed by the metaphysical power of the more obscure passages. . . ."

We referred previously to one aspect of the matter, quoting the dictum: "No one can equal Saint Thomas in clearness and simplicity, because he thoroughly understood what he was writing about; and above all because he be-

[2] *Catholic Herald*, April 19, 1968.

lieved." An author's trouble in understanding or, at times, his aberration of belief, are reflected in what he sets down. Here, as a sample, is Rosemary Haughton throwing light on the Gospel: ". . . we cannot even ask the Lord to have mercy on us because, being our conscious self, he is incapable of mercy. He is merely just. So at the end of the road that began with the search for man we find ourselves face to face with the devil. The devil, as a phenomenon of human life, is the dark, untameable area of unconscious life, but only *in so far as we are opposed to it* in our efforts to distinguish and discover ourselves."[3]

Mrs. Haughton, if I may give further illustration, writes of our Lord's words about eating His flesh and drinking His blood, and sets out to make His meaning clear in her own words since the original terms have lost their value "through the inevitable historical process of distortion brought about by the sustained though generally unconscious hypocrisy of religious people." She piles line upon line, the plain meaning never appearing, but does say, fairly: "It is hardly surprising that the Jews found this hard to swallow, in every sense."[4] She had written, a few pages before, that there was in the 'Roman Church' "exclusive emphasis on obedience, at the expense of personal honesty." What the poor old Church does, however, is to inculcate obedience, insist categorically on personal honesty, disallowing any appeal to situation ethics . . . and beg piteously for clarity . . . 'Let there be *light*!'

THE SAME LANGUAGE

The Popes have asked us to teach unchanged doctrine in understandable speech. Some writers are serving up pretentious obscurity, and we saw in earlier chapters the campaign to destroy traditional belief. The Pope has become alert to the danger in the search for "the literary forms of modern thought," and has extolled the dogmatic attitude which "does not allow ambiguity . . . and that guarantees . . .

[3] *On Trying to be Human,* p. 159.
[4] *Ibidem,* pp. 131-133.

the same truth . . . *the same language*, that of yesterday, today and tomorrow."[5] He was not urging us to bore people to death with Ciceronian prose but stressed the *sine-qua-non* character of the 'mots justes'. Three years later, he struck the required balance again: we were not bound to "a particular verbal expression," but "the dogmatic forms might be so intimately tied to their contents that each change either hides or provokes an alteration of the contents themselves."

Doctrine will develop, since it is living truth, but the use of established terms will be crucial, and re-expression must be viewed with the same caution as reinterpretation since it may *be* that. We are puzzled when, for example, Fr. N. Lash tells us in his essay *Dogmas and Doctrinal Progress*[6] that the dogma of the Assumption must be defined quite differently in other cultural circumstances. The dogma states a historical fact, that our Lady was taken up, body and soul, to God's presence. The Byzantine Father St. John Damascene, living twelve hundred years ago, in vastly differing cultural circumstances, wrote as most of us would happily today: "Raised, carried up to heaven above all the choirs of angels, Mary holds her place beside her Son." Fr. Lash's view makes no more sense than would a cry that the victory of William of Normandy in 1066 must be defined differently in our technological age. Again. Fr. Corbishley raises uneasiness about possible reinterpretation when he speaks of the doctrine of the Assumption as an "abstract, metaphysical doctrine."[7] Nothing could be more factual. *Veritas manet. . . .*

THE ENCYCLICALS

Now let us see what has been laid down in the encyclicals, how they are being disregarded, and, finally, what can happen as a result.

Pius XII, *Humani Generis*: "To be sure, all are agreed that the terms representing certain ideas, however much they may have been used in the schools, and even in the authori-

[5] *The Tablet,* August 14, 1965.
[6] *Doctrinal Development and Christian Unity,* pp. 21-22.
[7] *Catholic Herald,* October 31, 1969.

tative teaching of the Church, are nevertheless susceptible of further perfecting and polishing. . . . But the framework which has been built up, over a course of centuries . . . cannot be dismissed as resting on a flimsy foundation. . . . Are we to substitute for them guesswork of our own, vague and impermanent fashions of speech, borrowed from our up-to-date philosophies, which today live, and will feed the oven tomorrow? That were indeed the height of imprudence, the whole of dogma would thus become no better than a reed shaken in the wind."

Humani Generis was studiously ignored by many, and the result was reinforced teaching in *Mysterium Fidei*, fifteen years later: "This rule of speech has been introduced by the Church in the long work of centuries with the protection of the Holy Spirit. She has confirmed it with the authority of the Councils. It has become more than once the token and standard of orthodox faith. *It must be observed religiously.* No one may presume to alter it at will, or on the pretext of new knowledge. For it would be intolerable if the dogmatic formulas, which Ecumenical Councils have employed in dealing with the mysteries of the most Holy Trinity, were to be accused of being badly attuned to the men of our day, and formulas were rashly introduced to replace them. . . . These formulas . . . express concepts which are not tied to any specified cultural system. . . . They are, therefore, within the reach of everyone at all times and in all places."

Now there is an explicit order—"Keep to the accepted terminology!"—followed by a statement that any other course of action in writing of the Trinity in particular would be intolerable, plus an explanation—the terms are 'outside time,' that is, they do not belong to a dead language or a dying language, but are an immortal vesture of thought—truth has not petrified but been kept alive in them. "Certainly time has made many Catholic formulae . . . meaningless," wrote Mrs. Haughton,[8] but it is not what Paul VI taught. Now let us see what is being said in regard to doc-

---

[8] *Catholic Herald,* August 9, 1968.

trinal formulation of the Trinity in spite of the papal "Hands off!"

Tyrrell, writing in *Christianity at the Cross-Roads*, showed awareness of the problem of the development of doctrinal understanding, referring to Vincent de Lerins and the sound Catholic view that dogma in its early and later shapes shows "the difference between the boy and the man," but he was impatient of the whole topic: "We are referred at every turn to acorns and oaks and grains of mustard seed." Newman's measured doctrine was not nearly radical enough for his disbelief. Fr. Corbishley, in our time, has picked up the wrong simile, in his article *Dogma; Truth or Futility* in *The Universe* for August 25, 1967. Doctrines, he says, develop in the way in which an acorn becomes an oak-tree, which is highly misleading since an oak-tree is not recognisable as an acorn—there is no resemblance that the eye can instantly see. He should have followed Vincent de Lerins and compared the matter to the growth of a young lad into a mature man. One looks at his photograph and says, "He's put on weight, but it's him all right!" Then the author observed: "We say that a particular dogmatic formula 'enshrines' or 'expresses' some 'revealed truth.' Now, clearly the truth is not stated in one form of words in such a way that it cannot be stated in another form." The 'clearly' is unjustified. Then, of all examples, he picked on the Trinity, in spite of *Mysterium Fidei*. But, in fairness, let it be said that he did not attempt an alternative formula and that few of those who talk about re-expressing dogmas do essay to bell the cat.

But let us listen to bolder men. We take first John Baptist Walker's *New Theology for Plain Christians*, a book in which the author concedes that "the progressive Catholic, though verbally in agreement with his conservative co-religionist, may well find he has much more in common as regards his overall understanding of Christianity with a progressive Methodist or Baptist" (p. 82). The book carries the *imprimatur* of the Franciscan Provincial, and Fr. Michael Collins's review in *Furrow* (March, 1971) recommended it without reserve, especially for "the higher classes of secondary schools where young people need to be given an adult presentation of their faith." "Once we have assured *ourselves*," Mr. (as he now is) Walker asserts, "that what we want to say about God today is all of a piece with what the fathers of Chalcedon and Nicaea were trying to say, then we need no longer worry about making use of their terminology. We can forget words like 'nature' and 'person' and plunge further forward with our discoveries about God." (p. 33) "The height of imprudence!" Pius XII dubbed this sort of talk. "Intolerable!" said Pope Paul. But, once again, the advocacy of new terms went only as far as talk. Mr. Walker did not "plunge further forward" with "discoveries about God." The line was dead.

THE SOWER

It was pretty dead also in *that* number of *The Sower*, for all the dissatisfaction expressed with the Council of Chalcedon. Theologians, we were told by the editor, "are reluctant to say 'Jesus is God' full stop because most of the faithful usually misunderstand it. . . . We believe that God is in Christ." C. G. Armstrong took up the scent . . . "the person of Jesus is too rich to be adequately described in any one formula. . . . We must not think that we have adequately described Christ by monotonously repeating that he is truly God and truly man having two natures in one person. If such a formula no longer means anything to our contemporaries we have to reformulate the doctrine . . . the teacher should reserve the term 'God' for the Father." Then J. Weldon put Chalcedon in its place: "The Council gave the right answers to the questions that were being asked in those days. . . . The trouble is that we today find it difficult to understand what the Chalcedon Fathers meant. . . . Chalcedon assumes that we know enough about the nature of God and of man to be able to assert that the two can be united in one person. Can we make this assumption? . . . . The Chalcedon definition means nothing to people today because it follows philosophical categories which are completely outmoded. . . . The meaning of nature and person as used at the time of the Council is notoriously vague." And then, God bless the even vaguer man, he repeats (without acknowledgement) J. B. Walker's mistaken idea that, for scholastics, "In man it is the nature which acts, thinks, wills, understands, is conscious." If he had only stopped to think, he would have realised that down the ages, we say, "*I* believe . . . *I* understand . . . *I* disagree," attributing action to the person, not to his nature. Then H. O'Brien knocks in some of the nails: "Many Christians are dissatisfied with the forms in which the traditional belief in the person and work of Christ is expressed. . . . He was of one substance with the Father . . . his two natures, divine and human, existed in the unity of one person. Much of this presentation, it is felt, belongs to Christian myth. . . . Moreover, the traditional teaching assumes that we already know God and already know man to be able to conceive of their unification in one person. This assumption is false. . . . Christians today must do what their forefathers at the time of Chalcedon did in their day: re-think and re-formulate the doctrine. . . . They (modern theologians) believe that God was as fully present and active in Jesus as is possible for him to be in a finite human being. This is what they mean by the divinity of Christ, without having to use the abstruse misleading word, substance."

Does all this sound negative? Have the re-interpreters no positive new theology to give us, no light in the darkness? The answer is given at the end of R. Crumlin's article, after he has taught that Christ is living, Christ is becoming, Christ is Community: "As I read back over this I am struck again by the impossibility of trying to answer unanswerables. There is no answer, there are many answers, there is one answer." And he is dissatisfied with *Chalcedon?* If Tyrrell though hard-edged Catholic dogma 'infinitely inadequate', what would he have thought of this billowing, deadly miasma?

FR. AVERY DULLES, S.J.

One man, however, does seem to have tried to reformulate. I quote from *Triumph* (March, 1970): "In *Catholic Mind* for May 1969, an article entitled 'Dogma as an Ecumenical Problem' by Avery Dulles, S.J. (reprinted from *Theological Studies*, Sept. 1968) reads in part as follows: 'Many of them (Christians today) recite the orthodox formulas with so little understanding that their thoughts may well be heretical. When the modern Christian declares that there are three divine persons, he may well have in mind the modern psychological concept of person as an autonomous subject endowed with its own consciousness, intellect and will. Such a concept, consistently followed out, would lead to tritheism. God might be regarded as Siamese triplets! *To safeguard trinitarian orthodoxy*, one might raise the question whether it would not be *preferable to call God a single person with three modes of being.*' (italics mine)."

Here was a theologian who actually tried to restate in keeping with modern thought. The writer of the letter in *Triumph*, R. L. Davis, continued: "Well! What an extraordinary solution to a questionable problem this would be. '*To safeguard trinitarian orthodoxy*,' no less, it might be 'preferable' to substitute for the orthodox formulas from Nicea to Paul VI the thought and language of the oft-condemned heretic, Sabellius! Did I say 'solution'? I should say 'dissolution.' For, as Cardinal Newman observed . . . with the Sabellian interpretation, there remains no mystery." We round off this letter by consulting Ott's *Fundamentals of Catholic Dogma*, p. 50. He relates: "Sabellius . . . taught that in God there was one Hypostasis and three Prosopa . . . corresponding to His three different modes of Revelation . . . Sabellianism . . . was authoritatively condemned by Pope Dionysius (259-286). Dz. 48-51."

To clear our mouths of the taste that all this leaves, let us end this chapter by reading some lines written by Bishop Ullathorne at the first Vatican Council. . . . "During the last three Congregations one's soul has been literally bathed in theological light. And, as a rule, the listening assembly has been very silently conscious that it was giving the last touches to decrees of Faith that could never again be changed, and that were to stand, and to which the Church must stand, all days, even to the end of the world." So wrote a great Catholic, so wrote Newman's friend.

10

Campfire Stories
&
Historical Fiction?

Fr. John Symon's answer . . . is surprising in more ways than one. . . . First, is it really a good thing to describe the Old Testament as 'a varied collection of popular campfire stories, legends . . ' ? . . . Whatever the ancient books are, surely they deserve more respect. Furthermore, is not the whole tone . . . an open invitation to 'private judgment'—that modern curse so prevalent today?

P. S. HETHERINGTON,
Catholic Herald, April 26, 1968.

Similarly the Evangelists, full of His spirit and mind, might conceivably have been inspired to reveal Him to us, not in a strictly historical narrative, but in such fact-founded fictions as would best characterise and portray His personality to those who knew it not.

FR. GEORGE TYRRELL,
Lex Orandi, Chapter XXIII.

The primary purpose of the evangelists was not to write history . . . said Fr. Thomas Hanlon, professor of Scripture at St. Andrew's College, Drygrange. . . . Fr. Hanlon said modern biblical schol-

251

ars were in general agreement that many episodes in the New Testament, as in the old, did not necessarily portray historical events. . . . Sometimes their work might be compared to historical fiction—based on fact, but with the background reconstructed to present a vivid picture.

Scottish Catholic Herald, May 22, 1964.

This chapter wil be written with far less assurance than some chapters which have preceded, first, because the writer is aware that there is discussion among orthodox scholars on the points raised, and, secondly, because he is aware how ill-equipped he is to venture into the deep waters of Scriptural scholarship. It is many a long year since he listened to Dr. T. E. Bird, in Oscott, speaking with such love of God's Scriptures, and the exegetes have learned much since then, and the present writer has had little chance to assimilate it. But perhaps this can rank as an advantage: he may speak as one of the faithful whose consciences, an admonition of the Holy Office (June, 1961) stated, were not to be disturbed by strange assertions. And he is confident that many other priests will have felt the same anxiety and uncertainty. The aim of this chapter, therefore, is not in the main to prove something and disprove its contrary, but to express anxiety, to call for guidance, and, if any light is thrown in the process, so much the better—it will be a bonus on the side.

Concern is not the monopoly of the simple faithful. Cardinal Felici, writing in *L'Osservatore Romano* (November 28, 1968), warned: "one must also respect the dignity of those who seek and follow the truth taught by the authentic Magisterium and who therefore have the right not to be needlessly exposed to the risks of contamination or to what is more like an invasion of hungry wolves, who came clothed as lambs." He exemplified: "It is for this reason that we are astonished to hear, for example, that in an institute for the formation of priests, discussions were held between the students and young priests on the problem of the so-called 'demythologization' of the New Testament which some felt was necessary. . . . Does this mean that the clear precepts of the Council and the Bishops' Synod are no longer valid?"

Again, those who studied the report of the Commission of Cardinals regarding the Dutch Catechism, read there of a book which had appeared in Italy: "In that same book a wrong use is made of the opinions of some modern exegetes as to how St. Matthew and St. Luke wanted to present and explain the principal facts about the birth and infancy of Our Lord . . . the book itself dares to come to the conclusion, not without violation of the Catholic faith, that the faithful should now be permitted to believe in the virginal conception of Jesus not as a reality . . . but only as having a certain symbolic significance." "The catechism," the Cardinals imposed, "should offer no excuse for abandoning this factual truth . . . in opposition to the ecclesiastical tradition founded on Holy Scripture."

Here, then, doubt was thrown on the truth of Scripture. It happened again when *Herder Correspondence* for May, 1967, gave a précis of Dr. Schoonenberg's 'refutation' of the complaints of the Dutch traditionalists: "No doubt we hear often, in the . . . utterances of the councils and . . . popes, that Mary is 'virgin' and 'ever-virgin'. . . . But these titles are pre-supposed, and hence do not function, at least on this level, as trenchant answer in a debate. . . . That Jesus is the only-begotten Son of the Father does not exclude a human father. . . . There are reasonable grounds for thinking that there is not a universal consent today about the bodily virginity of Mary."

Can there be error in Scripture? As a student under Dr. T. E. Bird, I was taught an emphatic *No*, and, printed in the Douai Bible, we had the text of Leo XIII's *Providentissimus Deus* (1893) to guide us. A passage ran: "It is absolutely wrong and forbidden, either to narrow inspiration to certain parts only of Holy Scripture, or to admit that the sacred writer has erred. For the system of those who, in order to rid themselves of these difficulties, . . . concede that divine inspiration regards the things of faith and morals, and nothing beyond, because (as they wrongly think) in a question of the truth or falsehood of a passage, we should

consider not so much what God has said as the reason and
purpose which He had in mind when saying it—this system
cannot be tolerated . . . inspiration not only is essentially
incompatible with error, but excludes it as absolutely and
necessarily as it is impossible that God Himself, the supreme
Truth, can utter that which is not true. *This is the ancient
and unchanging faith of the Church, solemnly defined in the
Councils of Florence and of Trent, and finally confirmed
and more expressly formulated by the Council of the Vatican.*"

That is very firm teaching and, coming from the Holy
Father to the whole Church, carries tremendous weight, but
even weightier, of course, is the teaching of the infallible
Councils to which he referred. Anyone who wishes to attribute error to the Scriptures has not only a succession of
popes to confront but must also challenge the teaching of
General Councils.

In spite of this, *Lamentabili* (1907) had to condemn
this modernist error: "Divine inspiration does not extend
to the whole of Sacred Scripture so that it preserves each
and every part of it from all error." (Denzinger 2011.)

Once again, in 1920, the Papacy returned to the defence of the inerrancy of Scripture, this time in Benedict
XV's *Spiritus Paraclitus* in which he repeated the teaching
of Leo XIII about the absence of error, the impossibility of
error, and grieved that, though Leo's words had left no
room for ambiguity or quibbling, some priest-scholars "depending arrogantly on their own judgment" were ignoring
them.

To celebrate the fiftieth anniversary of *Providentissimus
Deus and*, in part, to refute a wild pamphlet published by
an Italian priest under the *nom-de-plume of* Dain Cohenel,
Pope Pius XII gave the Church *Divino afflante Spiritu* in
1943. The pamphlet had already been met by a letter of the
Biblical Commission dated August 20, 1941, and this letter
served as a draft for part of the encyclical. It was a 'liberat-
ing' document, loosening the reins on Catholic exegetes,
making it plain that they must take into account literary
forms of past ages, especially when dealing with historical
material. As Fr. Jean Levie wrote in *The Bible, Word of*

God in Words of Men (p. 142), "All were struck by the positive character of *Divino afflante Spiritu*, seeing it as an optimistic and trusting exhortation to work freely and fruitfully in the field of Catholic exegesis."

Pius XII said *Amen* to what Leo XIII had taught about error in Scripture: "We now set forth this by our authority also, enjoining that it be scrupulously maintained by all." He explained, at the same time, that we have to try to see what the writer was thinking in his own fashion in his particular epoch: " 'In the Divine Scripture,' observes St. Thomas, with characteristic shrewdness, 'divine things are conveyed to us in the manner to which men are accustomed.' For just as the substantial Word of God became like to men in all things, 'without sin', so the words of God, expressed in human language, became in all things like to human speech, *except error.*"

Divino afflante Spiritu was, Fr. Levie said, optimistic and trusting. Pius XII learned that his optimism and trust had been betrayed, since he returned to Scriptural questions in *Humani Generis* in 1950.

PIUS XII SOUNDS THE ALARM

"There are some," he said, "who make bold to overstep the warning landmarks which the Church has laid down. One especially regrettable tendency is to interpret the historical books of the Old Testament with overmuch freedom." The first eleven chapters of Genesis came "under the heading of history." "It may be true that these old writers of sacred history drew some of their material from the stories current . . . but . . . they did so under the impulse of divine inspiration, which preserved them from all error. . . . These excerpts from current stories . . . must not be put on a level with mere myths, or with legend in general. Myths arise from the untrammelled exercise of the imagination; whereas . . . in the Old Testament, a love of truth and a cult of simplicity shine out, in such a way as to put these writers on a demonstrably different level from their profane contemporaries."

His words did not encourage talk of "popular campfire stories, legends. . . ." A few lines further on, he laid down: "Be it known to all who teach in ecclesiastical institutions that they cannot, with a clear conscience, exercise the office so entrusted to them unless they dutifully accept the principles we have here set forth, and observe them strictly in educating their pupils."

In putting the Old Testament on a different plane from other historical writing of the time, he was recapping what he had said in 1943: "It (study) has now also clearly demonstrated the unique pre-eminence . . . which the people of Israel enjoyed in historical writing, both in regard to the antiquity of the events recorded and to the accuracy with which they are related—a circumstance, of course, which is explained by . . . divine inspiration. . . ." *Humani Generis* struck also at an old error: "Much that is maintained . . . is injurious to the divine authority of Sacred Scripture . . . they bring up again the old argument, so often censured, which contends that the inerrancy extends only to what it tells us about God, morals, and about religion." That old argument will rear its scarred head again in this chapter when we exemplify from modern writing.

THE FACTS BEHIND . . . .

I give now a sample of the kind of writing which causes distress to so many. Once again, we are thumbing the pages of J. B. Walker's *For All Men*. We read in the first chapter: "The facts behind the Bible story of the passover were probably something like this . . . One particular Spring the aftermath of the flooding was especially severe. But the Hebrews, well away from the flood area . . . remained unaffected by these plagues which seemed to have 'passed over' them as . . . they gathered again to eat their lamb. . . . Now was the time . . . for the Hebrews to make their escape. And if they took the route that lay over the mud flats at the neck of the Red Sea and crossed into the desert, the likelihood was that even if the authorities missed them and sent police in pursuit their chariots would never be able to cross the great swamp but would flounder in the mud. Moses had a further reason for confidence. He had lately been introduced to the cult of a new and invisible God, called Yahweh . . . by Jethro. . . . Perhaps, if the Hebrews dedicated themselves to this God, he would accept them as his people. . . . To emphasise their conviction, growing through the centuries, that only the all-powerful arm of Yahweh could account for the marvel of their escape . . . the Hebrew storytellers began to embellish their accounts of the passover with miracle and wonder, until finally the author of Exodus gathered together the various versions. . . ."

Walker has certainly piped us into the land of myth and campfire stories. Bishop Butler also seems to vary from Pius XII's doctrine, for he wrote (*The Inspiration of the Bible*, in *The Tablet*, February 3, 1968): "Much of the Bible is poetry . . . and it plainly incorporates, in the Old Testament, legendary elements . . . probably also myth. . . ."

THE HISTORICAL TRUTH OF THE GOSPELS

The Sacred Congregation of the Holy Office issued, in June, 1961, a further admonition: ". . . assertions . . . are being spread . . . bringing into doubt the genuine historical and objective truth . . . not only of the Old Testament . . . but even of the New, *even to the sayings and deeds of Christ Jesus*. Since assertions . . . of this kind are causing anxiety . . . all of those who deal with the Sacred Scriptures . . . should be warned always to . . . have before their eyes the doctrine of the Fathers of the Church and the mind and teaching authority of the Church, lest the consciences of the faithful be disturbed or the truths of the Faith be injured."

So far we have seen guidance and warnings given in 1893, 1907, 1920, 1943, 1950 and 1961. Scholars had been sufficiently warned but warnings alone do not ensure discipline. In Fr. Walter M. Abbott's *Documents of Vatican II*, the 'response' after the Constitution on Divine Revelation is given by Professor Frederick C. Grant, and he writes: "The Appendix to Cardinal Bea's *The Study of the Synoptic Gospels* . . . warns ordinaries . . . to 'Keep watch with great care over popular writings . . . on biblical subjects.' This is clearly censorship, and suffocating." This is all very well, but it seems to be suited to *Utopia*, which, by derivation, means 'Nowhere', rather than to the real world which is crammed with fallen nature and devoid of Pelagius's plaster saints and Rousseau's Noble Savages. Experience has shown time and time again the need here for the shepherds to protect the flock, and early experience at that, since 2 Peter 3.16 links wrong exegesis and destruction.

On April 21, 1964, the Pontifical Biblical Commission felt compelled to issue an instruction on the Historical Truth of the Gospels, and annoyed some Council Fathers by so doing, since the Council was at that time debating the constitution on divine revelation. The title of the instruction shows the main concern felt in Rome—as in the 1961 admonition, it guarded the "sayings and deeds of Christ Jesus." The labours of exegetes, it said, were all the more called for "by reason of the fact that in many publications, circulated far and wide, the truth of the events and sayings recorded in the Gospels is being challenged." Scholars were encouraged to study the type of literature adopted by the sacred writers, and allowed to seek out what sound elements there are in 'the method of form history' though warned of concomitant dangers. Three stages of transmission of Christ's teaching were enumerated—Christ's teaching of His apostles, their proclamation of the Gospel, and the writing of the evangelists, and, in dealing with the third category, there was emphasis on the need of getting at the mind and intention of each writer.

The instruction was, as such things so often—disappointingly—are, very general, but Cardinal Bea supplied an extensive commentary in *La Civiltà Cattolica* (Nos. 2735-6, 1964) which brought many things into sharper focus. *Herder Correspondence* (December, 1964) published a lengthy account of his commentary, and it is this I draw upon. It is not always clear if the Cardinal is being quoted *verbatim*, but it looks as if, for most of the way, his own words are being given. "The last twenty years have made such a reminder necessary and useful, he thinks, because in a number of recent writings the historical value of the Gospels has in fact been called in question . . . the Instruction . . . affirms that the Gospels are subject to the criteria of historical writing and at the same time are inspired by the Holy Spirit and therefore *immune from error.* . . . There is no question of a group of enthusiastic fanatics but of a strictly organized society whose very order derived from the *precision of its message* regarding the person and teaching of Jesus. That is shown, for instance, by the introduction to St. Luke's Gospel. He was not concerned to collect every possible story that may have been current regarding Jesus, *but with what eye-witnesses had handed down.* The terms 'witness', 'testimony' and 'bear witness' occur more than 150 times in the New Testament and mean *speaking from personal experience.* . . . From this it can be seen what is to be thought of the alleged creative activity of the original community in matters of doctrine. To the extent that there was any such activity at all, it was regarded as sectarian. Christian faith, on the other hand, rested on the testimony of the Apostles to what Christ had said and done."

We come then to a section headed *The Methods of the Form-History School* and read: "This school of exegesis is mistaken in taking as a principle that the similarities in form between the literatures of rabbinical Judaism and of Hellenism and short sections of the Gospels are to be interpreted as constituting a dependence of the Gospels on these literatures. In the East, literary form is chiefly determined by content. The real question is, therefore, to expound the content of the Gospels in its originality, *which has no parallels in the religious history of the age.* What is decisive is not similarity of form but the disparity of content, all the more so as the Apostles were concerned to transmit the words and deeds of Jesus *with the greatest fidelity.* . . . The Biblical Commission's Instruction . . . stresses that what the encyclical (*Divino afflante Spiritu*) said about the importance of literary types for the interpretation of the Old Testament *also applies to the books of the New Testament.*"

Later we read: "The apostolic preaching was certainly not intended to describe Jesus' life exhaustively or chronologically. The most superficial inquiry shows that the evangelists had no such intention either. *The aim was certainly an historical and biographical one*, but not the composition of a biography in our sense. The Apostles certainly intended, however, *to preserve the facts* regarding the life and activity of a real person as well as his teaching."

Truthfulness? Possibility of error? We read: "The truth of the account is in no way contradicted by the fact that the evangelists relate our Lord's words in different order and do not express what he said verbatim. . . . God is absolute truth and the Gospels are therefore not only historically true, humanly speaking . . . complete immunity from error. . . . Some do not do justice to inerrancy and the difference there is between it and the fidelity to truth which is possible, and required, in a purely human work. . . . The task of the exegete, therefore, is to discern the intention of the writer and his manner of presentation and not to term error what is only incompleteness."

Later we come to a warning, perennially relevant: "There is one apparent way of solving difficulties which must be resisted as a temptation. It is certainly not permissible to say that all that is necessary is to maintain the essential, the religious content, what concerns faith and morals; that the rest is only the mode of presentation . . . and therefore is not comprised in the inerrancy of Holy Scripture. . . . Christian faith does not consist in abstract principles and a theoretical doctrine, but *chiefly historical facts. . . .*"

Now that we have read of the Biblical Commission's concern about the way in which "the truth of the events and sayings recorded in the Gospels is being challenged," and Cardinal Bea's commentary that "the Apostles were concerned to transmit the words and deeds of Jesus with the greatest fidelity," we step into the Alice-in-Wonderland world of that issue of *The Sower* to see what the Modernists make of it all. The editor, Fr. Somerville, S.J., tells us that their edition of October, 1969, contained an article "following no less an authority than the Pontifical Biblical Commission which issued an important 'Instruction' on the gospels in 1964. We do not intend to repeat or summarise that article but simply to state some facts emerging from it which lead us to a better understanding of what a gospel is." And this is what he teaches us. . . . "Yet most Catholics take an over simple, almost naive view of the gospels. . . . The common simple view is that the four gospels are accounts of what Jesus said and did . . . this cherished view cannot stand up to scholarly criticism. . . . The gospels are entirely human documents, and therefore no more free from historical error than any other ancient document. . . . A gospel is not a life of Christ. It does not claim to report accurately what Jesus said and did." Reading this, could we find it in us to agree with Dr. Küng that there is untruthfulness in the Church?

To return to Cardinal Bea. . . . It was, he said, an 'illegitimate shortcut' to try to solve difficulties by limiting inerrancy to matters of faith and morals. That shortcut had been condemned in *Providentissimus Deus* in the name of "the ancient and unchanging faith of the Church," had been condemned again by Pius X in his address of April 17, 1907, to the cardinals in which he rebuked the errors of the Modernists—"to them inspiration is confined to the dogmatic doctrines, but these are understood just as they please", condemned implicity in *Divino afflante Spiritu*, and then explicitly in *Humani Generis*. We shall meet it again in a minute, but first let us say a word about the temptation to which a scholar may succumb when faced with a difficulty. Professor Butterfield, a professional historian, nevertheless expresses reservations regarding scholarship (*Op. cit.*, pp. 127-128): "great distress is produced amongst Christians and some harm is done to religion when too anxious an attempt is made to tie Christianity to the state of the various empirical sciences as they exist in 1849 or 1949 . . . . scholarship throughout history . . . has shown an aggressive tendency, so that in every age men claim that things are proved when they have not really been proved, or they make inferences which their apparatus and their evidence could never have qualified them to make." This is profoundly true, and it is the reason why a Catholic must not be cowed by a passing climate of scholarly opinion and abandon the guidance of the magisterium, betraying what Fr. Levie called "that religious recklessness that compromises the eternal faith on account of particular historical difficulties which may well vanish tomorrow" (*Op. cit.*, p. 157). Again he wrote: "The existence in every period of difficulties that cannot be resolved until a later age is a normal thing" (p. 198).

We have seen Tyrrell betray this religious recklessness, panicking while the scholars with faith tackled the new problems calmly, and we may set down here Père Grandmaison's definition of a Modernist: A Modernist is a man with a double conviction: first, that there can be real conflicts, in defined matters concerning the doctrinal or moral basis of the Christian religion, between the traditional position and modern findings; and, second, that, in that case, it is the traditional position which must normally yield to the modern through undergoing updating and, if necessary, radical change or rejection. (*Études*, 1923, t. clxxvl, p. 644.)

Fidelity to the magisterium has proved sound scholarship. Harnack's most famous phrase, uttered at the beginning of the century, was *Zurück zur Tradition*—Back to tradition! "The result," Pius XII said, "has been that confidence in the authority and historical truth of the Bible . . . has now among Catholics been wholly restored."

And, we add with respect, lost again. *Herder Correspondence* for January, 1965, revealed how traditional teaching was being brushed aside. Cardinal König and Bishop Simons "thought that the schema ought not to declare that inspiration preserves the human author from error. . . ." Other Fathers—for example, Bishop Philbin—urged the Council to defend the historical truth of the Gospels, above all of the accounts of our Lord's Infancy.

VATICAN II

What did Vatican II teach in the event? It ruled that: "In composing the sacred books, God chose men and . . . made use of their powers . . . so that with Him acting in them and through them, they, as true authors, consigned to writing everything and *only* those things which He wanted. Therefore, since everything asserted by the inspired authors . . . *must be held to be asserted by the Holy Spirit*, it follows that the books of Scripture must be acknowledged as teaching . . . *without error* that truth which God wanted put into the sacred writings for the sake of our salvation."

Now let us see what has been made of that last sentence, in the teeth of all past teaching. Dr. Hans Küng, who had maintained in *The Changing Church* that errors can easily be established in Scripture, has seized upon it to buttress his previous position: "In the face of all the conservative attacks . . . the historical-critical method has received explicit approval. Scripture is claimed to be inerrant only for religious truth and not for statements of a scientific or historical nature."[1] When Bishop Butler wrote on *Divine Revelation*[2] some weeks before Dr. Küng's article appeared, he quoted the vital sentence from Vatican II and added only the respectable gloss: "As St. Augustine pointed out . . . God did not intend to use Scripture to satisfy our natural curiosity about astronomy or cosmogony," which was in complete harmony with the mind of Leo XIII who had also drawn on St. Augustine and, in addition, summoned St. Thomas to witness that, as far as scientific matters went, the sacred writers "went by what sensibly appeared." Nevertheless, writing some two months after Dr. Küng's interpretation was advanced, Bishop Butler had moved over to Küng's camp: "The limitation ('for the sake of our salvation') means that we are committed not to a material but to a formal veracity of the Bible. The Bible, in other words, could contain errors without diminution of its inspiration, provided those errors were not in the field of the truth which is 'for the sake of our salvation.' "[3] Earlier in the article, he

---

[1] *The Sunday Times,* December 12, 1965.
[2] *The Tablet,* November 27, 1965.
[3] *The Inspiration of the Bible,* in *The Tablet,* February 3, 1968. *Lamentabili* condemned the Modernist proposition "Divine inspiration does not extend to the whole of Sacred Scripture in such a way that each and every part of it is preserved from all error." (Dz. 2011).

had written that scholars would not "find it easy to say that there is no material error at all in its pages."

When Bishop Butler categorically classed the phrase 'for the sake of our salvation' as a limitation, he begged the question. It could be such, but tradition and other reasons argue that it is not, and it looks as if he had succumbed to a temptation, experienced by him before, to make the magisterium yield to the cocksureness of today's scholars. As far back as ten years ago, he had written: "Our faith in the inspiration of Scripture does not compel us to suppose that the evangelists, taking over and editing traditional materials which were of very various provenance and unequal historical status, were miraculously enabled to raise every element in these traditions to a level and a context of exact factual correspondence with the details of what actually occurred . . . between the end of the Last Supper, and the Way of the Cross. . . ."[4] It is rather cryptic, but most readers would take it as viewing that there was error of fact, and not merely incompleteness of detail, in the Gospels.

Fr. Joseph Blenkinsopp, S.D.B., writing on *Rethinking Biblical Inerrancy*,[5] laid a finger on one flaw in the Küng-Butler interpretation. "Today," he wrote, "we are more than ever convinced that God revealed his redemptive purpose through events. . . . There is therefore no question of religious truth over here and historical truth over there—in which respect Küng's statement referred to is rather misleading. There is no way of abstracting the 'message' . . . from the history, which means that the divine guarantee of inerrancy must cover the interpretation of events found in the Scriptures." This carries an echo of Cardinal Bea's "Christian faith does not consist in abstract principles and a theoretical doctrine, but chiefly historical facts. . . ."

The weight of evidence provided by the history of the Council's text is also against the Küng interpretation. The original text was not 'for the sake of our salvation' but 'pertaining to our salvation' and 184 Council Fathers asked that the phrase should be dropped for the precise reason that it

[4] Cf. *The Tablet,* July 29, 1961.

might be taken as restricting inerrancy to faith and morals. The Theological Commission dragged its feet, and, on Octoberber 8, 1965, a group delivered a memorandum to the Pope, claiming openly that the phrase had been deliberately inserted to restrict inerrancy in a way contrary to Catholic teaching. After an investigation, the Pope sent observations on this and other matters to the Theological Commission. He said that the matter involved "great responsibility for him towards the Church and towards his own conscience." The Commission was asked to drop the expression "truth pertaining to salvation" from the text. After discussion and voting, the Commission adopted the text as we now have it.[5]

To see what had, or had not, been effected, we compare the two texts:

Early Text	*Final Text*
"The books of Scripture must be acknowledged as teaching . . . without error the truth pertaining to salvation."	". . . without error that truth which God wanted put into the sacred writings for the sake of our salvation."

When one compares the two versions, one sees that a tightening has taken place in order to placate the Pope and the traditionalist section of the Council, but one detects still some foot-dragging on the part of the liberals. The text could have been sharper and have met more fully the wish of the Vicar of Christ. If the Council had dropped the dangerous phrase as requested, instead of replacing it with an improved one, there could have been no misrepresentation. As it is, we know in what sense the Bishop of Rome gave his seal to this decree, and the Church's full teaching shines out in the assertion that the sacred writers "consigned to writing everything and only those things which He wanted," so that everything asserted by them "must be held to be asserted by the Holy Spirit," and any phrase which may seem ambiguous must be interpreted in line with tradition. As the Council laid down, "The living tradition

[5] *The Rhine Flows into the Tiber,* pp. 179-182.

of the whole Church must be taken into account," and the matter is "subject finally to the judgment of the Church."

We can, I think, see Bishop Butler moving towards 'the left' in the Sarum lectures which he gave in 1966, the year following his traditional gloss and Dr. Küng's untraditional one, lectures which have been published as *The Theology of Vatican II.* He wrote, "But for an age as conscious as our own of the extremely human and contingent character of literary records, an age so suspicious of miraculous claims and so sensitive to the approximate character of human evidence, the notion of inspiration, especially when it is spelt out in terms of 'inerrancy', is hardly marketable at all" and he mentioned that some of the Council Fathers were anxiously aware of this. But this anxiety smacks strongly of an inferiority-complex in the presence of humanism, a concern with what the neighbours will think instead of with truth. Inspiration raises Scripture above the level of 'human evidence' and removes the 'contingent character', but the notion admittedly is not widely marketable; it has not been so for a long time. It is not credible to a world without faith, but what bearing have market-indices on truth?

The Bishop goes on to deal with further words of the Council decree, which I give in Fr. Abbott's version: "Holy Mother Church has firmly and with absolute constancy held, and continues to hold, that the four Gospels . . . whose historical character the Church unhesitatingly asserts, faithfully hand on what Jesus Christ . . . really did and taught for their eternal salvation. . . . Indeed, after the ascension . . . the apostles handed on to their hearers what He had said and done. This they did with the clearer understanding which they enjoyed after they had been . . . taught by the light of the Spirit of truth. The sacred writers wrote . . . always in such a fashion that they told us the honest truth about Jesus. For their intention in writing was that either from their own memory . . . or from the witness of those who themselves 'from the beginning were eyewitnesses . . .' we might know 'the truth'. . . ."

This could not be more emphatic . . . the evangelists taught us the honest truth, passing on eye-witness accounts of what Jesus really did and said, and they did this with the especial assistance of the Holy Spirit. There is not much sympathy displayed there for talk of 'historical fiction.' Bishop Butler comments that the affirmation of the historical character of the Gospels was due to a last-minute intervention, and it was indeed another 'correction of course' by the helmsman of the barque, one which would anger the 'liberals'. Cardinal Cicognani announced that Paul VI "could not approve a formulation which leaves in doubt the historical character of these most holy books," and the addition was made.[6]

Fr. Blenkinsopp remarked, "Christianity is based on actual facts, and the gospels put us in contact with these facts." This is a vital truth, and the Council is of the same mind, stressing that the Gospel history is 'Gospel truth.' Here Bishop Butler seems to waver again and try to side-step the import of Vatican II's words, judging that the Council is teaching that "the gospels are, by and large, valuable documents for the knowledge of Christ's historical life," "By and large"? This is to water the Council's wine. "Always in such a fashion. . . ." cried the Council. "By and large," the Bishop has amended.

We come now to Bishop Butler's handling, in his Sarum lectures, of the passage on which we have read his and Dr. Küng's comments of 1965, and this is to move from the particular topic of the New Testament to the Scriptures in general. We repeat the passage from Vatican II with its preceding sentence: "in composing the sacred books, God chose men . . . they, as true authors, consigned to writing everything and only those things which He wanted. Therefore, since everything asserted by the inspired authors . . . must be held to be asserted by the Holy Spirit, it follows that the books of Scripture must be acknowledged as teaching firmly, faithfully, and without error that truth which God wanted put into the sacred writings for the sake of our salvation." Studying this, and other passages in Vatican II's decrees, the reader should bear in mind the fine words of

---

[6] *Ibidem,* pp. 179-184.

Fr. Henry St. John, O.P., (*The Tablet*, March 28, 1970):
"constant emphasis must be laid on the fact that each of the
documents of the Council is promulgated by the Church as
its day-to-day teaching through the universal Catholic episcopate under the leadership of the pope in a General Council,
speaking with the authority that this implies and expressing
what belongs to the People of God as a whole. . . ."

The Bishop's summing-up of the Council's words is: "In
other words, the criterion of the truth of scripture is not one
of material accuracy but of formal relevance." This stretches
the meaning of what the Council taught and approximates
to a false antithesis. When God sets down truth for the
sake of our salvation, there will be both accuracy *and* relevance. God will, however, let His authors write according
to popular appearances when mere science is concerned, and
so Augustine and Aquinas taught—Bishop Butler tries to
'use' them—but they would have recoiled at a suggestion of
factual error or yarn-spinning in Gospel incidents; and they
would not have swallowed a literary 'end justifies the means'
excuse. Anatole France, in the epilogue to *Vie en Fleur*,
tells his readers how he invented details to bring out the
true nature of his characters, and comments, "I believe that
no one ever lied with a greater regard for the truth." It
does not sound a suitable frame of mind to attribute to
either the Holy Spirit or an Evangelist. Catholics must give
full value to the teaching that the authors wrote "only those
things" which God wished, so that "everything asserted by
the inspired authors must be held to be asserted by the Holy
Spirit."

Bishop Butler then writes in rather baffling fashion:
"Underlying this distinction"—i.e., between material accuracy and formal relevance—"there is a distinction between
two concepts of truth. Truth for the Greeks is that which
gives legitimate satisfaction to our intellectual curiosity. . . .
For the Bible and for Christianity truth is above all the
genuineness of the manifestation of God's saving purpose."
He thinks that this distinction solves the alleged *impasse*
between inerrancy and scientific scholarship. But he has
not given Everyman's truth; neither concept of truth as given

above gets down to what truth *is*. "Legitimate satisfaction
to our intellectual curiosity"? A visit to the theatre satisfies
intellectual curiosity about a play . . . but truth remains un-
defined. Again, what is meant by "genuineness" in the second concept? Surely both a Greek philosopher (not a sophist)
and a Christian-in-the-street would concur that truth is the
apprehension of reality by our intellect, and the correspondence of speech and writing to actuality. That is Everyman's
truth—what Jesus "really did and taught," "the honest
truth," and we must not imagine that because Pilate, two
thousand years ago, asked "What is truth?" and did not wait
for the Son of God to answer, that nobody then knew, or
cared, what 'true' meant. People were as hungry for the facts
then as now, and it was a pleasure to find Archbishop Ramsey
of Canterbury saying: "I have read Bultmann. I think I
could take an examination on Bultmann. I think his demythologization is based on the fact that he thinks the primitive Christians did not take history as seriously as I think
they took history. I think we ought to take history very
seriously, because the primitive Christians took history very
seriously." (Interviewed by Ved Mehta; cf. Ved Mehta, *The
New Theologian*, p. 76.)

Any 'impasse' between inerrancy and scholarship will
not be resolved by a nebulous distinction between ideas of
truth. It will be solved by the discovery of truth, for the
Bible and the Church have a knack of being proved right.
When Loisy published *L'Évangile et L'Église*, von Hügel
wrote to him: "I have read your anti-Harnack up to page
140. It is quite simply superb. Never have you done anything stronger, more beautiful," but, when the second edition was being prepared, the Baron suggested that the author
should add a note to say that there was a 'historical nucleus'
in St. Mark's Gospel, only to be told that there was no such
nucleus. Now, in 1972, we read; "Bible experts in Rome believe that a Spanish Professor's claim that he has found an
extract of St. Mark's Gospel among the Dead Sea Scrolls
may give a new direction to New Testament research. . . .
If the thesis is accepted, New Testament theories will have
to be changed. St. Mark will have to be regarded as a writer

contemporary or almost so with Christ. Scholars will also have to revise their ideas about the order in which the four Gospels were written.[7]" So much for the fluctuating Stock Exchange of scholars' ideas!

We must bear in mind what the Pontifical Biblical Commission counselled in 1964 to "those who write for the Christian public at a popular level"—"Let them regard themselves as in duty bound never to depart in the slightest from the common doctrine and tradition of the Church." We proclaim, then, in the words of the Instruction, that "the Gospels were written under the inspiration of the Holy Spirit, and that it was He who preserved their authors immune from all error."

SOME MODERN WRITERS

Vatican II taught the necessity of taking into consideration literary *genres* in the Bible, "for truth is . . . expressed in a variety of ways, depending on whether a text is history of one kind or another, or whether its form is that of prophecy, poetry, or some other type of speech . . . due attention must be paid to . . . the customs men normally followed at that period . . . all of what has been said about the way of interpreting Scripture is subject finally to the judgment of the Church. . . ."

The key to many problems may lie in the matter of literary forms, but there is a danger that these will serve as a blanket to cover wild exegesis or disbelief, and this is where the steadying hand of authority is vital. We read earlier the remarks of J. B. Walker concerning the facts behind the passover story. Here now is Fr. Paul de Surgy writing in *The Mystery of Salvation* (p. 59): "Between . . . the miracle of the exodus, and the details which are manifestly the embroideries of the imagination, there is an area in which it is impossible to determine exactly what is historical truth . . . if God had judged it good to reveal exactly which parts are history and which imagination, he would not have had these traditions put down in epic framework." Again,

[7] *The Daily Telegraph,* March 17, 1972.

on page 63: "it matters little, therefore, whether . . . some details betray a certain imagination or exaggeration . . . (the wall of water to right and left, the 'not so much as one of them remained' which reflects the usual optimism of victory communiqués. . . .)." Is this legitimate comment or disbelief? And, if the sacred writer tipped a load of campfire stories into the measure of truth to produce an epic, and this was the known procedure of his day, how did the story come down among the Jews as factual account? Would not a wink have accompanied the tall yarn?

And so to the New Testament again. . . . If we look at Mr. Derek Lance's *What is Christianity, 11-16: First Year*, a handbook used by many teachers, we find on p. 200 that he leans explicitly on Fr. Avery Dulles. We read: "The gospels are not scientific historical accounts of the event, nor biography in the modern sense." This we concede, but the careful insertion of the word "scientific" and the qualifying phrase "in the modern sense" must not hide the fact that their historical and biographical character are firmly laid down by Popes and Council. Mr. Lance continues in a veir which recalls Loisy and his friends: "they are professions of faith of the early, believing church." (See various propositions condemned by *Lamentabili*.) He supports this by a quotation from Fr. Dulles: "They aim to transmit not a photograph of Jesus as he might have appeared to a detached observer, but a portrait of Jesus as understood by the believing church." A false trail has been laid by the intrusion of the word 'photograph'. St. John had no camera and yet he preached that "which we have heard, which we have seen with our eyes, which we have looked upon and our hands have handled" (1 John 1:1). St. Irenaeus told us of the vivid memories that he carried from his younger days: "For the things one learns when one is young become one with the soul and unite themselves with it, so that I can say in what place the blessed Polycarp used to sit in order to speak, how he came in and went out, what was the character of his life, his physical appearance, the talks he had with people, how he told of his relations with John and with the others who had seen the Lord, how he reported their words. . . . I

have kept them in memory, not on paper but in my heart."
And not in a photograph! St. John's memories would be as
vivid, and, though he gave us no physical description of
Jesus, he gave us the 'honest truth' that he clearly remembered. And so did Matthew, while Mark and Luke recounted
the stories of eyewitnesses. Mr. Lance has given us the
Loisy, not the Vatican II, Gospel.

THE INFANCY NARRATIVES

Loisy, in *L'Évangile et L'Église*, Section 1, *The Sources
of the Gospels*, Chapter III, wrote of the Infancy Narratives:
"The very nature of their subject, the critical examination
of the two versions . . . and an analysis of evangelical tradition, make it impossible to regard them as a definite expression of historical memories." Mr. Lance has not the same
sweeping confidence, but, on page 125 of his book, we come
upon a passage dealing with the Magi: "It is impossible
to say who these Magi were. . . . Some people even doubt
whether this passage in Matthew represents an actual event
and suggest that it is a story put in to bring out a particular
theological truth about Christ." (Anatole France's "no one
ever lied with a greater regard for the truth"?) He adds,
"Matthew, like the other evangelists, is not concerned with
writing a factually correct biography of Jesus." 'Biography'
is the false-trail-word here since it suggests an exhaustive,
chronological account. Matthew *was* concerned with writing
down the facts and the Holy Spirit saw that he did so.

Fr. Dulles more than once uses a word in this way to
distract us from the real point. On page 35 (*op. cit.*) he tells
us: "The Gospels do not profess to be memoirs or even, in
the modern sense, biographies." Memoirs or biographies . . .
not exactly! But history . . . yes! On page 39 we learn that
"Mark is no more interested in writing an impartial historical account than the other Evangelists." The trick lies in
the word 'impartial'; since they were committed to the Son
of God, it is suggested that they could not write objective
truth. Yet disciples can tell the honest truth, while Fr.
Dulles himself can be inaccurate and fail to provide an 'im-

partial historical account.' On page 77: "Face-to-face com-
munion with the risen Christ fashioned them into new men."
But it was the Holy Spirit Who, at Pentecost, blew away the
Old Adam. Again (p. 83): "when the high priest asks Him
whether He is Son of God, Jesus replies evasively, substituting in His reply the term 'Son of Man.' " But Matthew,
Mark and Luke provide the answers, "Thou hast said it,"
"I am," and "You say that I am." Once again (p. 87) Fr.
Dulles claims that "Jesus does not seem to have openly
taught that He was God." "Openly" holds the ambiguity.
We know that the Jews twice took up stones to kill Him because of claims made under enemy pressure (St. John 8 and
10).[8]

Now let us introduce 'midrash' in a passage from an
article of shining common-sense, *Language, Truth and Theology*, by Fr. John Bligh, S.J.[9] He wrote: "it is now being
said by many Catholic writers that 'the infancy narratives
are midrash.' Some of them mean that the infancy narratives
are packed with allusions to Old Testament prophecies and
types. . . . The Jewish and Protestant writers . . . who
started the fashion of calling the infancy narratives 'midrash'
mean that they are non-historical—they are pious legends
modelled on Old Testament stories which themselves contained a good measure of folk-lore and legend. Catholic
teachers who use the term 'midrash' of the infancy narratives can hardly complain if they are understood to be saying
that the infancy narratives are imaginative creations. . . .
But St. Luke presents these narratives as a reliable account
of what actually happened, based on the reminiscences of
eye-witnesses."

---

[8] Mr. de Rosa has created, in this context, an Aunt Sally for the
pleasure of knocking it flat. In *Christ and Original Sin* (p. 6), he
wrote: "The suggestion that Jesus went around claiming to be God
is, to the mind of contemporary theologians and exegetes, oversimplified." But so, surely, is the suggestion that apologists went
around suggesting that Jesus went around . . .

[9] *The Tablet,* November 11, 1967. That *Sower* (p. 84): "The infancy
stories are frequently taken to be narrating miraculous events as
if they were historical. There is reason to doubt whether the events
were either miraculous or historical."

EYE-WITNESSES OR NOT?

Vatican II widened St. Luke's claim to extend to all four evangelists. Yet Dom Placid Jordan, in *The Divine Dimension* (p. 188), contradicts the Council, asserting that "the four gospels, with the possible exception of St. Matthew's, are not eye-witness accounts of Jesus' life. To the synoptics Jesus was truly man, not God-man." And, if we turn to Fr. Symon's *Catholic Herald* column for December 18, 1970, we read: "There is a tendency to assume that, if we accept scholarly doubts about the details of Jesus' appearance to the shepherds or the Wise Men, we will end up by denying the central beliefs of our faith. This is very far from being true. . . . For Jesus' birth and early years very few eye-witnesses, if any, were available." How does he know? His "if any" cannot be squared with the Council's doctrine, and would not one eye-witness, our Lady, suffice? On April 30, 1971, Fr. Symon was at it again: ". . . in what are called the infancy narratives several secondary details are not intended as an exact account of what happened at the time of Jesus' birth. . . . The details are chosen to illustrate the religious meaning of Our Saviour's mission in a way that could be understood by the people of the First Century." Yet we recall that there was a Divine Author who wrote for the men of all centuries. On December 25, 1970, Fr. Symon had written "that we can serenely continue to profess our faith and at the same time believe, or disbelieve, all kinds of peripheral stories. Whether these *myths* (italics mine) belong to the first century or the twentieth, they do not affect the central message of the gospel." I submit that we cannot serenely profess faith at variance with the teaching of the magisterium.

"The details are chosen. . . ." he wrote, and in the first article quoted he explained this: "Matthew and Luke might have confined themselves to the bare facts but. . . . Around the central facts they wove a number of other incidents, not so as to deceive their readers, but so as to explain through symbols the meaning of Jesus' mission." But, we ask, did they not in fact (on this hypothesis) deceive their readers?

There is no hint in the early Christian writers that we are to take the infancy narratives with a pinch of midrash; they have come down to us as being as authentic as the crucifixion. Where does one draw the line? And is all this attitude any more than another Tyrrell-flight in panic before aggressive scholars? Perhaps the true diagnosis is to be found in Père Grandmaison's definition of a Modernist.

Fr. Raymond Brown, S.S., contributes in *Jesus, God and Man* (p. 42)—"The present chapter will . . . admit the possibility that statements attributed to Jesus . . . were not uttered by him. . . ." and (p 92): ". . . there is a core of historical material in the fourth Gospel, but . . rethought in the light of late first-century theology." (A core only? When may we then say, "Jesus said. . . ."?)

This type of writing causes concern. The Pontifical biblical Commission's Instruction is all the more necessary because "in many publications, circulated far and wide, the truth of the events and sayings recorded in the Gospels is being challenged." Yet it is the exegetes who are doing the challenging, with popular writers picking up the doubts and broadcasting them, smiling affectionately at the 'myths.' Myths, *Humani Generis* said, "arise from the untrammelled exercise of the imagination; whereas in our sacred books, even in the Old Testament, a love of truth and a cult of simplicity shine out. . . ."

Part of the difficulty experienced by the non-exegete is that the mass of evidence cannot be presented to him in a few pages. That is why he may do injustice to the expert's work. Yet, making every allowance, it does seem that Dr. Strabismus is to the fore in scriptural commentary. Fr. Blenkinsopp (*art. cit.*) tells us, for example, that a German Jesuit, Fr. Norbert Lohfink, "argues that it is no longer possible to regard the individual writer as the subject of inerrancy . . . only . . . the final sense given to every part by the Christ-event is inerrant . . . it is not what anything in the Bible *meant* which is important, but what it *means*."

Even when we deal with the work of orthodox writers, the argumentation (as far as space allows it) often seems so uncertain; the grounds for statement seem insecure, and the disagreement among experts deepens our sense of uncertainty. One cannot help thinking of the way in which Ronald Knox played games with Higher Criticism in *Essays in Satire*, and one wonders if the scholars have been becalmed too long in a dead sea of scrolls. Even occasional judgments of that fine writer, Fr. (now Cardinal) Jean Daniélou, leave one with a mind full of queries. In his *The Infancy Narratives*, we read of the Annunciation: "Luke's presentation . . . contains certain elaborations, certain features borrowed from earlier biblical stories . . . there is a recognized literary form for describing annunciations . . . Luke undoubtedly put this word into the mouth of the angel with the intention of showing us . . . it is very probable also that Luke's description of the Annunciation was largely inspired by Daniel, especially in regard to the choice of the name of Gabriel for the angel. . . . The technique is very similar to what we find in the canticles Luke gives in the following chapters. We know that this was a literary convention very common in Judaic and Judeo-Christian writings of the time—these *misrashim* based upon Scriptural quotation. . . . Since the passage in question is by no means Lucan in style, it seems most likely that it is a *midrash* of Isaiah 9 dating back to the early Judeo-Christian world. That certainly is what Bultmann seems to prove." (pp. 24-34)

Then, writing of the appearance of the angels to the shepherds, the same book explains (p. 62): "Luke is here making a major theological statement: that the infant is divine. The form in which that statement appears would seem, however, to be derived from Qumram representations of the apocalypse." Or, later (p. 63): "The presence of other liturgical hymns in Luke's infancy narrative—not only the *Gloria*, but the *Benedictus*, the *Magnificat* and the *Nunc Dimittis*—would lead us to think with Riesenfeld that the *Sitz im Leben* of these accounts in the primitive Church was the liturgical assembly."[10] I quote one or two more sentences: "It looks as though Luke has translated the histor-

[10] See also the interesting article, *The Magnificat and Benedictus*, by Dom Edmund Flood, *The Clergy Review*, March, 1965. A number of scholars ascribe the *Magnificat* to Elizabeth!

ical fact of the payment of a poll-tax into a general census" (p. 67). "That Joseph fled from Bethlehem to escape Herod's massacre is part of the original historical truth. But that the place he fled to was Egypt is questionable" (p. 83). ". . . it is very probable that the *midrash* on the star, with its leading the Magi from Jerusalem to Bethlehem and stopping over the spot where Jesus was, was inspired by Balaam" (p. 84). "Matthew must have here been projecting onto the childhood of Jesus a situation that only existed later on" (p. 92). "So the idea that the Magi were pagan seems to be Matthew's own contribution to the story—once again a projection onto Jesus' childhood of a later situation. . . ." (p. 94). "All this leads us to see the *Nunc Dimittis* as a very old Judeo-Christian hymn which Luke puts into the mouth of Simeon" (p. 110). "Clearly, the source of this account is Mary's evidence, but Luke certainly did not hear it from Mary herself" (p. 117). (Why *certainly?*)

This is precisely what may be covered by the Council's mention of literary types but, if it is, and these views (expressed by a traditionalist) are correct, then writers and preachers are in an unhappy position. If the evangelists wrote along these lines, they did not—one hopes—deceive their first hearers. However, as our idea of honest narrative is different, we would deceive our listeners, as we were deceived, if we spoke about the appearance of the angels to the shepherds, or Mary bursting into the *Magnificat* or the Magi plodding along after the star. As far as one can ascertain even the earliest Fathers swallowed the stories as un-retouched reportage. One wonders uneasily if the experts have not wandered through the Looking-Glass, since they pass naive judgments. Professor Barclay of the Church of Scotland, for instance, asserts that in our Lord's day people didn't ask of a story if it was true.[11] If they didn't, they weren't 'people.' Our faith in experts has been badly shaken. The Piltdown skull is still grinning at them.

[11] Cf. *The Sunday Post,* March 21, 1965.

11

Nullus Adam

All faith is in Jesus Christ and in Adam.

Pascal (Quoted from *Francis Thompson* by Agnes de la Gorce.)

What truly is the point of departure of the enemies of religion for the sowing of the great and serious errors by which the faith of so many is shaken? They begin by denying that man has fallen by sin and been cast down from his former position. Hence they regard as mere fables original sin and the evils that were its consequence. Humanity vitiated in its source vitiated in its turn the whole race of man; and thus was evil introduced amongst men and the necessity for a Redeemer involved. All this rejected, it is easy to understand that no place is left for Christ, for the Church, for grace or for anything that is above and beyond nature; in one word the whole edifice of faith is shaken from top to bottom. But let people believe and confess that the Virgin Mary has been from the first moment of her conception preserved from all stain; and it is straightway necessary that they should admit both original sin and the rehabilitation of the human race by Jesus Christ, the Gospel, and the Church and the law of suffering. By virtue of this, Rationalism and Materialism are torn up by the roots and destroyed, and there remains to Christian wisdom the glory of having to guard and protect the truth.

POPE ST. PIUS X, Ad diem illum, 1904.

Catholic Truth for the autumn of 1967 contained a review of Mr. de Rosa's *Christ and Original Sin* by a headmaster, Mr. D. C. Grainger, and its opening sentences can be fairly classed as devastating. Mr. Grainger quoted from the book this sentence—"There is no subject more liable to cause teachers to tear their hair out and children to profess a belligerent unbelief than original sin"—a fevered assertion which conjures up a picture of the St. John Bosco Guild in despair and children manning the barricades. He then remarked: "But that is not the experience of one of the 24 Catholic members of my very experienced staff. I passed the book around. The general comment was: 'I wonder if he believes in original sin at all.' . . . . vastly more attention should have been paid to the traditional teaching of the magisterium."

Reading that comment, I was reminded of what Newman said of the *sensus fidelium* when writing, in *On Consulting the Faithful*, of the fourth century troubles: "I mean . . . that in that time of immense confusion the divine dogma of our Lord's divinity was proclaimed . . . and (humanly speaking) preserved, far more by the 'Ecclesia docta' than by the 'Ecclesia docens'; . . . it was the Christian people who, under Providence, were the ecclesiastical strength of Athanasius, Hilary, Eusebius of Vercellae . . . who would have failed without them. . . . I argue that, unless they had been catechised, as St. Hilary says, in the orthodox faith from the time of their baptism, they never could have held that horror, which they show, of the heterodox Arian doctrine."

"I wonder if he believes in original sin at all" might seem an unfair reaction, since Mr. de Rosa wrote explicitly: "I have wanted, as far as possible, to stand apart from the controversies still raging and to describe them as objectively as I could. . . ." It is, however, fairly rooted in the trend of the book. Fr. Winstone, in his laudatory review, was of opinion that "He is preaching others, not necessarily himself, but it is not difficult to detect where his sympathies lie." That is putting it mildly, since Mr. de Rosa works with might and main to make the new doctrine of original sin seem the only tenable one. But he has wanted to stand to the side, as a ventriloquist does. It is true, of course, that the new doctrine is derived; like all our reinterpretations, it comes from abroad.

Over four hundred years ago, the Council of Trent groaned to find old errors regarding original sin rearing their heads again (Denzinger 787), and pronounced an anathema on those who disputed the need to baptise infants (Denzinger 791). On March 31, 1967, *Time* magazine reported: "Dutch theologians also reject original sin as an inherited spiritual stigma on the soul. . . . For that reason, some thinkers question the need for infant baptism." So we are back *there* again. Now let us draw on Mr. de Rosa for a few quotations to see what 'they' are saying nowadays. "The idea of two primitive ancestors at the beginning of the human race, they say, is most unlikely. The paradisal state . . . in Genesis is really a projection, not a piece of history . . . there will be a state like this in the future. . . . According to Dubarle: . . . 'what the text describes is the effect of a countless multitude of individual sins . . . not a strictly individual event but a universal condition passed on by inheritance . . .' . . . Scientific findings make it impossible to accept the classical teaching on Adam and Eve . . . Original sin is what results in us by reason of our birth into this condition of sin. . . ."

What has been said there is: the human race did not come from Adam and Eve (polygenism is in and monogenism out); the story of the fall, as given in Genesis, is incredible—man's natural perfection lies ahead, not behind (evolution presupposed, with some dependence on de Chardin); original sin must therefore be given a different meaning; it is not Adam's sin passed on, but the general sinfulness of the world into which we are born, to which sinfulness we in turn contribute. "The first sin (or sins) was not of decisive significance" (p. 133).

Now, first of all, have scientists established that the human race springs from a multitude of pairs, not from one couple? They have not, as Mr. de Rosa admits. ("Science cannot say definitely that mankind arose from many couples. Monogenism cannot be absolutely ruled out. But the spontaneous assumption of scientists as scientists, in accord with the acknowledged norms of evolution, is that the human race evolved from numerous couples. This assumption is very widespread in the academic world."—pp. 108-109. One must comment: spontaneous assumptions do little credit to science.) A fuller picture is given in Fr. de Surgy's *The Mystery of Salvation* (pp. 22-23), his opening quotation being from de Chardin's *The Phenomenon of Man*, p. 188: " 'If the science of man can say nothing directly for or against monogenism . . . it can on the other hand come out decisively, it seems, in favour of monophyletism (a single phylum).' As Père Dubarle wrote recently: 'everything seems to indicate that there is enough indetermination in what palaeontology can tell us to be able to uphold . . . the religious affirmation that there was a first single human pair". Even if, as Mr. M. C. Davies of Nottingham University affirmed in *The Tablet* for June 30, 1966, *most* biologists vote for polygenism, yet genetic arguments are available to show that monogenism is feasible and possible (see *Some Considerations about Polygenism*, by John J. Rourke, *Theological Studies*, 1965, 26: 407-416).

Fr. de Surgy continues: ". . . how are we to resolve the dilemma—monogenism or polygenism? If one takes chapters 2-3 of Genesis in isolation, it is possible to say, despite the general term used to designate man, that the author took Adam and Eve to be specific individuals, not collective beings. However this is not sufficient to settle the question finally, for it does not seem as though the writer had the question of polygenism in mind." (How could he have had, one is driven to ask, when, under divine inspiration, he was teaching to the contrary?) "We may say, therefore," Fr. de Surgy continues, "that his text as we have it deals with a single pair, but that, apart from the tradition of the church which is the only infallible interpreter of the word of God, it is not a complete answer to the problem. In reality, if we are to put the problem properly, we must not be content to take this text in isolation, but must see it in relation to all the biblical texts, which, taken together, present Adam as a specific individual (for instance, Rom. 5:12ff.), to the patristic commentaries in which Adam is also held to be a definite person, and, above all, to the documents of the magisterium, and especially the fifth session of the Council of Trent on original sin." This is the true Catholic approach; the matter can be settled only by scripture and tradition as interpreted by the teaching authority.

THE ENCYCLICALS

What, then, does the *magisterium* teach in the matter? We will not go first to the ancient councils but to the teaching given in our lifetime. What do we, as Catholics, know about original sin? Pius XII answers in *Mystici Corporis* (1953), an encyclical to which Mr. de Rosa made no reference: "We all know that the father of the whole human race was by God constituted in such an exalted state that together with the life of this earth he would have transmitted to posterity also the supernatural life of heavenly grace. But after Adam's unhappy fall the whole of mankind, infected by the hereditary stain, forfeited its participation in the divine nature and we all became children of wrath. Nevertheless . . . the Word of the Eternal Father took to Himself of the race of Adam a human nature . . . so that from the new and heavenly Adam the grace of the Holy Spirit might flow into all the children of the first parent." That is what "we all know"; that is the *sensus fidelium* common to Pius XII, Mr. Grainger and his 24 teachers. And it includes: (1) Adam was the father of the whole human race; (2) he was created in perfection; (3) all mankind inherited the stain of his sin.

We pass on to *Humani Generis* (1950) which attempted to stamp out renascent errors. After referring to evolution, Pius XII taught: "There are other conjectures, about polygenism (as it is called), which leave the faithful no such freedom of debate. Christians cannot lend their support to a theory which involves the existence, after Adam's time, of some earthly race of men, truly so called, who were not descended ultimately from him, or else supposes that Adam was the name given to some group of our primordial ancestors, since there seems to be no possible way in which such a view can be reconciled with what the sources of revealed truth and the utterances of the Church's teaching authority lay down concerning original sin, which stems from a sin really committed by one individual, Adam, and which, handed down to all by procreation, is lodged in everyone as his own." There we have several points of teaching: (1) As Fr. Karl Rahner phrased it in *Theological Investigations* 1, Chapter 8, *Theological Reflexions on Monogenism*, p. 233: "What is said of polygenism . . . is that it is not a free opinion in the Church, it cannot be held" or, page 235, "The clear intention of the encyclical is to exclude polygenism from theology." (2) Adam was an individual man, not a group. (3) Catholics may not hold the polygenistic view since it seems at variance with what Scripture, tradition and the utterances of the magisterium teach. (4) Adam's sin is historical. (5) His sin is passed to us by blood descent.

It is interesting to se how Mr. de Rosa deals with this teaching. As remarked, he did not refer to *Mystici Corporis*. Though he devoted some sixty pages to Original Sin in Part III of his book, he did not give the full text of what the Pope said, brief as the passage was, though he found space for 24 lines from Bishop Robinson's *In the End, God* about the myth of Adam and Eve, a passage which, he felt, would "be acceptable to many of the modern Catholic theologians." He appended a rider that "*Humani Generis* is a pastoral decree suited to its time" and then confirmed a suspicion, aroused by the quotation from the encyclical, that he had not a copy. He did this by writing that his modern theologians "pointed out that he (Pius XII) had not quoted a single document (say, from Trent) nor a single verse from Scripture (say, from Romans 5) as proof that the matter was already beyond dispute. If anything, he was himself personally in favour of closing the door to polygenism. Nevertheless he certainly didn't lock the door." "If anything" is wonderful!

It is certainly true that the Pope did not *quote* a single document or Scripture text. We have to remember that *Humani Generis* did not tackle this one topic alone but covered quickly a whole range of false scents and therefore could not tackle any one in great detail. But what the Pope did, as Mr. de Rosa would have known if he had consulted *Humani Generis* at first hand, was to append to his teaching a footnote referring the reader to Romans V, 12-19, and Trent, session V, can. 1-4, the verses and Council that he was said not to quote as proof that polygenism was ruled out. These references are supplied in the C.T.S. translation and are part of the original document (A.A.S. 42-1950 - 567).

Is it quite honest to write: "In short Pius XII didn't open the door to polygenism. If anything, he was himself personally in favour of closing the door . . . Nevertheless he certainly didn't lock the door"? The last part is true; Pius did not lock the door but slammed it hard and the sound echoed through the Church. He did not declare the view heretical but *untenable by a Christian.*

THE ADDRESS OF 1966

We move on to an address given by Paul VI to a gathering of theologians on July 11, 1966. Mr. de Rosa mentions it on page 74, giving it less than five lines. "These limits," he quotes, referring to what is allowable to theologians, "are drawn by the living teaching authority of the Church, which is the supreme norm for all the faithful." That is all; he does not think it worth printing what the specified authority taught that day. *Herder Correspondence*, May, 1967, in an article *New Thinking on Original Sin*, at least gave 16 lines to the Pope's words, but they merit much more.

"Catholic doctrine on original sin," Pope Paul said, "was reaffirmed in the Second Vatican Council. . . . Thus in the dogmatic Constitution *Lumen Gentium*, in full consonance with divine revelation and the teaching of the preceding councils of Carthage, Orange and Trent, the fact and the universality of original sin are clearly taught, as well as the intimate nature of the state from which mankind fell through Adam's guilt: 'God the Father did not leave men, fallen in Adam, to themselves, but ceaselessly offered helps to salvation. . . .' "

"It was logical that a reference . . . to the dogma of original sin should be made in the pastoral constitution *Gaudium et Spes* . . . it is not surprising that the document . . . should point out the sad consequences of original sin which were already denounced in lively and effective terms by the Apostle in the letter to the Romans, although the council, following the example of St. Paul himself, does not present original sin as the sole source of mankind's ills. . . ."

". . . In explicit terms the constitution itself in Chapter 1 (*De humanae personae dignitate*) referring tacitly to Genesis and the doctrine of the Council of Trent, indicates the first man's sin as the principal source of the moral disorder existing in mankind. . . ."

"As it clearly emerges from these texts to which we considered it fitting to draw your attention, the second Vatican Council did not aim at deepening and completing the Catholic doctrine on original sin, *already sufficiently declared and defined . . . in the Councils of Carthage (418), of Orange (529) and of Trent (1546).* It only wanted to confirm it. . . ."

"Catholic exegetes and theologians are therefore granted all that liberty of research and judgment which is demanded by the scientific nature of their studies. . . . There are limits, however, which cannot and must not be overstepped by the exegete, the theologian and the scientist who really intends to enlighten his own faith and that of other Catholics. These limits are marked by the living magisterium of the Church, which is a proximate norm of truth for all the faithful. . . ."

"Convinced therefore that *the doctrine of original sin both regarding its existence and universality, its character as true sin even in the descendants of Adam and its sad consequences for soul and body, is a truth revealed by God in various passages of the Old and of the New Testament, but especially in the texts you well know, of Genesis 3: 1-20, and of the Letter to the Romans 5: 12-19,* always take care, in scrutinizing and specifying the meaning of Biblical texts, to observe the indispensable norms which stem from the *analogia fidei,* from the declarations and definitions of the above-mentioned councils and from the documents issued by the Apostolic See. . . ."

"It is therefore evident that the explanations of original sin by some modern authors will seem to you irreconcilable with true Catholic doctrine. Starting from the undemonstrated premise of polygenism, they deny . . . that that sin from which so many cesspools of evil have come to mankind was . . . the disobedience of Adam, 'first man' . . . committed at the beginning of history. Consequently these explanations do not even agree with the teaching of Scripture, of sacred tradition and the Church's magisterium, according to which the sin of the first man is transmitted to all his descendants not through imitation but through propagation . . . (Cf. Council of Trent, 5th session, canons 2-3)."

"But even the theory of 'evolutionism' favoured today by many scientists and not a few theologians owing to its probability will not seem acceptable to you where it is not decidedly in accord with the immediate creation of each and every human soul by God, and where it does not regard as decisively important for the fate of mankind the disobedience of Adam, universal protoparent (cf. Council of Trent, session 5, canon 1)."

There mankind has been given a resounding reaffirmation of eternal truth, and it is not surprising that Mr. de Rosa did not think fit to quote it. This edification, building-up, rather than Bishop Robinson's demolition, is what should shape a Catholic's thinking. It condemns the host of modern theologians whose views Mr. de Rosa propounds. "It is therefore evident that the explanations of original sin by some modern authors will seem to you irreconcilable with true Catholic doctrine." And the references to Vatican II are a healthy reminder. Adam, said *Gaudium et Spes*, section 22, was the first man, and man would have been immune from bodily death if sin had not entered the world (section 18).

Clear as the Pope's address was, it still found Catholics to diminish its force. Fr. John Russell, S.J., writing on *Evolution and Theology* in *The Tablet* for September 16, 1967, said: "The most important pronouncement on original sin since 1950 was an address of Pope Paul VI . . . This reaffirmed, substantially, the teaching of *Humani Generis*, but with the significant exception that polygenism was not specifically mentioned." The following week, Fr. Vincent J. O'Brien,

C.M., dealth with the mis-statement: "Does not the Pope's use of the terms 'Adam, the first man,' 'Adam the universal protoparent,' and 'the first man's sin' imply a rejection of polygenism? And surely the latter is 'specifically mentioned' in the following passage: '. . . starting with the undemonstrated premise of polygenism, they deny. . . .' "

THE CREDO OF THE PEOPLE OF GOD

Paul VI raised his voice, two years after his address of 1966, "to give, on behalf of all the People of God, a firm witness to the divine Truth entrusted to the Church to be announced to all nations", saying that he wished his profession of faith to be explicit "in order that it may respond in a fitting way to the need of light felt by so many faithful souls. . . ." This is what he proclaimed as the faith of the Church, to settle any dispute about the doctrine of original sin: "We believe that in Adam all have sinned, which means that the original offence committed by him caused human nature, common to all men, to fall into a state in which it bears the consequences of that offence, and which is not the state in which it was at first in our first parents, established as they were in holiness and justice, and in which man knew neither evil or death. It is human nature so fallen, stripped of the grace that clothed it, injured in its own natural powers and subjected to the dominion of death, that is transmitted to all men, and it is in this sense that every man is born in sin. We therefore hold, with the Council of Trent, that original sin is transmitted with human nature, 'not by imitation, but by propagation' and that it is thus 'proper to everyone'. We believe that Our Lord Jesus Christ, by the sacrifice of the Cross, redeemed us from original sin and all the personal sins committed by each one of us. . . ."

Once again the Holy See repeated the unadulterated word of tradition. The Bishops' Synod also deplored the way in which truths of the faith were being called into question, including the mystery of original sin. Yet it remains true that many Catholics do not give firm assent of mind and will to the teaching of the magisterium, or minimise the duty of doing so. Here is Fr. Symon, writing in the *Catholic Herald* for February 12, 1971: "Needless to say the Church remains attached to the traditional way of expressing our faith in original sin. Just as St. Paul, in the Epistle to the Romans, speaks of Adam as one, so too does the Second Vatican Council and, in his 1968 'Creed of the People of God,' Pope Paul VI." Then we are treated to a bathetic conclusion: "If a Catholic is satisfied with this more usual way of expressing the Faith, there is no reason whatever why he should now abandon it." The true conclusion should, of course, have been that a Catholic is bound to accept this teaching, and may not abandon it. But the bathos in the conclusion can be traced, on a re-reading, to what preceded. First, there was a mistake of fact. Fr. Symon wrote earlier, "Over the last 20 years, since Pius XII wrote on the subject, it has been suggested that there is another possible explanation. According to this view the human race would first have appeared as, say, perhaps a dozen or a hundred men and women." In fact, however, Pius XII knew of this explanation and scouted the suggestion that "Adam was the name given to some group of our primordial ancestors." But the rotten beam in Fr. Symon's structure appears as a *suggestio falsi*, when he states that the Church remains "attached to the traditional way of expressing our faith in original sin," which is echoed later in "this more usual way of expressing the Faith"—the false underlying assumption being that that is *one* way of expressing the Faith but others might be equally orthodox. The Church is attached to that expression of the Faith because she is attached to the doctrine, and no one, the Popes have made clear, has come up with another orthodox way of interpreting the doctrine. A Catholic has no option; he cannot hold the views now being propounded in defiance of tradition and magisterium. I have not read, or seen, *The Theology of Original Sin*, by Fr. E. Yarnold, S.J. one of the signatories of the Windsor Agreement, but was saddened by Fr. Maurice Nassau's review of it in the *Catholic Herald* (May 26, 1972). He wrote: "It is clear from the book that a great deal of thought has to be devoted to the whole question of Original Sin before modern interpretations can be fully accepted but, as Fr. Yarnold points out, there is much in them that can be commended. There has, for example, in the past been far too much emphasis placed on the first sin and the historical origin of the human race." By Popes and Councils?

Before going back to see what the Councils taught, we draw attention to false trails which are being blazed. Pius XII taught in *Humani Generis* that original sin is passed on to us by procreation, by blood descent—the teaching of Trent which Paul VI repeated in 1966 and again in the 'Creed of the People of God.' Yet de Rosa (admittedly writing before the papal 'credo') quotes, on page 20 of his work, from Rosemary Haughton's *On Trying to be Human*: ". . . it is thought of as being transmitted in the process of generation, not (as it must be) simply because that is how human beings are. . . ."

Rosa locuta est. Vatican II, however, impressed in *Gaudium et Spes* that man would have been immune from bodily death if he had not sinned (as the *Credo* also taught), and we shall contact this point again when we come to the decrees of Carthage and Trent. Mr. de Rosa, on the other hand (pages 104, 105) gives as worthy of consideration views of Claude Tresmontant and Dubarle affirming that we need not accept this teaching.

TEILHARD DE CHARDIN

A third false trail: on page 132 our author quotes from Fr. T. Corbishley's *The Contemporary Christian*: "It is no exaggeration to say that, in the sphere of the physical sciences in relation to theology, no single man has done as much as Teilhard de Chardin to prepare the way for a new presentation of the immutable truth entrusted to the Church." But it must be countered that Teilhard had no place in his scheme for the doctrine of original sin; he jettisoned it, for those who spoke with him tell that he inclined to the view that it was only an early state of physical imperfection. It is typical of the way in which re-interpreters clutch at straws that the writer went on to note hopefully of Pope Paul's 1966 address: "in the final draft the qualification of the 'first man' as applied to Adam is put within inverted commas!" As it happens, the first use of the term is without inverted commas, the second use has them since it is an explicit quotation from *Gaudium et Spes,* and the third use is again without them. "I have come to the conclusion," wrote Fr. de Chardin in *Stuff of the Universe,* "that . . . a whole series of reshapings of certain representations or attitudes which seem to us definitely fixed by Catholic dogma has become necessary if we sincerely wish to Christify Evolution."[1] In 1924, he wrote to a friend: "One of my papers (in which I expounded three possible lines of my search for a way of representing original sin) has been sent to Rome. I do not know how. The censor is naturally astounded. I have got off with the comment that I am 'Heretical' or that 'I have a screw loose'—I have leave it to you to choose which.' "[2] "Christianity," he wrote in a letter in 1953, "will only recoup its power to influence the world when it . . . sets itself to the task of rethinking the doctrine of original sin in terms of progress rather than of a Fall . . . original sin is nothing more than a by-product of evolution."[3] Already, in 1920, he had written: "There is not, strictly speaking, a first Adam,"[4] and, two years later, "Adam and Eve are the images of humanity on its way to God. The beatitude of the terrestrial paradise represents the salvation which is constantly being offered to all. . . ."[5] He felt, however, that Catholic thought was flourishing in spite of the Vicar of Christ—"In the course of the last fifty years, I have watched the revitalisation of Catholic thought and life taking place around me in spite of all the encyclicals."[6] Such words do not flow happily and humbly from a Catholic pen, but they help to explain why Teilhard is so popular in some circles today and why, whatever Fr. Corbishley may have written about 'immutable truth,' the Holy Office ordered in 1957 that de Chardin's works were to be withdrawn from the libraries of seminaries and religious institutes and from Cath-

---

[1] See the article *The Strange Faith of Teilhard de Chardin,* by Henri Rambaud, p. 36, in *Approaches,* March, 1966.
[2] *Ibidem,* p. 54.
[3] Cf. *The One and the Many,* by Donald Gray, p. 57.
[4] & [5] *Ibidem,* p. 63.
[6] *Approaches,* March, 1966, p. 38.

olic bookshops in Rome. In 1962, this was followed by a declaration that his works were "replete with ambiguities or, rather, with serious errors which offend Catholic doctrine."

THE COUNCILS

Pope Paul declared that the Second Vatican Council considered that the doctrine of original sin was already sufficiently declared and defined in the Councils of Carthage, Orange and Trent. It is time now to read the conciliar decrees, and we first draw attention to the healthy reminder of Fr. P. Schoonenberg in *Man and Sin* (p. 158): "The shepherds of the church, the bishops around the pope, provide an irreplaceable guidance, so that their teaching authority is the clearest realization of the assistance of the Holy Spirit promised to the whole church. Within the believing and listening church their function is to teach."

Carthage (418 A.D.): "Whoever says that Adam, the first man, was made mortal, so that, whether he sinned or whether he did not sin, he would die in body . . . let him be anathema." (Dz. 101.) Canon 2: "Whoever says that infants . . . ought not to be baptized . . . that they draw nothing of the original sin from Adam . . .let him be anathema. Since what the Apostle says, 'Through one man sin entered into the word, and through sin death, and so death passed to all men, in whom all have sinned' (Rom. 5:12) must not be understood otherwise than as the Catholic Church . . . has always understood it." (Dz. 102.)

Pope Zosimus approved the doctrine of Carthage and so it gained immeasurably in weight. As it said that St. Paul's words in Romans 5 must be understood as the Church has always done, it is deplorable to find the Dutch catechism teaching: "At first sight it seems that his intention is to stress the fact that it was through one man that sin came into the world. But the repetition of the word 'one', occasioned by the view of world history as it existed in Paul's time, is only part of the literary dress, not the message. What this difficult passage teaches us is that though sin and death ruled over mankind, grace and eternal life, the

restoration, has come in greater abundance through Jesus. . . .
This most moving text of Scripture can never be replaced as
a summary of how man stands before God. But it can and
must be replaced as a description of the beginning of mankind." (Catechism, pp. 262-263.) "Adam," the bishops
had taught on the preceding page, "is Man . . . It is only with
chapter 12, where Abraham appears, that we begin to make
out historical figures." (From *Humani Generis*: ". . . the
first eleven chapters of Genesis . . . do nevertheless come
under the heading of history. . . .")

Orange (529 A.D.): Canon 2: "If anyone asserts that
Adam's transgression injured him alone and not his descendants, or affirms that bodily death certainly, which is the
punishment of sin, but not sin, which is the death of the soul,
passed through one man into the whole human race, he will
do an injustice to God, contradicting the Apostle who says
'Through one man sin entered the world, and through sin
death, and thus death passed into all men, in whom all have
sinned' (Rom. 5.12)." (Dz. 175.) Boniface II confirmed
this teaching and so it became 'Catholic' in authority.

So we come to the General Council of Trent which had
to deal with a list of thirteen heresies relating to original
sin, among which we find a new wave of Pelagianism and,
rather unexpectedly, an allegation of Erasmus (remembered
by Queen's College, Cambridge, as the man who left behind
a giant corkscrew) that Romans 5 did not mention original
sin. The topic was treated in Session V. Canon 1 reads: "If
anyone does not confess that the first man Adam, when he
had transgressed the commandment of God in paradise, immediately lost his holiness and the justice in which he had
been established, and that he incurred through the offence
of that prevarication the wrath and indignation of God and,
hence, the death with which God had previously threatened
him, and with death captivity under the power of him who
thenceforth 'had the empire of death' (Heb. 2:14)—that is,
of the devil—and that through that offence . . . the entire
Adam was transformed in body and soul for the worse, let
him be anathema." (Dz. 788.) Adam, then, was created in
"holiness and justice," and death was the result of his sin.

The Dutch bishops challenged this on page 269 of their catechism, teaching: "And as regards man himself, we need not imagine that he once existed in a state of paradisiac perfection and immortality," their novel view being "propounded in the light of our present view of the world, as a world in a state of growth and evolution" (p. 268). The influence of de Chardin is strong there.

Canon 2 lays down: "If anyone asserts that the transgression of Adam harmed him alone and not his posterity, and that the sanctity and justice, which he received from God and lost, he lost for himself alone and not for us as well; or that, when he had been defiled by the sin of disobedience, he passed on only death and bodily suffering to the whole human race, but not sin also, which is the death of the soul, let him be anathema, since he contradicts the Apostle who says . . ." and once again we have Romans 5 (Dz. 789).

Canon 3 begins: "If anyone asserts that this sin of Adam, which is one in origin and transmitted to all, and which is in each one as his own by propagation, not by imitation, is taken away by . . . any remedy other than the merit of the one mediator . . ." and deals out the familiar anathema (Dz. 790). Canon 4 echoes Carthage, insisting on the necessity of baptism even for new-born babies. (I would note here that J. B. Walker, in *New Theology for Plain Christians*, p. 90, holds that infant baptism is undesirable.)

The conciliar teaching has been echoed in our time by Pius XII, Vatican II, and Paul VI. Fr. Schoonenberg, whose words regarding the irreplaceable guidance of the magisterium have been cited, unhappily provides one more example of the flimsiness of the arguments advanced in favour of novel interpretation. We have seen Trent speak of Adam's sin as "one in origin." Fr. Schoonenberg writes (*op. cit.*, p. 175): "When the encyclical *Humani Generis* quotes the doctrine of Trent . . . *it is a remarkable fact* (italics mine) that it does not mention the formula 'origine unum' . . ." What a non-argument that is, when the encyclical said: "Original sin is the result of a sin committed . . . by an individual named Adam"! If that is not the equivalent of "one in origin," words no longer hold any meaning. After much detailed study of Scripture and Council texts, Fr. Schoonenberg comes to the conclusion that "there is a presumption in favour of the classic doctrine of original sin. . . ." But, as the Church's teaching is infallible and the original meaning of a doctrine must be retained, there is infinitely more than a presumption.

Chip, chip, go the hammers of the modern theologians as they labour to find out how much of doctrine they can knock away. "It is clear, however," Fr. Schoonenberg admits (*op. cit.*, p. 173), "that for the Council (Trent) and for the whole thinking of the church, the universality of original sin is determined by the fall"—but this does not deter him; it makes the attempted reinterpretation all the more challenging. "They throw over the definitions of the Council of Trent by misrepresenting the whole nature of original sin" was the warning given by *Humani Generis*. But, Mr. de Rosa claims, "There has been . . . a discernible growth of courage among the theologians responsible for this delicate venture" (*op. cit.*, p. 92), and unfamiliarity with *Humani Generis* hid from him that he was verifying the prediction of Pius XII that "the views which are put forward obscurely today . . . will be proclaimed tomorrow, by other, bolder spirits, openly and extravagantly."

"Both the magisterium and those who listen to it must realise that what matters is not to cling to a formula, but to be faithful to a message." So Fr. Schoonenberg (p. 168). But, if he had listened to the magisterium, he would know that formula and message are often inseparable and the papal verdict must be accepted when it refuses a doctrinal divorce. All the picking away at doctrine . . . was St. Augustine led astray by a faulty translation ('in quo omnes peccaverunt') and did the Church follow him into error? Can we strip the lamina of essential doctrine from a lamina of faulty presupposition? . . . is therefore unavailing. The modern theologian can make a case of sorts, of course; he is not a fool. But he cannot in the end judge the case, having no divine jurisdiction. Cleverness is never enough, as most of the heresiarchs have been talented and educated men.

The theologians continue to question and modify. A. M. Dubarle suggests that Pope Paul in 1966 relaxed the rigour of Pius XII.[7] Fr. Karl Rahner (*Evolution and Original Sin* in *Concilium*, 1967) moves from the position he adopted in *Theological Investigations* and in doing so underlines the ephemeral character of expert opinion. So continues the confrontation with what *Herder Correspondence* (May, 1967) dubbed "the deep blue sea of apparent papal intransigence", though the papacy is the rock on which the changeable sea smashes. The result is that more and more of us are becoming aware that theological writing is tending to grow sterile at the best. In his day, St. Thomas More grew weary of theological argumentation which, he said, was "like one man milking a he-goat while another held a sieve."

If the theologians, the goat and the sieve could all be kept in quarantine, the Church could afford to smile at them, but the doubts and the denials escape and affect even our schools. I quote now an account, provided by a headmaster who is not given to exaggeration, of the chat that he had in the staffroom with the Reverend Religious Inspector before Father went round the classes. They got on to the topic of catechetics and here is a passage from the conversation:

Priest: "Of course, you understand that salvation is material?"

Head: "Oh! What about the soul?"

Priest: "The soul . . . I don't know what that is."

Head: "And when the body dies?"

Priest: "When you're dead, you're dead."

Head: "What about Purgatory, prayers for the dead?"

Priest: "Well, I don't know about Purgatory. I suppose you could pray for the dead. God probably foresees these. But we look forward to the resurrection of the body really."

Head: "Spirits, angels . . . are they out?"

Priest: "Well, I think we can forget them."

[7] *Le Monde,* August 6, 1966.

Head: "What about the recent amendments to the Dutch Catechism by the Commission of Cardinals?"

Priest: "These old men mean well. I wouldn't pay any attention to them.

Head: "It's a bit difficult these days in school. I will follow the Church but not opinions which don't appear to have official backing."

Priest: "Don't worry about dogma. Very little is needed. Eighty per cent of your teaching should be aimed at material advancement of people . . . social work, etc."

Head: "Isn't this just humanism?"

Priest: "The only thing that separates me from humanists is one phrase: 'For God's sake!' "

"And so," the headmaster concluded, "it went on. I'm afraid that I'm going to stick to the Faith as I know it until the Bishop says otherwise. Do you recognize this stuff?" Yes, indeed, we recognize it, and many would say that the good headmaster should have forbidden the priest to teach his schoolchildren . . . but Catholics have grown up to respect, not suspect, priests. We like our nuns to be positively Catholic too. The *Catholic Herald* for November 8, 1968, printed an interview with a nun, dealing with her catechetical work, and she was happy to say that "now there is very little difference between what is taught in Religious Education in a Protestant school and a Catholic school." As a profound philosopher once observed, the mind boggles.

12

Alter Christus?

*There can be no communion between the Catholic
Church and a heresy which fights against Christ.*

St. Athanasius.

*The devotional Christ is totally incredible . . . .
Jesus is a stage prop for the pageantry of the Ro-
man Catholic Church. If it hurts any to read this,
I hope it hurts a lot.*

FR. JOHN MCKENZIE,
Critic, September-October, 1971.

At a retreat which I attended in recent years, the Jesuit
retreat-Father spoke of the childhood of Jesus, and of how
He "advanced in wisdom," and said that Jesus' knowledge
would probably be in accordance with His era, that He would
think the earth to be flat. Moreover, St. Joseph or our Lady
might occasionally have to give Him a thrashing; that is a
normal way to learn. If it had been fitting to debate in
chapel, his listeners might first have replied that good parents
thrash only because of delinquency—and surely our Jesuit
was not alleging that Jesus was guilty of moral fault. The
Jesuit might, of course, have knocked the wind out of our
sails by retorting that he *was*, since, in notes taken at the
lectures of Fr. H. Richards in New Zealand (July, 1972), I
read: "The speaker quoted Hebrews 4:15, omitting from the
phrase 'like unto us in all things, without sin' the words
'without sin' and remarked afterwards that some of his hearers
had not noticed the omission, which, he said, was delibe-

rate." And, though it has been revived in our time, the view that Jesus' human knowledge was limited was fathered by the first Modernists and has been condemned (Dz. 2032-2034).

Baron von Hügel tries to blind with historical science in his 2nd series of *Essays and Addresses* (1904): "As historians, we now know that the institution of the Church is far less directly and completely attributable to Our Lord than used to be believed. . . . This same historical criticism is demonstrating, with apparent ruthlessness, the limited and non-infallible character of Our Lord's recorded manifestation of human knowledge. . . ." Reading this confident assertion, one would imagine that one was listening to a scientist who had established his contentions by rigid experiment in the laboratory; one would never suspect that the man was recounting mere conjectures; yet so it was.

GOD IN FANCY DRESS OR FATHER CHRISTMAS

Ved Mehta, in *The New Theologian* (p. 9), writes of Bishop Robinson's *Honest to God*: "The style of the book, like that of a schoolboy's composition, was showy—bulging and straining at almost every point with far-fetched analogies constructed for purposes of polemics: 'The traditional supranaturalistic way of describing the Incarnation almost inevitably suggests that Jesus was really God almighty walking about on earth, dressed up as a man. . . . He looked like a man, he talked like a man, he felt like a man, but underneath he was God dressed up—like Father Christmas.' "

We have echoes of this polemical 'guying' in Catholic books like Mr. Lance's *What is Christianity*: *11-16*, in which he draws upon Mr. de Rosa's *Christ and Original Sin* (he also drew upon Fr. Dulles and Fr. H. Richards, establishing the cross-infection which takes place). On page 128, he produces his lampoon of the Catholic view: "Christ is regarded as not *really* a man. Jesus is God only *acting as if he were* a man. Jesus would be seen rather as, in the words of Peter de Rosa, 'God in fancy dress.' The infant Jesus, it would be thought, only pretended to be helpless and ignorant and the man Jesus pretended to suffer and be afraid and to pray. He could have used his 'God power', but did not, so as to give us an example. But this will not do at all:" Certainly it will not do. He has drenched the belief in Christ's omniscience in clumsy sarcasm shot through with confusion. If Christ chose to veil His knowledge, it is illogically deduced that He pretended to suffer. Doubt is cast also on His power to avoid suffering if He so wished, though Jesus revealed that, if He asked, His Father would send more than twelve legions of angels to His aid immediately (Matt. 26:52).

We pass on to J. B. Walker's *New Theology for Plain Christians*, still on sale in Westminster Cathedral. He pours scorn on the traditional belief (p. 20): ". . . it was claimed . . . that he 'beheld the face of God continually', just as the blessed do in heaven . . . except when he deliberately switched off this 'beatific vision' in order to suffer the pains of his passion." Here is 'guying' plus confusion once more. In spite of the crude remark about 'switching off', it *was* claimed that the beatific vision was uninterrupted. The author continues: "The synoptic gospels themselves clearly imply that he only gradually came to understand about his mission and about the suffering it would bring . . . though there is general agreement among Roman Catholic theologians that Jesus must always have been in some way aware of his special relationship with God as Son to Father . . . this awareness does not necessarily mean that he knew consciously who he was and what he was meant to do. . . ." (One might compare the teaching of the old anti-Arian warrior, St. Fulgentius: "It is . . . quite incompatible with the integrity of the Faith to assume that Christ's soul did not possess a full knowledge of its divinity, with which, according to the Faith, it physically possesses one person."[1])

St. Fulgentius, who suffered so much for the doctrine of Christ's divinity, has laid his finger in that passage on the key to the matter under discussion. There is only *one* Person in Christ, our Lord's human soul being united to the

---

[1] Ludwig Ott, *Fundamentals of Catholic Dogma*, p. 163.

divinity in the hypostatic union. When, therefore, Jesus said "I", God spoke, and the 'knowing subject' was God, even when God was using a human soul, brain and memory. This is why an attribution of ignorance to Jesus seems to shake the pillars of belief in His divinity. Tradition also attributed to His created soul a continual beatific vision of God in whom we all live and move and are. The apostles had worked out no Christology, but, when He told them that He came from the Father into this world, they responded: "Now we know that thou knowest all things" (John 16:30), and St. Peter backed up the sincerity of his act of love with, "Lord, thou knowest all things" (St. John 21:17).

Two reflections are called for. First, human personality and knowledge are deep mysteries to us, so that we are in the dark regarding our own consciousness. Inevitably, we shall be pressed in by greater mystery when we consider a divine Person. Our human reason will hardly be able to formulate the right problems, far less come up with the sound answer, and we must accordingly speak with utmost humility. In the most reverent sense, God alone knows. Secondly, as Fr. Brown wrote in *Jesus, God and Man* (p. 42): "the biblical evidence does not decide the theological problem or conclusively support one theory over another." That means that the debate cannot be decided by scholarship since texts are in the hands of both sides; the magisterium, echoing tradition and *sensus communis*, is our only safe guide.

THE LIGHT OF THE WORLD, IN THE DARK

Fr. Brown wrote (p. 102): "A Jesus who walked through the world knowing exactly what the morrow would bring, knowing with certainty that three days after his death his Father would raise him up, is a Jesus who can arouse our admiration, but still a Jesus far from us. He is a Jesus far from mankind that can only hope in the future and believe in God's goodness, far from a mankind that must face the supreme uncertainty of death with faith but without knowledge of what is beyond. On the other hand, a Jesus for whom the future was as much a mystery, a dread, and a hope as it is for us and yet, at the same time, a Jesus who would say, 'Not my will but yours'—this is a Jesus who could effectively teach us how to live, for this is a Jesus who would have gone through life's real trials."

This verdict seems to be as detached from reality as it is possible to be. First of all, generation after generation of Catholics have believed that Jesus knew all things, including the details of the future. In the chapter *The Consciousness of Christ*, in *Facing the Truth*, Fr. D'Arcy concedes: "All theological works and orthodox lovers of Christ have laid stress on his obedience, but they usually presuppose that from the beginning he knew with certainty all that was to happen to him." Fr. Karl Rahner makes much the same claim in Volume 5 of *Theological Investigations* (Chapter IX): "Theological tradition attributes a knowledge to Jesus as man which embraces and exhausts all past, present and future reality, at least to the extent in which these realities are related in some way to Christ's soteriological task. . . . This theological tradition furthermore attributed to Jesus—from the very first moment of his human existence—the possession of the direct vision of God as it is experienced by the blessed in heaven." He adds, "Such statements sound almost mythological today when one first hears them; they seem to be contrary to the real humanity and historical nature of Our Lord"—but there is no reason why they should sound stranger today than at any point in history. St. John Vianney, St. Thomas More, St. Bernard, St. Augustine knew just as much about men and life as we do.

The point that I am making here is this: it is of no value to write that a Jesus Who knew everything would be "far from us", "far from mankind." Through the ages the saints have held this view of Christ, and He was very close to them. Would Fr. Brown suggest that He did not "effectively teach" them and our parents how to live? Fr. D'Arcy rightly spoke of 'orthodox lovers' of Christ. The poor labourer, for instance, pouring out his love at the foot of the statue of the Sacred Heart, did not feel that Jesus was remote and alien. If asked, he would have replied that Jesus' knowledge of His passion-to-come made His suffering all the more protracted and His love more signal. And, if anyone had dared breathe of a Christ-in-the-dark, of a holy home in Nazareth resounding to a thrashing, of a Jesus Who did not know Who He was or where He was going, he would have disowned this other Christ. *Alter* Christus . . . but not the Christ of Catholic belief. Mr. de Rosa (or his modern theologian) says, ". . . there were many things of which he was ignorant and towards an understanding of which he had to grope in the dark . . . his awareness of being God's Son had to mature, become explicit, as time went on. . . . None of this will lessen our respect for our divine Redeemer" (*op. cit.*, pp. 13-14).[2] He does not see that he has already diminished Him.

Fr. Hans Urs von Balthasar, in *A Theology of History*, p. 33, writes of our Lord: "It would be better to compare him to an actor playing a part for the first time, receiving it by inspiration, scene by scene, word by word. The play does not exist in advance, but is conceived, produced and acted all in one." It would be better only if it were true; Jesus was not an 'actor' to whom guidance was doled out but, in Him, a human spirit was linked to a divine in hypostatic union. It is such novelties which cannot satisfy our faith although the article *New Thinking about Christ*, in *Herder Correspondence* (July-August, 1967) tried to convince us that "we cannot remain content with some of the theories about Christ's knowledge which have become almost traditional in our textbooks and have been favoured by some recent statements of the teaching authorities." Somehow the validity of the teaching of the magisterium was not depreciated by *Herder's* assurance that "recent Roman Catholic thinking on christology brings it very close to the best of modern Protestant thought."

We have seen Mr. Walker sceptical about Christ's possession of the beatific vision always. Mr. de Rosa shares the same scepticism. On page 4 he tells us "from the middle

---

[2] His colleague, Fr. H. Richards, wrote in *that Sower:* "Jesus was limited . . . in power, in health, in knowledge, in foresight, in the understanding of a situation . . . He had to search his way painfully into the unknown future, making decisions which he was not always sure were the right ones."

ages there was a great devotion to the passion and cross"
but that "there grew up simultaneously . . . a theology of
Christ which put him beyond all human efforts at identifica-
tion and imitation." (Poor Thomas à Kempis and his *Imitation of Christ!*) He continues: "To him was attributed the
beatific vision of his Father from his conception. . . . Such
things were thought to be entailed by Christ's divinity. . . ."
Then, on page 63, "They (theologians today) react strongly
against the picture given in some devotional works. . . .
Christ was not a *comprehensor*. . . ."

Mr. de Rosa makes the belief sound like something possible only in a more primitive age: "According to most theologians of an *earlier period*, Jesus had the beatific vision of
God in his earthly life" and Brother Gabriel Moran, in
Theology of Revelation, p. 69, sings in unison: "Whereas
medieval theology thought . . . we realize today that . . . ."
but Pius XII lived in our day and so we come to what he
wrote in *Mystici Corporis* (1943): "He is adorned with all
those supernatural gifts which accompany the hypostatic
union . . . and 'all the treasures of wisdom and knowledge
of God' abound in Him. He also enjoys the beatific vision in
a degree, both as regards extent and clarity, surpassing that
of all the saints in heaven . . . the loving knowledge with
which the divine Redeemer has pursued us from the first
moment of His incarnation is such as completely to surpass
all the searchings of the human mind; for by means of the
beatific vision, which He enjoyed from the time when He was
received into the womb of the Mother of God, He has forever
and continuously had present to Him all the members of His
mystical Body, and embraced them with His saving love. . . .
In the manger, in the Cross, in the eternal glory of the Father,
Christ sees and embraces al lthe members of His Church. . . ."
Thus, Pius XII repeated a traditional belief so strong that
Suarez judged: "I regard the contrary opinion as . . . bor-
dering on heresy."

In the article already mentioned, Fr. D'Arcy draws on
a contribution by Fr. John Bligh, S.J., to the *Heythrop
Journal* (October, 1968) and writes: "Becoming man . . .
this knowledge is laid aside . . . He emptied himself. . . .

Father Bligh argues that this emptying was . . . maybe of his knowledge too. . . . It is chosen ignorance which makes him suffer humanly when his loving intentions are thwarted: and it is not without desolation . . . that he realises finally that it is by the cruel death of the cross . . . the Father's intention of the salvaging of the world is to be accomplished." It is all very well to write in this way of "chosen ignorance", but *we* must not choose ignorance. *Lamentabili*—by condemning Modernist propositions regarding Christ's knowledge—has instructed us. We pin on to *Lamentabili* the answer given by the Holy Office in 1918 to three questions put to it. The answer was *NO* and the tripartite question was if the following propositions could be safely taught: (1) "It is not established that the soul of Christ, while He lived among men, had that knowledge which the blessed or *comprehensores* (those who see God) have;" (2) "The view cannot be considered certain which holds that Christ's soul was in no respect ignorant, but knew all things in the Word from the beginning, past, present and future, or all things which God knows by the knowledge of vision;" (3) "The view of some recent thinkers, which holds that Christ's soul had limited knowledge, is no less acceptable to Catholic schools than the belief of earlier writers asserting His universal knowledge."

Mr. de Rosa, I note, has returned to the theme of the limitation of Christ's knowledge, in *God our Saviour: A Study of the Atonement*, but the answer as to whether this can be safely taught was, in 1918, *No*. Since then *Mystici Corporis* has made it doubly certain that the answer will remain *NO*. Pius XII reaffirmed this in the encyclical *Haurietis Aquas* in 1956. Finally, those who wish to study recent attempts to square traditional views with more 'modern' re-examination should consult the article *Knowledge of Christ* in *A Catholic Dictionary of Theology*, Volume 3. There they will find Rahner, Lonergan and Reidlinger wrestling with the problem. My purely personal opinion is that the problem 'throws' them all, that man is here out of his depths. Man cannot plumb his own consciousness. How can he expect to dissect that of the Second Person of the Trinity?

13

Reprise

*At least five times, therefore, with the Arian and
the Albigensian, with the Humanist sceptic, after
Voltaire and after Darwin, the Faith has to all
appearance gone to the dogs. In each of these five
cases it was the dog that died. . . . There are
people who say they wish Christianity to remain as
a spirit. They mean, very literally, that they wish
it to remain as a ghost. But it is not going to
remain as a ghost. What follows this process of
apparent death is not the lingering of the shade;
it is the resurrection of the body. . . . Day by day
and year by year we have lowered our hopes and
lessened our convictions; we have grown more and
more used to . . . dilution, to dissolution, to a
watering down that went on for ever. But Thou
hast kept the good wine until now. . . . (The Catholic Faith) was supposed to have been withered up
at last in the dry light of the Age of Reason; it was
supposed to have disappeared ultimately in the
earthquake of the Age of Revolution. Science explained it away; and it was still there. History
disinterred it in the past; and it appeared suddenly
in the future. To-day it stands once more in our
path; and even as we watch it, it grows.*

G. K. CHESTERTON, The Everlasting Man.

I have set at the head of this chapter a great and heart-
ening passage from *The Everlasting Man* to remind us that
we must deal with our renovator-innovators firmly, but not
despondently. It is easy to become despondent after spend-

ing much time in their company, as we have done in these pages, but it would show a lack of sense of proportion really to take them *seriously*. Shaking a metaphorical spear at the Cardinals, Tyrrell cried out, "It is they who are in peril, not we!" but history has laughed at the poor man. The Modernists are born losers since their thinking, as Archbishop Goodier told us, betrays "an intellectual and moral disease." Thus Charles Davis points to the seeds of self-destruction in them: "because of their paradoxical position, people who hold more or less the same views as I do and yet remain within the Church seem to suffer distorting effects on their thinking. I get the impression at times of a tension, a forced carelessness, an uneasy subtlety or ingenuity in arguing." It is no wonder, then, that a contributor to *The Experience of Priesthood*, presumably speaking of the shaky circles in which he moved, remarked: "The happy and fulfilled priest is the exception."

They are sad men, and they should be sad because all through this book we have collected their admissions that they are at variance with their fellow-Catholics, that they are weird mutations. Some, like Tyrrell, could hug to themselves the comforting thought that they were the minority of "able and cultivated minds," but still the admissions of odd-man-out keep appearing. If we take Berengarius as a Modernist born out of due season, we hear him denouncing the "opinion of the mob." Then, taking Fr. Coventry as in some respects Modernist, we hear about the imbalance "in the popular mind." Fr. Bullen laments that "many people," "young people especially," believe in a change of physical reality in the Eucharist. *The Sower* is upset because "people for centuries have thought that Jesus is God," and "most of the faithful usually misunderstand it." It shakes its head because "most Catholics" take "the common simple view" that the gospels are accounts of what Jesus said and did, the "cherished view." And when it comes to the question of our Lady—Chesterton called attack upon her "the little hiss that only comes from hell"—then we are told mournfully that the question of the Virgin Birth "arouses among Catholics such emotions as to prevent objective judgement." Fr. Somerville, as we saw, is very up-stage about what "the vast majority of the faithful think of the Christian life"—believing, keeping Commandments, going to the sacraments. And Fr. McBrien came down heavily on "the more conventional Catholic understanding of papal infallibility," while Fr. Schoof could find only two countries, plus one hanger-on, where the new theology, could take root. One is left with the impression that, when they meet, it is for a good cry . . .

With God's grace, most of those who are troubling the Church now will come to their senses and their knees, but, for those who are obdurate, there is a parable worth meditation. It appeared in Mr. Philip Toynbee's review of three books, one of which was Rosemary Haughton's *On Trying to be Human*, a review which bore the caption *The God that Failed*.[1] It tells how the members of the Christian Club, in Pall Mall, began to experience doubts about their club. They couldn't see God with their telescope and so they decided to dig a tunnel and seek Him below ground. They dug and dug, coming on electric cables, water pipes and sewers. . . . "But these warnings that others might have been there before them were resolutely disregarded. With eager shouts of 'I am becoming even more radical than you,' they vied with each other in the zeal with which they drove their tunnel further" . . . and further from the Christian Club. Finally, they hacked their way into a smoke-filled room; "their spades had broken through into the smoking-room of the Atheists' Club. . . . Needless to say, these crestfallen adventurers were made very welcome." We may add that other Catholics would dig in other directions, some landing in the Anglican Club, others in the No-man's-land where you feel closer to God on a mountain-top than in a church.

And still, in the Church, the truth shines warm for those who hold to her teaching. Reading the words of St. Gregory of Nyssa "For now the Gospel glory of the true Sun sheds its brightness on all within the house," one might be tempted to assume that he lived in a 'patch of peace.' Not so: thanks to the machinations of the Arians, he led for some years such

[1] *The Observer,* June 21, 1968.

a vagrant life that his friend St. Gregory of Nazianzus likened him to drift-wood tossed up and down by the waves. Yet the storm-racked House was to him dazzling in its brightness . . . as it is to us. Those who remember the golden age (as it seemed) between the two waves of Modernism may well pray:

"Fair the day shine as it shone on my childhood—
Fair shine the day on the House with open door!"

but we must not be so naive as to imagine that tranquillity is normal to the Church. "Simon, Simon, behold Satan hath desired to have you. . . ." and Satan is determined to have us yet. He was a murderer from the beginning and a liar, our Lord said, and he ever returns to his attack upon truth, ever attempts to shift the Rock. At the time of the first Modernist infection, Gaetano Negri wrote memorable words: "In the modern world, which is whirling round dizzily, only the Church is strong enough to stand still, since the reasons for her stillness are not passing, relative considerations and interest, but a 'motionless end of eternal wisdom' (Dante)." There is profound wisdom in the words, and yet the Church stands still only as a healthy growing tree stands still, bringing out blossom and bearing noble fruit in due season—"inter omnes una nobilis; nulla silva talem profert fronde, flore, germine." When each storm abates, the truth seems to shine more warmly and the purified Church appears more beautiful. "We have grown used," wrote Chesterton, "to dilution, to dissolution, to a watering down that went on for ever. But Thou has kept the good wine until now."

Index